I

OF

INNOCENCE

I WAS ADOPTED BY A CHILD ABUSER

DAVID WILDE

Death of Innocence

This book was first published in Great Britain in paperback during August 2020.

Email: ads2life@btinternet.com

ISBN: 978-1-9161803-2-1

PREFACE

I have changed the names of my adoptive parents and have sought to camouflage any aspects of the following account, to protect me from slander or libel, and to protect others who may not wish to be identified. It is written in the sincere hope that it will expose the system and the people in it who were instrumental to what can only be described as a devastating adoption and a destructive upbringing and the '*Death of Innocence.*'

I suspect there are many other victims, who like me have suffered in silence throughout their lives and although frighteningly painful, I guess I'm lucky to possess the ability to write it all down, even though somewhat disjointedly at times; not to mention the fact that it has taken 69 years for me to gain the courage to do so.

I sincerely hope that the following book will offer a cleansing process and hope, to those who find themselves isolated with no answers or apologies for their pain. And to all others who are drawn to the injustice and need to react in order to stop the torment of young lives; remember that life was meant to be a gift and not a nightmare.

INTRODUCTION

"Anyone can have a child and call themselves 'a parent'.
A real parent is someone who puts their kids above their own selfish needs and wants"
... Unknown

My account is a roller coaster in places but I hope that ultimately you will see that good can come out of the worst of situations and that the seemingly unsurmountable can be overcome. Importantly I want you to see how the establishment has failed me and countless others and I hope it opens everyone's eyes to how we shouldn't unquestioningly go along with what they say is right.

I've often wondered what my 6-week old self looked like as I have no photos and certainly no memories, but I'm told I was cute and probably was as it was often only the cute ones that were adopted in those days. In fact, my adoptive parents later adopted another child, only to return it some weeks later as they wanted one with different colour hair!

It's probably just as well that I didn't know what was happening to me as I couldn't have done anything about it, and at least I am spared around three years of memory. Nothing could have prepared me for my new life as it wasn't the stuff that brochures are made of. My adoptive father had been pushed into adopting me by my adoptive mother, in the belief that he couldn't father children of his own and once I was in the nest, she fell pregnant and I was essentially surplus to requirements. Basically, that's what instigated the reign of terror by my adoptive father as I was a constant reminder of his inability to father a child, which when combined with his uncontrollable rage and paedophile tendencies made for a deadly mix.

Far from being given a forever family, I had been stripped of everything that was my very being; years later I even found out that my name had been changed from John to David, and my birth certificates lost so that new ones were produced. To this day I am still unsure if I was born in 1948 or 49. Thanks to my birth mother I have never been able to trace my real father as she didn't name him on the certificate and even when I found her years later she wouldn't reveal his name. Worse still the adoption society had failed to check the applicants properly and I was placed with candidates that were not only mentally unsuitable but also medically so, as my adoptive father had TB which he subsequently passed on to me.

I have spent many hours in later life, contemplating and trying to understand how it was possible to be placed into a new home at such a young age, with apparently so little thought and preparation. I'm sure that many of the decisions made, were done so in the belief that they were in my best interests and what I find so desperately upsetting is that I am probably one of a huge number who were dealt such a deadly blow by the inappropriately named civil service. I can see no civility in their behaviour and they did me a great disservice.

I can however understand that there were many and varied problems in the 40's and 50's that were not really understood, most especially concerning the displacement of thousands of children in the evacuation procedures of the second world war. We were just a commodity to be given away into families that thought they wanted us, and it conveniently relieved the burden on the post war state.

It's then no wonder that as a young child at school, I started to fabricate the truth about myself, which was meant to bolster up my less than perfect beginning and blot out the real truth of what was going on at home. When you are constantly bombarded with cruel and heartless words such as "You were not born to us,"...... "We didn't create you," ......"You're just a little bastard whose real mother didn't want you;" you have to find a safety mechanism. Mine ultimately became school, education and a thirst for learning which has never left me and even now is my escape; learning is my therapy.

This book is all about my early life and how I dealt with the constant barrage of abuse from my adoptive father, and how I overcame it all to find a kind of peace. If you're looking for a blow by blow account detailing the sickness and depravity of his paedophile behaviour, then this is not the book for you. I will tell you of his physical abuse and allude to the former as I still find it too painful to think about. I will share the pain of growing up; of being bullied; of serendipitous meetings with people who would help me shape my life; and ultimately how I escaped the torment of my so called 'father.'

A bad adoption is capable of creating excuses with little or no effort, the simple fact is that understanding the truth to invoke changes, means understanding life stories, even if they are difficult to hear. It seems to me that adoption regards itself as a preselection process; one that is rarely agreed by people who have considered the consequences should it go wrong, which sadly it often does. Even now it hurts me to consider what was said to me at the age of five when my adopted father screamed out that I was, "No different from a dozen tomatoes on a market stall, and that they could have picked up any one of them," even now these words always made me feel worthless.

I truly hope that you will enjoy the following pages which in places will make you laugh, and I hope you will better understand that not all forever families are forever and that it is possible to be isolated twice! It is clear that the lack of information and support available to the Barbara and Leslie, was due to the fact that in general, people in adoption societies came from secure families and as such had no idea that things could go wrong, or even what such problems might be.

I was a small lamb, given to a pack of wolves who knew that the lamb was not old enough to understand why its mothers comfort was essential to its survival. All people have opinions, and opinions are only viable if they are assisted by agreement. The real problems were that human beings only ever know 1% of the facts before any constructive decisions are made, resulting in devastating consequences.

Chapter One

"If you can help a child,
you don't have to spend years repairing an adult."
... ***anonymous.***

I suspect that Margaret like many adoptive parents was shown a picture of a three week old baby, with little or no hair, rosy cheeks, and the glimpse of a windy smile (not so different from how I look now really), and on seeing the picture she was completely overtaken with the prospect of adoption. Len and Margaret had wanted a child from the first day of their marriage, or rather Margaret had. The most destructive hurdle to this outcome was that Len was suffering from Tuberculosis at the time, having been resident in a sanatorium for several months prior to the adoption. A fact which the adoption society either missed, or only realised when it was too late to turn back the clock. I was therefore a prime target for infection with an immature immune system, probably undernourished and definitely innocent at the age of six weeks. This negligent oversight not surprisingly led to my being diagnosed with the disease at just ten-months of age, destined to spend the next ten years of my life as a virtual cripple unable to breath or even walk properly without severe chest pain and dangerous breathing difficulties.

I am guessing that there would have been a cover up by the public servants who operated the adoption society. As they would find it difficult to avoid the fact that I had contracted the same disease that Len my new adoptive father had been suffering from for several years, and who must therefore be the source of the infection. To this day I remain astonished that the emphasis was to preserve the public servants' position; as no action was ever taken, nor questions asked as to how a young child had contracted such a dangerous disease. Again, I can only guess that my demise had eroded the system's integrity, which created the necessity to take the actions needed to cover up the truth. The adoption society had simply failed to vet the family properly, and therefore exposed me to a disease that left a large patch on my lung, making it difficult for me to breath, and leaving me unable to join in with sports when I went to school. Their failure committed me to years of treatment at a place called the Groby Road Isolation Hospital in Leicester, a two-storey isolation block that was not at all a pleasant place, especially for a small child. My first meaningful recollection in life was at the age of three, traveling up to the hospital on a Midland red bus with Margaret my adoptive mother. Their prescribed methods were archaic and sometimes extreme, with most of them being far from effective. I can remember lying on a mat with dozens of older people doing breathing exercises week after week after week, and never really understanding why. I being the youngest of them all attracted perhaps a little more attention than the mature people who had been infected, but there were no dedicated children's sessions as there would be today.

I'm not sure which part of the adoption service was meant to protect me from such a blunder, but I know from the records that Margaret was told my condition wasn't considered to be very serious! Which I guess perfectly protected the society and all those connected. Tuberculosis is and remains a serious infection in any form, but then back in the early 50's it was technically very difficult to treat, with terrifying symptoms especially at such an early age. Knowing her as I did even at that age, I suspect that being told it *wasn't considered serious*, would have relieved her guilt. She was a kind woman who was dominated by Len, and as such she would have leaned towards blaming herself for what had happened. I can almost guarantee that deep down she would have known I had become a victim of neglect via a system that simply cared more about its position than the welfare of a young child. I further suspect that the society would have threatened to remove me from the family in the event of any real controversy anyway, which would have provided the perfect platform for Margaret to become totally silent. In the 1950's most people believed in the system, as the war had provided little else to believe in and suffering was accepted as normal life. Without a psychological outlet to express her fears, Margaret was on edge virtually all the time, and I continue to protect her memory for several reasons which I will tell you about later.

It was a year after the adoption, that Margaret unexpectedly fell pregnant by Len, which then removed the endless questions of guilt for both his illness, and his suspected subsequent sterility due to the infection. This immediately fuelled his feelings against the unwanted adoption as he was no longer an inadequate male and I was simply a reminder of his broken ego.

Like most children my real cognitive behaviour started at around the age of three, when I became much more aware of what was going on around me. I was able to think and reason for myself and I was very perceptive. I can vividly remember Len becoming increasingly verbal and violent, raging for several hours a day and threatening to get rid of me like some kind of unwanted guest. Looking back, I can only guess that my illness had become an issue for him, the visits to hospital and my constant wheezing being a daily reminder of what had really happened. I was a reminder of the doubts that had previously been cast over his masculinity, as Margaret forced him to adopt simply on the grounds of his inability to produce a child. It is then not difficult to understand that once Len had been able to father his own child, he had no further use for me as I reminded him of his former inadequacy. I can remember sensing strong feelings of resentment coming from him; my hostile parent, and I never felt comfortable being around him ever again.

Len went to work every day which lessened the atmospherics, and in a sense served to bond me slightly to Margaret, and it's true to say that over the months I did become closer to her. I think she knew that adoption was different and that I was second best for Len, and definitely a threat; completely different to his own son. As my mind developed along with my mental perception, my eyes swelled up in the realisation that this was not about a future anymore; it was about Len, and his son who had cleaned up the accusations to make him whole again.

Margaret and Len's own son was just three days old when she had been allowed to leave the hospital, and I'm sure that bonding with him was not in any way the same as her forced attempt to bond with me. I suspect that by this time even she had realised it would never be possible to become close to me with Len breathing down her neck all the time. It was obvious he would feel cheated should she divide her affections equally.

As a toddler I can remember her talking to a friend saying that when the doctor handed over her son for the first time, there was an immediate recognition that he was part of her and she of him. I can now fully understand and respect what she was saying but at the time I didn't, and it just served to fuel the uneasiness in my developing mind. I can see now that I must have presented a huge problem for both me and her, as we were both frauds in our own way; misfits with consequent problems constantly looming in the midst of her own son's existence.

With the pressure of Leonard's demands, her life was torn down the middle, trying to be a mother to her own son whilst at the same time trying to be a mother to a stranger. It's not something she would have admitted at the time, but I'm sure she was ashamed of that unplanned and challenging beginning. I know this because just three days before she died, she apologised to me for all that had happened in putting me with Len.

I was a myth which demanded that she should bond with me regardless, and I felt that she often wondered what was wrong with her because it wasn't working. I could see and feel that she was going through the motions, staring at my face whilst she fed me, carrying me around when Len wasn't looking. Then one day I felt a change in her, as she woke up in the light of the startling conclusion that I did not in any way feel like part of her; and both she and I knew deep down that I never would. It then became very clear that she was in the middle of a battle in which Len was both the security and the destruction of her dreams.

I'm not trying to labour the point; but I need to set the stage for this book, and it is important to pay particular attention to the bedrock of the ensuing problems, in the hope that they will be fully understood by all. I also needed to provide clarity both to the story and to the integrity of me the author, as this subject can be seen as controversial; to which many will want to hide their faces and pretend that it never happened

I am not in any way resentful, even though it has been recorded many times that babies show obvious responses to a mother; crying or not crying, or dramatically calming when soothed by her. In my case due to the pressure of Len, Margaret was never able to naturally feel that personal communication and response towards me. Therefore, there was never that automatic encouragement and feeling of closeness that parents derive from caring and playing with their child. I have no idea how Margaret coped with that, as her task was at best overbearing and at worst impossible.

It is also recorded in many papers that children raised in orphanages stop responding to adult attention because they learn that their efforts don't work; which over time became the profile of Len, and therefore my early life could well have been in an orphanage. I remember that Margaret was reluctant to make eye contact with me for fear of reprisal from Len, and he and I both became locked in a survival mode in which contact turned into abuse of the most hideous kind. I have read many times, *we all like people who like us*, but as I was to find out, it's a two-way street; for if I didn't look at Margaret, Len concluded that I didn't like her and vice versa. For him this was the perfect excuse to implement his regime of pure hell and reprisal.

I understand it can be very difficult to build a meaningful relationship with children who are adopted, especially past early infancy, but in my case, it really didn't matter as Len had already commenced his secret reign of terror against me. Even then I must have known that in such a position it was virtually impossible to create a stable environment, as the bumpy beginnings failed to forge any form of security. As soon as I could speak, I developed a stutter which gripped me until my early teens; in short, my life was a huge mess.

I have read that things can go horribly wrong with children who have experienced very difficult beginnings, and they can develop a condition known as *reactive attachment disorder*, a frightening and daunting diagnosis. Children with this condition can appear to have no conscience and are invariably unable to appreciate the consequences of reactive behaviour. Over time, it can become a struggle to trust anyone when living in a permanent state of fight or flight, with destructive consequences attached to every action and every breath. I feel sure that as time went on, I was prone to lash out at both Len and Margaret, as I had become very difficult to control. I am equally sure that consequent of my deprived beginnings, together with the need for emotional control, I developed an eating disorder which was the result of being force-fed meat, and to this day I suffer from mild bulimia and slight OCD.

From the age of three, Len would derive great joy from attacking me when no one was looking, and his son Paul became a weapon for my destruction; if Paul had a problem, it was automatically my fault and I was punished accordingly. Strangely I was aware that having two such young children in such a difficult environment would make things very difficult for Margaret. Looking back now I can see that it would have become hard for her to like, let alone love me, and caring for me became exhausting for her and I guess demoralizing at best. It is not then surprising that I developed much more mental energy than the rest of the family, purely as a defence mechanism, which resulted in my requiring very little sleep. I am still looking for excuses for Len and his hate, which is why I have spent many hours trying to analyse the facts in favour of both Len and his wife, but the injustice is not just about them but about the entire system that created the beginning of my life and the later extraordinary story.

I can remember that open affection began to feel terrifying to me and set off some fairly large but escalating problems. The real problem was that such a condition was injected by the poison of what had become a particularly unbalanced family, who found themselves in a subliminal situation that they could have neither understood nor controlled?

Paradoxically, sometimes the safer a child feels, the more a young child can feel threatened, but in my case, I never felt safe and always felt threatened. Looking back, my adoptive parents should have been given a trial visit and been monitored before any real commitment was made, but the people running the society had neither the skills or understanding of the facts and I guess are currently drawing their retirement benefits unaware of the damage they must have inflicted on thousands of innocent children.

CHAPTER TWO

"Dreams are often most profound
when they seem the most crazy"
*... **Sigmund Freud***

I opened my eyes slowly and could hear Paul screaming in the bed next to me, my heart jumped as I totally knew what was coming next. Len burst into the room and tore me from the sheets, and I felt a hard thump as my head hit the carpet, close to the bed legs. I was sweating with fright as if someone had turned up the heating, and my heart was bursting through my chest. All I could think of was hiding away, and underneath my bed presented the perfect hideout, so I quickly scrambled into the semi darkness to avoid the impending blows.

I could feel a large hand trying to grab me by the leg, and I reacted by frantically kicking and screaming. By this time, I was wailing with fright, and the tears were flowing down my face like rain. "No, no," I screamed; but he eventually secured a firm grip on my leg and yanked me out from under the bed. By this time Paul had stopped screaming; his face turned to a distinct look of achievement bathed with importance.

Len, as was normal, tugged on my pyjama trousers and ripped them off me, and then tore off my underwear to land his flat hand hard on my bare bottom. As soon as I started crying, he was always very careful to immediately blame me for what had happened.

"Now look what you made me do" he would say adding to my confusion, as I was never sure how I had made him do anything. My backside had a red imprint of his hand stretching from cheek to cheek, and it stung with excruciating pain which I manged to hide from him, fearing he would top up his efforts again.

"Get up" he screamed. "Stop crying, or I'll give you another one; which will hurt me more than it will hurt you."

I had grown used to his clichés, as everything always turned out to be my fault. I stood up straining with the pain and struggling to stop crying. He pushed me out of the bedroom to the top of the stairs and started shouting again.

"Why do you cause so much trouble, what did I do to deserve you?" he bellowed. "Why don't you just go away?"

He pushed me again and I lost my grip on the stair rod and went flying down the stairs. "Are you drunk" he screamed after me. "Can't you stand up properly?"

Margaret appeared at the bottom of the stairs and for some obscure reason asked, "What's he doing on the floor? What happened?"

"Stupid boy was messing about at the top of the stairs and fell," Len shouted out to drown her questions.

I kept quiet and said nothing as I knew that by this time his anger would have tempered, and that provided I said nothing I would emerge relatively unscathed. Paul was by this time smiling with triumph, bathing in the power that he had developed to increase his importance and nurture his presence in his family. Len with a look of triumph in his eyes ordered me back up the stairs again and into the bathroom, which automatically started me sweating and my speech became broken and nervous.

For some reason he liked to use a flannel on my body, which was as cold or as hot as he could possibly make it, and then he would bitterly complain if I uttered a single word about what he was doing. I thought it was perfectly normal for him to be doing what he was doing, and only much later did I realise it was perverse and that he was enjoying every action.

Len having decimated the early morning, screamed out that it was breakfast time and I braced myself to pay strict attention to his tormenting rules. He assisted Paul down the stairs and sat him on his chair, which was elevated to the correct height by a cushion, whilst I was almost thrown into position. The height of the table and my lack of cushions meant that my bowl of cornflakes was positioned just at eye level, making it very difficult to stop my arms from flying about as I tried to eat them; which in Len's eyes was a cardinal sin. I sat there nervously, waiting for him to stir his tea and attack my hand with the hot spoon. The anxiety was killing me as the heat from the spoon never failed to make me cry. Then as if by reflex I started to whimper.

"Shut up," he screamed, "or you won't eat anything!" I held my breath and grimaced to camouflage my fear, but that didn't work as he attacked from the side with a hot spoon, instantly making me scream out and cry again.

"Right! that's it," he declared, "it's under the stairs for you," and in a flash I was incarcerated again.

Under the stairs had become my haven, a place where I felt safe. The door was almost triangular, shaped to contour the stairs, with a wire flipper thing in the middle that stopped flies from entering the cupboard. This provided the only passage of air that entered my cage and looking back I can't imagine how I survived with so little oxygen to breath, but I did. I seemed to spent more time under the stairs than in the outside world, usually being deprived of meals, so I had taken to storing food under there. I hid it away at the furthest point of the stair angle, right at the pointy bit. My favourites were Wagon Wheels and Mars Bars which I admit were stolen from a tin in the kitchen cupboard. Like most youngsters my age I liked fizzy drinks and my favourite was Tizer, which again I had acquired from the pantry whilst no one was watching. It was a strange life and I always felt very confused, but not fully understanding my confusion, it always made me panic when dealing with the isolation and uncertainty.

I was nearly four years old and my head was not in tune with the reality of my situation yet. What was happening and why, were questions far reaching from the actual immature facts. I placed my hand against the mesh ring that allowed cold air to cool me and peered out through the hole in an effort to find a calming thought to help me cope when it inevitably happened again.

My tears had dried into crusty streaks that ran like train lines down my face, and I felt my eyes twitch as I struggled to find the daylight in my cage. I needed to escape but I was trapped; the darkness of the cupboard and the single strand of light that cut the black like a laser beam, always prompted the need to run as hard and as fast as I could, but there was nowhere to run, and the door was bolted anyway.

My mind drifted until I could feel the sun beaming down on my face as I leaned against a broken fence which was connected to a badly malformed tree that had long since stopped growing. The water running by at my feet chattered incessantly as the pebbles moved under its never-ending flow, and as I turned my head, a sea of sunflowers was dancing majestically in the summer breeze. For some strange reason I developed the uncontrollable desire to run as fast as I could, and as I did so the sunflowers would move frantically as I sped my way through the field. The flowers towered above me like giants with caring faces that seemed to smile down to protect me. Then hidden in a private place awaiting my escape, was a small yellow spaceship with a glass dome, and one very large lever situated in front of the dark brown seat. There was a red button on the side of the craft that I somehow knew would open the glass dome and protect me. I pressed it and with a strange hissing noise the dome opened, and I climbed in and pressed the green button that lay on the floor by the seat, and the dome closed.

My eyes were glistening with excitement as I pushed the lever and the craft shot forward at breath taking speed, the yellow in the sunflowers turned into streaks of speeding light as the craft gained lift and hurled me into space. I sped on, and as if by magic a large purple globe appeared before me and drew the craft towards it. A sliding door hissed, and my vehicle was taken into the globe. Digested in golden strands of happiness, I smiled with sparkling enthusiasm as I knew what was about to happen and climbed out of the craft to take my place on a small bright yellow chair formed in the shape of a dome.

As I sat on the chair there was a swishing sound and a small round vent opened in the globe to release a purple smoke that was as thick as vines, as it clung to the air that I was about to breath. My lungs inhaled the thickness of each plume and my childhood frame descended into a perfect sleep that seemed to last for ever, and upon waking with bright eyes I climbed back into the craft and pulled the lever backwards and it rose up again to speed me back to the dark cupboard under the stairs.

As I woke up from my dream, my mind was calm, my eyes were dry, and I had developed a way to combat the lunacy of a truly terrible situation that would recur on numerous occasions.

CHAPTER THREE

"Nothing will benefit human health
and increase chances of survival of life on Earth
as the evolution to a vegetarian diet"
... Albert Einstein

It was November 4th and the sun was shining through a steamy grey sky; Margaret was preparing food for the following night's bonfire night celebrations and the kitchen was filled with strange smells that were almost frightening to me, as I had never been to a party before and the prospect seemed both alluring and exciting. I felt nervous as Len had told me they were going to burn a man called Guy on the bonfire, and I was uneasy that if things went wrong it could easily be me.

Everything was focused on tomorrow night and the thought of rockets and spaceships filled my mind with complete enchantment, but also concern coupled with excitement. Margaret grumbled at the amount of people who were likely to turn up, which set my mind wondering what fireworks were really all about, as they were only a distant memory from last year. I was told there were friends coming with small children who I could play with, and it was clear that bonfire night was going to be a big thing. It was Len's night of the year when he took complete control of everything; I had been warned to be very good.

I was also vaguely aware that last year Mrs Peat's family who were essentially pyromaniacs and lived next door, had built an enormous bonfire and Mr Peat set off all the fireworks they could get their hands on as quickly as possible. I could also remember that their garden was much too small for the fireworks, and his shed burned down consuming most of his privet hedge with it. My mind was full of what might happen, and my childish thoughts enveloped a fantasy world that created excitement and fear. Mrs Peat had a son called Geoffrey who was handicapped, although I had no idea what that meant at the time. All I knew was that he made me laugh and was never nasty to me, so he had become a good friend.

I woke up early on bonfire day and I could hear the thud of raindrops beating on the window. Len was shouting at Margaret and his voice engaged me with immediate discomfort as I knew he was in a bad mood. I peeped through the curtains to visit the day, which was desperately disappointing, and instinctively knew that the party was less that secure from pending problems, in which I would most probably become embroiled. I crept down the stairs hoping that Len would be too engaged in the day's festivities.

Margaret was setting the table in preparation for her feast. She had starched a gleaming white tablecloth with such zeal that it stood up by itself on the four pleated corners. I knew she had worked hard on its whiteness, as the box with the robin on it was nearby. A box that had prompted me many times to attempt to draw the little bird; but my efforts were in always in vain, as Len would find the drawings only to look at them with distain declaring them rubbish and taking great pleasure in throwing them away.

It was clearly to be a grand occasion as elegant cups and plates were arranged with white serviettes at each place setting, and special knives and forks had appeared which I had never seen before. Each chair was carefully set in position, and Paul's chair elevated to the correct height with his customary cushions. Suddenly Len appeared and screamed, "Get up the stairs. NOW!"

I did so as quickly as possible fearing being flung down the stairs again in another improvised flying lesson, but amazingly he didn't follow me as was usual, and the relief brought an invisible smile to my face. I was beginning to like bonfire night and my zeal for the pending party increased.

By now I had mastered washing and drying myself in the mornings, fearing Len and his actions against me. I was also very good at dressing as quickly as possible which also helped to prevent him attacking me. I looked down at myself, relieved and inwardly smiling as I had completed the task without a single problem. Silently I crept back down the stairs and Margaret presented me with a bowl of cornflakes, with strict instructions to eat them at the kitchen table. To my enormous relief, Len was virtually non-existent as he had temporarily abandoned his quest against me in favour of his bonfire night duties.

The day drew on and the rain subsided, the sun came out to dart it's rays with meridian splendour into the sky. It was to be a memorable day as I dared to look forward to my very first bonfire party; my mind was excited at the prospects of a painless day.

Evening came, and the night sky was cloaked in black to the point of obscurity when the doorbell rang, and the first guests arrived. It was Geoffrey and the Peat family; Mr Peat with his wife, Clifford their son, and Eileen their daughter who was clearly reluctant to be present. Geoffrey was very excited as he nibbled on a piece of dry bread dropping crumbs on the floor as he did so. As if by reflex, fearing problems, I knelt down and captured each one with the precision of a scientist watching bacteria swarm and multiply in a drop of water.

"Hello Geoffrey, are you looking forward to the party," I exclaimed.

"Yeth I amp" he replied in a broken language which I had learned to fully understand.

"Let's go and play hide and seek shall we, as I know it always makes you laugh." I said to him. "Yeth agrite" he answered, "you sthart coutog and I'd go and heide."

He always hid in places where I could see him, and I tried to compensate for this, as he was a good friend who never ever tried to hurt me.

"Found you," I laughed, as he stood by the front door in full view. He burst into uncontrollable laughter which always made me feel good.

"Yer tern nouw," he cried. So off I went to hide with slightly more precision than his own effort, but not too hard as he had been known to wander several streets away, and dozens of people ended up searching for him.

By this time the front room was full of people, many I had never seen before, and Len addressed them inviting the gathering to go into the garden whilst he burned the man called Guy. Due to the rain most of the bonfire was damp and after several attempts it still refused to ignite so Len reverted to petrol in the hope that he could overcome the problem. He poured quite a lot of petrol on the pile and then lit a match with the most startling effect, there was a big flash and Len vanished in a bright light. The fire did start though, but Len was forced to spend some time remodelling his hair and eyebrows as both were badly singed.

At the age of three and a half I had no idea who *Guy Forks* was or why anyone would want to burn him, nevertheless Len's bonfire flash had adjusted his thoughts to himself and as a consequence I had become unimportant, which was good, and I could start to relax a bit. He again addressed the party and reported to them that the fireworks were about to begin and that he was in complete control of the display. I had no idea what was involved but if the previous fire lighting flash was anything to go by, it sounded dangerous to me, so I held Geoffrey's hand and we hid behind the garden shed.

Len had gone to great lengths to measure the distance from his firework display to the party guests for safety reasons, but he failed to calculate how far a jumping jack could jump. In those days the fireworks were very powerful; the bangers were called cannons for obvious reasons and the jumping jacks could reach extraordinary heights. We all stood frozen with bated breath as Len lit a jumping jack; bang, bang, bang it went and homed in on Geoffrey who was not at all pleased at the pyro attack. It attained its highest altitude and jumped down Geoffrey's welly, still banging and sparking as it went. Geoffrey screamed with pain and jumped around in time with the jumping jack which really looked very funny to me and I couldn't help laughing, not really understanding how serious it was. Luckily the jumping jack had almost stopped jumping, and fortunately Geoffrey had some very thick socks on, so he survived the attack, but Len immediately scorned me for laughing. He waited until the display was over and no one was looking, then ceremonially pulled my trousers down and landed a very painful blow to my bare backside. I managed not to cry though, or it could have been much worse.

It was then that Margaret unveiled her dining table *Fit for a King* as she put it, and some sat around the table, whilst the others, mainly the grown-ups were standing. Margaret had made some minced meat topped with dumplings that floated in the brown liquid, like shipwrecked victims. The smell was horrendous, and it tasted even worse. I took a spoon full of the meat, but it tasted so bad that I chewed and chewed it thinking that if I kept doing that I wouldn't have to eat anymore.

A shiver ran through me as Len looked at me in anger and demanded that I stopped messing around with my food. The spoon was snatched from my hand hurting me in the process and he started to try and feed it to me. I tried to push it away from my mouth, turning my head as I did so, and to my horror the brown mess splattered and stained the snowy white tablecloth. I knew that I was about to find myself in a very bad place; turmoil and terror gripped me, and I had no idea what was coming next as the tablecloth was totally ruined. My heart pounded as he scooped me up and took me into the kitchen, closing the door and shutting us away from prying eyes. There was a pan with some extra mince on the cooker that hadn't been used. He glared uncontrollably, and my face hurt as he wrenched open my mouth to fill it with the meat. I could hardly breath as my eyes drifted upwards in pain, breathing became difficult and I coughed and choked, tears streaming down my face. I was literally drowning in meat; shaking so badly I started to wet myself as he spooned yet more into my mouth and held it closed with his hand.

"P-please s-stop" I begged as I started to wretch… "p-please stop your hurting me, my t-tummy hurts." Which wasn't surprising as I was literally crying brown meat from my eyes, and my nose was burning with the flow of the greasy liquid that was running down my face. I was shaking and screaming for help, but no one came. Even my ears had meat in them, and the smell was so bad that I started to be sick again.

"Now look what you've made me do! Why don't you just go away leave us now," he seethed. His words loud enough for me to hear, yet not so loud that the guests would hear through the closed kitchen door.

He dragged me upstairs like a rag doll and attempted to clean up the mess. He changed my clothes and washed away the evidence then calmly brought me back downstairs and apologised to the party for the upset I had caused; making sure they all knew I was adopted and that it was difficult to know what someone else's child would do. I found it difficult to talk and still shook from head to toe; this was the day I began to stutter. No one ever guessed what had happened, except Geoffrey who somehow knew, because he was crying for me; he was a good friend.

From that date to this, and with Margaret's support, I never touched meat again. I often smile as it turned out that vegetarianism was the way to go, so Len really did me a great favour although he never knew, albeit his methods left much to be desired. It's strange how life can scar us from such a young age, as even to this very day I also find it very difficult to sit at a table with a starched white tablecloth!

CHAPTER FOUR

"Keeping an active mind has been vital to my survival, as has been maintaining a sense of humour."
... ***Stephen Hawking***

Shortly after my fifth birthday I was off to primary school for the first time. I had been looking forward to it for ages as my entire mind was set on being away from Len. All my thoughts were about me; me escaping, me learning, and me just being able to be me. But even me being me made me anxious.

I was still traveling up to Groby Road Hospital every week for breathing exercises, to help with the effects of the tuberculosis I had contracted from Len. I was too young to really understand why I was going there, nor how serious tuberculosis was, and it's only been in later years that I've understood the severity of it. All I knew was that I couldn't run or walk very fast as it hurt my chest and made it difficult to breath. I guess I must have realised there was a connection between this and the visits to the hospital, but it was a lot for a five-year-old mind to take in and the visits made me anxious. The exercises hurt, and I couldn't understand why I had to do them.

"Will I be able to play with the other children at school without it hurting?" I asked myself. I knew I could play with Geoffrey, but he was different.

For some time now I'd found it increasingly difficult to talk without stuttering as my years with Len had badly affected my speech, although I had no idea how much so. My enforced vegetarianism and the events that led to it caused me to suffer well beyond the effects of my disease, causing side effects that are more serious than I could have ever imagined. Every mealtime was traumatic, waiting for the inevitable hot spoon, the clip across the ear, the dig when I wasn't looking. I dreaded Len noticing that Margaret no longer put meat on my plate in an effort to be kind. All of this made me very nervous and extremely angry, to the point where I wanted to speak but the words became mixed up in my anger and I now found it very difficult to speak at all without stuttering which was very embarrassing. The more anxious I was the worse my stutter became; I was caught in a vicious circle.

I kept on asking myself in the silence of my mind; what was school going to be like? Would I be good at learning? as everything I tried to do up until now was either scorned or destroyed by Len. But most importantly would there be anyone there that I could relax with; any friends like Geoffrey? Geoffrey was the only one I could speak to without stuttering and so he was very special indeed. I don't think Len liked Geoffrey very much as he was always telling me that I had found a friend who was ideal for me, and I instinctively knew he was telling me that I was also not very smart. I didn't understand what handicapped meant but the word was often bandied around. All I knew was that Geoffrey was honest and never lied; Geoffrey could do a thousand-piece jigsaw in a few hours when other normal people took days, so he couldn't be that stupid could he I reasoned?

It was five o'clock in the morning and I was up dressed and ready to go. I was being very careful not to make much noise as I knew that Len had been working hard last night and I had been warned not to disturb him, as he needed to sleep. My mind was full of what ifs? I had a quiet breakfast with Margaret and Paul and then it was time to set off. My head was oozing with uncertainty as I crept out of the door with Margaret who was going to take me to the school.

I had no experience at all of school life because Len couldn't afford to or didn't want to send me to a nursery school; but in fairness Paul wasn't sent either. This was my first big challenge in life, and I remember thinking that I was leaving a bad home and I needed to be strong and independent. I knew I would be meeting different people, but I was scared they all might be like Len. I was looking forward to learning but had no idea what I was going to be doing, and something in me was also scared of being with other kids. I never felt good enough, as Len was always telling me to be like Paul and I simply wasn't.

I climbed on the bus grabbing hold of the shiny pole that squeaked with the sweat on my hands. Margaret insisted that we sat on the long seat just inside the bus, and I pulled myself up to dangle my legs over the edge, like icicles struggling to hang on, as the temperature changes and they melt away. I needed to cry for some reason, as I instinctively seemed to know that school could very easily present more problems; bigger than the ones I had grown accustomed to. I knew that I would have to work, as Margaret had explained what was likely to happen to me, and as I had no memories of happiness, I felt little loss of the past; just uncertainty of the future. The journey took forever, "It's much slower than my spaceship ever took," I thought. Suddenly the conductor pulled the cord and the bell rang with a frightening clang bringing me out of my daydream, 'Ding Ding' and the bus came to a stop outside the school.

There is a problem with being so small on a bus when grown up people stand up all around you. It feels like you have been tossed into a dark cave with very little air to breath, surrounded by musty smells and a smoky odour that clings to your nose like a bowl of putrid meat. Tightly gripping Margaret's hand, we entered the large metal gates that led to a building with coloured bricks that glistened in the sunlight. There was a huge green door with a brass handle that had been polished until it shone like the stars in the sky. We entered and walked along a very long corridor that was decorated with painted pictures of every subject imaginable. There were faces with bright blue eyes and pink skin, there was one with a black face that had a spike through its nose, another had lots of trees and sunshine in it which made me feel calmer.

We eventually came to another door that had shiny sign on it. Margaret read the sign to me, "It says Head Mistress," she said, and the door opened to reveal a very old lady darkening the entrance.

"Good morning and what is your name?" she enquired.

"D-D-David" I stammered.

"And how old are you?" she asked.

"F-f-f-f-f-five," was my eventual reply.

I was very embarrassed and finding it difficult to answer her, I could feel the heat rising in my face and I wanted to run away. My face must have spoken to her as she abandoned any further questions and led us to a classroom. On seeing the classroom with so many children in it, I again became scared, because my social skills were at that time zero.

In the corner I could see a boy sitting on his own, almost isolated from the class by his position. She pointed towards him, "Sit down next to Peter," she said.

I crept into the space next to him and slid into the very small hard chair. There was a terrible smell that immediately stung my nose, and I began to feel sick; it was coming from Peter and I soon realised why he was isolated from the rest of the children. Peter looked terrified; I think he knew he smelt and as he tried to talk to me, he burst into tears. The head mistress left the room escorting Margaret with her, she turned and waved through the window of the door and the day began.

"And who are you?" boomed a powerful voice from a man I later came to know as Mr Deacon. "Stand up and introduce yourself please."

Shaking I struggled to stand up as the platform on the twin desk was very small, but eventually I moved into the walking area. "D-D-D-David," I stammered. The name had taken ages to say and the entire class started to laugh.

"Sorry I didn't Hear that," boomed out Mr Deacon, having clearly seized a chance to escalate the fun

"D-D-D-D-D-David," I spluttered again, each letter more difficult to force out of my mouth than the last. I tried again, "S-S-Sorry, D-D-D-D-D-David." But by this time the entire room was in uproar and some kids were almost falling off their seats with laughter. My mind was in turmoil and I wanted to vanish, to become invisible. Then something changed in me and I also started to laugh, laughing so hard until I cried. I guess it was an attempt to camouflage the real tears.

Like a switch, the room slid back into silence leaving only me roaring with laughter.

"Did you enjoy that" barked Mr Deacon.

"Y-y-y-yes," I spluttered and the whole room burst into laughter again.

"Well David, welcome to our gathering and what would you like to do today?" he asked.

I had no idea how to answer and I knew that whatever I said would be funny, so I mumbled, "P-play p-please."

"P-play!" he exclaimed. "We don't p-play here," he said, cruelly mimicking my stammer, "what about drawing a p-picture?"

"Y-yes p-please," I sprayed, and everything went into turmoil again.

I was always keen to draw and paint, but Len would find my efforts and declare them rubbish, ripping them up to destroy them. So, after a time, whenever I drew a picture, I would rip it up myself before he could. I had no idea if my efforts were good or bad, but I did enjoy drawing. We all gathered around a large square table, and huge sheets of thick grey paper were placed in front of us, along with five colours on a pallet; red, blue, yellow, black and white. The smell from Peter was all but forgotten, as he sat by himself in solitude with his drawing paper, a virtual leper in a colony of kids led by Mr Deacon.

My mind started to race; and I could see my spaceship appearing on the paper before me within a sea of sunflowers. I could feel the tree that I had relied on so much and smelt the water that moved the pebbles under my feet. I picked up a brush and moved it over the paper, the tree grew with fiery expectation and the sunflowers reach for the sky by the inspiration of my excited brain. The sky was blue with fluffy white clouds and I carefully placed my spaceship hidden but visible within the towering flowers. I have no idea how long my dream escape took to create but looking up at its final creation the entire class gathered around me in awe of my effort.

I prepared to answer the questions as best I could when one little girl called Lynda exclaimed that what I had created was very good, another boy called John was keen to know if the spaceship was real.

“N-no,” I stammered, “it it’s in my h-head, but it h-helps me es-escape,” and this time no one laughed, not a single child uttered a word.

I picked up my paper and walked over to Peter who was still sat alone and still smelling. Then in a clear voice without a single stammer said, “I did this for you Peter. It’s a present to make you happy.”

… And that was my first day at school.

It’s good to know that this sort of behaviour is outlawed today, but something inside of me screams out that we all need to battle with our problems. Although such methods are frowned upon today, this baptism of fire turned out to be a brilliant way for me to conquer mine. I had gained respect in a sea of uncertainty which was to grow in later years beyond my wildest dreams.

The next day I was very keen to get out of the house and rose early, Len was in a bad mood and insisted on washing me, today he chose a particularly hot flannel. He always paid special attention to my private parts, although to be very honest they really weren’t very private to me and I had no idea of the implications of his actions at that time. I screamed out with pain as he splashed hot water over my legs.

“Shut up, stop that noise or you’ll feel the back my hand,” he growled.

That was enough to stop me in my tracks. I gritted my teeth and held my breath to force the silence that he had demanded. It worked, and I began to dry and dress myself hoping that he would not try and assist me in any way. Margaret called to say that breakfast was nearly ready, and I moved carefully to the top of the stairs, when all of a sudden, Len appeared behind me and pushed me in the back to hurry me up as he was late for work. I held on to the banisters to prevent myself from falling and slowly made it to the bottom without further incident.

I could feel my body getting hotter as the dreaded breakfast time drew nearer, Paul was already elevated to his privileged position as I cautiously climbed on to my chair. At eye level, I gazed at the bowl of cornflakes with the same caution as a mouse staring face to face with a dangerous cat. Yet again my eyes started to glaze over, and a tear trickled down my cheek. "What's the matter with him" snarled Len, "what have I done now?"

Margaret glanced at him and calmly poured some milk into my bowl and thrusting a spoon into my hand she gave me a secret smile with a calming glow. "Eat up now or you'll be late for school," she said.

Len was busy heating up his teaspoon and I moved my hands over the top of the table in the hope of preventing the attack and with a defeated look he abandoned the assault and carried on drinking his tea. "I have to rush," he exclaimed and jumping up from the table he hurriedly put on his jacket to quickly exit the back door.

He was gone, and the relief was instant as my face began to shed its grey terror. I was never sure if Margaret was aware of what was happening, but I knew that the coldness of my fear vanished when Len was not there. Paul had been playing with his food, flooding the table with limp cornflakes and tepid milk casually mixed with broken bits of toast. I never really understood why he was allowed to make such a mess without being told off, but he always did; looking triumphant and privileged on almost every occasion.

Margaret scooped Paul up to clean him down and put his jumper on and we set off for the bus stop which would take me to school. The bus pulled up and I gripped the pole to climb aboard. Margaret spoke to the conductor and I sat on the long seat but this time I was alone; Margaret had left me and asked the conductor to make sure I got off at the right stop. My mind slipped away to what had happened the day before, and for some strange reason I wondered if

Peter would still smell, as I wasn't keen to sit next to him if he did, because I hated feeling sick.

Suddenly my thoughts were disturbed by the ding, ding as the bus came to an abrupt halt, and I could see the large school gate through the window that towered over my slight frame. "Come along then sonny" said the conductor, as he assisted me off the bus, and I gingerly walked through the gates with a feeling of immense uncertainty of the pending day.

Everyone was playing on the grey tarmac, and there were crates containing tiny bottles of milk stacked up by the door that I thought led to my classroom. For some reason I was intrigued with the bottles of milk and slid one out of the crate having never seen one so small before. It had a coloured top with a hole in it and the thick almost yellow cream had vanished leaving only the bland white.

"What are you doing?" shouted in a deep voice, "they aren't for you, you're not allowed to open them yet! You naughty boy."

I was devastated knowing that I hadn't opened it and turned around to see Mr Deacon standing there with a frown on his face. "I can see you're going to be trouble my lad," he said, "put it back. NOW!"

I carefully slid the bottle back into the crate and stooped ready for my punishment, but it never happened which was strange; no smack with the back of his hand, no hot spoons, no more screams; just silence, and the matter was over. I glanced back at the crates to see lots of tiny birds pecking at the bottle-tops to get at the cream, and I knew Mr Deacon was aware that his outburst was not in any way called for, realising that I was not guilty as charged. I think that was the first time I ever witnessed justice and truth, and it was to grow with me as the days passed by.

Mr Deacon then grabbed a large bell and shook it to create the loudest clang I'd ever heard, and then blew on a whistle which screamed like a frightened mouse being chased by a big cat. “All in please!” he shouted, and everyone formed lines which represented the class that they belonged to. I however, had no idea which was my line until I picked out Peter, by both sight and smell, as everyone continued to avoid him. I took my place in the line and one by one we all filed into the long corridor which eventually led to my classroom.

Mr Deacon soon appeared, “D-David,” he said, clearly intent on continuing his mimicry from the day before. “S-sit by P-Peter today.” I took my place next to Peter and immediately started to feel sick again. The class commenced, and Mr Deacon started to hand out a writing book to each person in the room, but there weren’t enough to go around. He drifted towards me and looked straight at me.

“D-David” he said, intent on further ridicule, “I want you to go to the class next door. Knock politely, then enter and ask Mrs Scupholme if she has any more writing books please.”

I was immediately terrified as the heat rose in my body, but I was more scared of not doing what he demanded. I lifted myself up from the chair, walked over to the door and opened it to find myself in front of another door, which I knocked on with my shivering clenched hand. “Enter,” came a voice from within, and in I went.

“Yes, what can I do for you?” exclaimed Mrs Scupholme.

” Mm Mr D-D-D-Deacon w-w-wants to know if y-you h-have any w-w-w-writing b-books p-please.” I eventually managed to say.

By this time, I was shaking as the entire class was beginning to break into volatile laughter. Mrs Scupholme beckoned me forward to her desk. “Now s-l-o-w-l-y; what can I do to help you?”

“M-m-m-m-m-m-m,” I started, and burst into tears with complete frustration.

“What’s your name?” she asked in an attempt to calm me down.

"D-d-d-d-d-d," I began, and again the words just wouldn't come out.

"Donald?" she asked.

"N-n-no," I attempted to reply.

"Derek?"

"N-no," I replied.

"David?" she finally offered.

"Y-y-yes D-D-David," I burst out.

The entire class was in fits and she demanded that everyone stopped laughing. She smiled and calmly said "Try again, but s-l-o-w-l-y this time."

I took a deep breath looked straight into her face and slowly uttered "Mr Deacon n-needs some more writing books p-please."

She went to the cupboard and returned handing me some books. "You're a very brave little boy!" she said, stroking my hair, and I took them and left the room.

I was both puzzled and excited, but I never forgot Mrs Scupholme. Thanks to her and to another of my teachers I eventually trained myself to speak properly.

Every year Len would arrange a holiday during the summer, and we usually went to Wales. His favourite place was Abersoch in the north, but this year he'd chosen Tenby in the south for some reason. I didn't really want to go but Margaret had been busy preparing to go away, saying it would be nice to go away, "As a family." I sensed that she would be heartbroken if I tried to refuse or kicked up a fuss about it; apart from which there was nowhere that I could stay anyway. It was the last day of School and everyone was excited about the extended holidays, except for me, as I was terrified of spending every day with Len; although I really had no idea of just how long the holidays would be. School finished early and I had boarded the bus after what seemed a very short day, clutching my end of year folder. As usual Margaret was waiting at the bus stop and I handed it to her with a degree of excitement as everyone seemed pleased with my performance.

When we got home, Len had taken a brief look at my work and then hidden it away without making a single comment. He was far more involved with preparations for his *gift of a holiday* in Tenby, as with regimental accuracy he had timed everything to the second. Even Margaret was inspected to make sure that the sandwich boxes were correctly labelled, especially mine, which was always made up from less expensive food. On this occasion they were a mixture of egg and cheese, with mine having far less filling than the others. Len insisted I was given margarine instead of butter and had barred me from having Heinz ketchup a long time ago, in favour of a cheaper brand that was for my use only.

By the next morning, he had packed his Hillman Minx estate car with total precision, and we all climbed in to take up our designated places for what Margaret has said was to be a *very long journey*. The summer sun was beaming down as we set off and the heat was making the air in the car almost unbreathable, as in those days there was no such thing as air conditioning. I wound the window down in the back of the car, hanging my hand out to direct the air flow into the car. In my mind, my hand was a bird flying free as the air pushed it back and forth, flapping faster as Len gained speed. Paul and I were sat in the back and I had been placed behind Len's seat which was pushed back as far as it could go, giving me very little room. It also placed him close enough to land a blow on me almost at his leisure, and I sat there considering what might happen if he got cross about anything.

Both Paul and I had wound the windows down to try and cool ourselves, when suddenly Len grumbled, "Who's opened the window? It's causing a draft and it's almost impossible to hear myself think." It didn't dawn on me that I was under attack; as Paul was playing flying birds as well, when suddenly Len launched his hand from the side of his seat and landed a blow on my head. It was impossible for me to avoid it, as I was pinned in between an array of bags and holiday gear, along with the fact that his chair was perilously close. "Did you hear what I said? Close the window NOW," he boomed.

Paul looked over at me with a privileged look as he continued to enjoy the open window on his side; whilst over on my side I strained on the handle to wind my window back up again. The journey was long, tiring and threatening, as I could feel Len planning his next attack against me. I sat silently trying to predict what would happen next, as his actions became a progression of deliberate hatred. I felt such an urgency for it to finish, but for all the wrong reasons. I should have been excited for the journey to end and for the holiday to start, but I just wanted it to finish so I could escape Len's reach.

As we neared our destination Len and Margaret set up a kind of game which became a competition between Paul and myself, it was called, *The First to see the Sea,* and I was reasonably willing to get involved as it relieved the boredom and presented few possibilities for a stealth attack from Len. I pulled myself up to glance out of the front window in a childish attempt to see the horizon that would contain my first glimpse of the sea, when to my astonishment it appeared unexpectedly. "I I've seen it f-first," I shouted excitedly.

Len ignored my call and snarled, "Stop cheating," before landing me a backhander, as I was perfectly positioned in the centre of the car.

Eventually Paul squealed out with excitement, "I've seen it!" pointing with a gleam in his eye, and everyone clapped; apart from me.

Len looked in his rear-view mirror and adjusting it to focus it on me, "That's what you get for cheating!" he snarled and looked away again.

We drove into the campsite late in the day as it had taken hours to reach our destination. I was completely worn out with the anxiety of the journey and pretended to be sleeping, as I'd worked out that I was less likely to come under attack if my eyes were closed. Margaret had been very quiet, and I could feel her remorse at the injustice of Len's behaviour, as she quietly leaned over to wake me up. "We're here," she whispered. "Wake up, look the caravans are over there."

Len had gone over to the campsite office and was grinning as he returned, clutching a key for the caravan with the number 214 engraved on a round disk that was tied to it. He had also been given a map of the site, with detailed directions; as he had been informed that there were well over 1000 caravans on the site and therefore the map was essential to locate the correct one. We drove around for what seemed to be a very long time, and eventually Len reversed the car at the side of caravan 214, which was identified by a sticker fixed to the front window.

We all piled out and one by one, the contents of the car were transported to the caravan and the cases unpacked to be neatly placed in our designated wardrobes. When we'd finished, I opened the door to go outside and look around as I was uncomfortable with my surroundings. Len and Margaret were too close for comfort, being only feet away from the bunk bed that had been allocated to Paul and I. The air was cooled by the sea breeze, and as I had walked over the grass it squelched and slopped about, as the caravan was located on what I have since realised was reclaimed marshland although at the time it was just wet to me. Len called me in, and we sat around the table to finish off our lunch boxes, which by that time had become dry and tasteless. Margaret had boiled a kettle after Len had switched on the gas supply, and surprisingly things had become uneventful for a change. We all went to bed early that night at Len's insistence, as he had told us tomorrow would be the start of his profiled adventure and gift to us all; including Margaret.

Morning came, and I could hear the sound of vehicles traveling up and down the road. There was no window next to the bed, so I slid out of the bottom bunk to open the curtains. Paul had demanded that he slept on the top bunk which I was delighted with, as the prospect of being dragged from that elevated height had filled me with fear. Len started up almost as soon as he had opened his eyes. "I don't want any trouble!" he snapped, pointing and prodding me with his finger.

I looked up at him and I could see that he was not in a particularly good mood and prepared myself for the coming day. We ate our breakfast, and to my surprise he didn't launch any stealth attacks with hot teaspoons when Margaret wasn't looking. Despite my earlier misgivings, the day was turning out ok as we set off for the beach armed with our buckets and spades. It was a pleasant beach, but the site office had warned Len there were thick clumps of oil around that had contaminated the beach and warned him to keep the kids away as it was difficult to remove and probably harmful to a child's health. Len had drilled it into me that if I became stuck up with oil, *there would be trouble*, and so I prowled about cautiously before I dared sit down on the sand.

I was really keen to build a sandcastle and I started to dig in the slightly damp sand which was ideal, and I began to build a fish shape with a bucket eye. Len came over to help Paul who was complaining that his bucket was faulty, demanding that mine was much better. Margaret was laying down on a towel snoozing, so didn't see when Len deliberately trod on my fish. "Whoops! I'm so sorry," he grinned sarcastically, "Look what I've gone and done!"

I didn't really care as he'd spent forever trying to destroy almost everything I'd ever done, "It It's ok," I sighed and started to form the shape again. I was getting very hot, so I went to Margaret to ask if I could go and paddle in the sea; "Yes," she replied, "As long as I can see you," and I ran excitedly to the water's edge. There was a rock jutting out of the water and I decided to sit down on it, dangling my feet in the water to cool them down. It was peaceful there and I could see Len playing with Paul and Margaret who waving to make sure that I could identify her on the crowded beach. I jumped up to dodge a big wave and stepped in something sticky that made my foot drag about in the water. When I looked down, I was terrified to see a big splodge of oil clinging to my foot. I tried to pull it off but all that happened was my hands became stuck up as well. I was wearing a tee shirt and my next reaction was to wipe my hands on it in an attempt to clean the tar from my hands, causing things to go from bad to worse. Not only did I now have tar on my foot, it was on my hands and shirt as well! I started shaking with fear as I knew Len would welcome the opportunity to punish me, but I had no idea how he would take his revenge.

I slowly walked back to Margaret, smeared from head to foot with thick black tar; trembling at what might happen to me. Len took one look and went barmy, "I told you!" he shouted. "But you don't listen to anything you stupid fool!"

"I I'm really s-sorry," I spluttered and started to cry.

Len was a smoker and always carried a tin of Ronson lighter fuel with him and he dragged me back to the caravan and squirted the lighter fuel on my hands which stung and made things much worse. He rubbed so hard that my hands started to hurt, and I pulled away from him fearing that he would subject my feet to the same punishment.

Margaret came running up as she heard me wailing, "God! Len!" she screamed, "he's only a child. What are you doing squirting that lighter fuel on him?"

Len glared at her and snapped, "He's mad! Uncontrollable! All he ever does is cause trouble."

Margaret walked over to the camp office, where they recommended some cream to remove the tar. It turned out I wasn't the only kid that had fallen foul of the gluey black mess, and she managed to clean me up surprisingly quickly. Len however wasn't finished yet as he ranted and raved and started to push me about. I was becoming scared and my speech had broken down completely; rendering me unable to say even one word. The day had vanished, and dusk had fallen before Len finally calmed down and I was so sad and ashamed of what I'd done that I opened the door to get some air and walked out across the soggy grass. I wasn't gone for that long, but upon my return Len had locked the caravan door and I couldn't get in no matter how much I rattled it. As I tried in vain to open the door, I could hear Len inside screaming at Margaret, "I can't stand it anymore, he's got to go!"

Panicking and unable to keep still, I walked round and round the caravan wailing and crying for them to open the door. I must have walked around for several hours as the half-light of dusk had now turned a deep dark black as night set in. I could feel my skin itching and stinging, but the door remained locked. I was becoming really scared, as not even Margaret had offered me comfort, in what was becoming a desperate situation. Then eventually I heard her shout,

"I'm letting him in! So, you'd better get used to it!"

And with that, the door opened, and the light illuminated the swarms of mosquitos flying around in the night air.

As she drew me into her arms, I was horrified to see that I was covered in bites; so many that it wasn't surprising my body was one massive itch. I remember her screaming at him as she showed him the bites, but he just grinned, and said, "Serves the little bastard right!"

I was so badly bitten that Margaret called an emergency doctor and they covered me in a pink lotion. The doctor told Margaret that this part of the site had been a marsh and that's why the caravans were usually cheaper to rent. "He's not the first little lad to be bitten," he said, "but he's certainly one of the worse cases I've seen."

The rest of the holiday was painful as the bites took ages to heal and my skin was covered in blemishes that continued to itch for days, leaving red bumps for weeks after. I think I must be susceptible to mosquito and midge bites, as even now I'm always the first person to get bitten if there are any around, and the bites invariably turn nasty.

The holiday ended, and eventually we all piled into the car to suffer the return journey which seemed to take twice as long to complete as the journey there. I was still covered in spots when I went back to school, but Len must have given them a satisfactory explanation as no one mention or uttered a word.

Upon returning to school after the holidays Mr Deacon insisted that everyone in the class did sports. His particular preference was football for the boys, and he produced some strange looking boots with several round studs nailed into the soles. They had miles of laces which were very hard to tie up, and everyone in the class struggled to secure them properly. Margaret hadn't given any thought to games at all, as she knew that I couldn't run very well, and clearly abandoned any possibility of my playing football. Mr Deacon found some long shorts and a shirt with green and black squares which were much too big for me, but he insisted that I took part. So, I reluctantly put them on and walked on to a large field to take up my position with the team looking like a scarecrow. I didn't realise how important winning was to a team of kids, and that anyone who let the side down would be automatically ostracized.

Mr Deacon stood by, to do what they called a kick off, he blew a whistle and Keith Wadsworth kicked the ball to his friend and the game began. It was very muddy, and I was dreading the ball being passed to me, but inevitably James kicked the ball to me, and I managed to control it. I started to run but the pain in my chest really hurt and my breathing sounded like a sea lion with a sore throat. I tried really hard to run but I just couldn't, and the ball was taken off me by a member of the other team who immediately scored a goal. Everyone in my team turned on me as I had clearly let them down, no one had any idea of my tuberculosis and that I was having breathing exercises, because no-one had ever told them how bad my chest was. I struggled up to Mr Deacon and with a strained stammer shouted "P-please sir can I stop p-playing now?"

My breath was rasping like a lumberjack's saw and my chest was so bad that it was pushing me forward making my head hang down. "No, you cannot," he shouted and blew his whistle with a deafening scream.

I struggled back to my position by the goal post and stood there all but paralysed with the pain and a boy called Keith ran by me and kicked the ball into the net for a second time. I knew that I had totally let everyone down, and I needed to tell them that it was my breathing that had caused it, not me, but I didn't know how.

"D-David," taunted Mr Deacon, "what are you d-doing, can't you see the ball, it's the r-round thing made out of leather?"

At that point someone kicked the ball hard and it powered straight into my chest. In those days the ball was made out of very thick leather with ridges and stiches to hold it together and was heavy unlike it's modern counterpart today. With a thud it hit me, and I fell to the ground in pain screaming and flooded with tears. I struggled to my feet in time to take a further blow from another well position ball which knocked me down again. Despite the pain I realised that I was being attacked deliberately and struggled off the field to sit by a spectator. I think my team lost by five goals to zero; and I was dubbed as the reason for that embarrassing defeat. Mr Deacon glared at me in a manner befitting Len's reactions, which drained me of both energy and dignity for weeks after.

Mr Deacon then blew his whistle to end the game and everyone left the field, and we were all led into a large room with a yellow tiled wall and told to take off our clothes. My heart stopped as everyone stood naked in front of me, I didn't feel comfortable and my mind lost complete control whilst I trembled, and the tears flooded down my face.

Everyone lined up and the shower sprays started with a giant hiss, the command was given to slowly walk through whilst Mr Deacon scrutinised the gathering to make sure that everything went smoothly. By this time, I was shaking uncontrollably, and Mr Deacon advanced with an outstretched hand to push me into the shower. I cowered down as close to the floor as I could, but he managed to grab my arm and pulled me back up again. I could sense that he was angry, and he lashed out with his hand on my bare bottom which stung, but nowhere near the pain that Len could inflict.

"Get Up," Mr Deacon shouted, "and stop being silly."

Still shivering with everyone looking on I slowly stood up and he grabbed my neck and pushed me into the shower. It was hot but nowhere near the temperature I was used to, which came as a pleasant surprise as I had expected it to be much hotter. I walked through virtually alone, and Mr Deacon met me with a large white towel and wrapped it around my body. "Are you ok now?" he exclaimed.

I didn't answer as my mind was so full of unanswered questions and my chest was beginning to hurt again. I somehow knew that I would have to explain why I had acted as I had and sat down to try and prepare my head for what was to come. I dressed myself as quickly as I could, and we were all led back to the classroom. Mr Deacon singled me out and sat me in front of the class on a small chair.

"Tell me what that was all about please," he asked, momentarily forgetting to mock me.

"I I d-don't know," was the squeak that came out of my mouth.

"What d-don't you know, t-tell me?" he said, returning to his affected stammer, and I burst out crying again.

My stammer had yet again given rise to various chuckles in the class, but most were sitting in silence, trying to work out why I was forced to sit there.

"Go back to your desk and open your writing book and stop making trouble, as you are disrupting the rest of the children," he snarled.

I slid into my chair knowing that the smell would get stronger as I became closer to Peter. I had no idea why, but Peter was smelling extra strong even though he had just walked through the shower.

"Right," said Mr Deacon, "we are going to learn how to write our names," and he chanted a tune "ABCDEFG, HIJKLMNOP, QR, STU, VWXYZ," which we all had to remember and sing back to him.

By this time, I had calmed right down embroiled with the prospect of being able to write my name. Some of the children could already write as their parents had practiced with them in preparation for starting school. It became urgent for me to understand how to do it, and so I shut everything out but the task at hand, which I had long ago learned how to do. Even Peter's smell became invisible as I recited the letter tune over and over again. After a considerable time had elapsed Mr Deacon homed in on me. "Stand up D-David; sing me the letters of the alphabet"

I could see them in my head and each letter became a sunflower as I quickly ran through the field. I took a deep breath and sang… "ABCDEFG, HIJKLMNOP, QR, STU, VWXYZ," without even one stutter. "How did I do that?" I thought, both shocked and surprised and so I think was Mr Deacon.

The school bell signalled the day had finished and we all filed out of the classroom and passed through the towering gates. I stood by the bus-stop lost in my excitement of the alphabet tune which had totally infected my brain. The bus chugged up and I could hear the familiar bell dinging to bring it to a halt. One ding to go, and two to stop. I grabbed hold of the shiny pole and pulled myself on to the platform taking care to sit on the long seat as Margaret had insisted.

The conductor pulled the cord and off we went. I was still mesmerised with the alphabet song which by this time had become second nature to me. I have no idea how I missed the stop, but I suddenly saw Margaret waving as the bus went by. The conductor realised that it was my stop and pulled the cord to bring us to a sharp halt; and climbing off the seat he lifted me to the ground below.

Margaret was frantic, "What were you thinking, you naughty boy?" she shouted.

"I I was l-learning the alpha alphabet s-song," I tried to tell her, but my broken words did nothing to calm her.

"Let's get you home my boy. You wait until I tell your Father!" she snapped.

I could feel my face turn grey with the heat rising in my body. My eyes clouded over, and I began to scream along with a torrent of tears uncontrollably flooding down my face. Paul was clutching an ice lolly, too preoccupied to notice what was going on. I was screaming even louder, and Margaret was becoming more embarrassed by the moment as she shuffled by Mrs Peat's House and fumbled with the key to open the back door. "Stop it now, what's the matter with you!" she shouted.

I was so mixed up that I couldn't answer, and she ordered me up the stairs to my bedroom. The bedroom was not my favourite room as it was Len's chosen point of attack, it had become his battle arena in which he could isolate his actions from the rest of the house. I lay on the bed listening for his car, waiting for the sound of the front door opening and his booming voice. Suddenly I could hear him growling like a lion about to slay its prey as Margaret recited her story of what I had done on the bus.

"I told you!" I could hear him shout out, "we don't know where he came from. He's not ours, he's just a big mistake!"

I could almost feel the pain to come, as he thundered up the stairs. "Right! In your own words. What have you been up to?" he demanded.

I had no words to answer him, I had no idea what to say so I just kept quiet. He demanded that I removed my short grey trousers and my underwear, and then as hard as he could he landed a blow on my bottom that stung so much that I started to wet myself. "You dirty boy! Why don't you just go leave us, we don't want you," he snarled.

I ran to the toilet, but he put his foot out and I tripped and fell to the floor. I was so scared that I could smell poo and realised that I'd messed myself. By this time, I was frantic and completely out of control as Margaret came running up the stairs.

"What are you doing Len?" she snapped at him. "This isn't right he's only a little boy, he's petrified," she said as she scooped me up and took me to the bathroom to clean what had become a complete mess.

"We don't need him here. Just get rid of him, he's a mistake!" Len shouted after her.

CHAPTER FIVE

"Whatever words we utter should be chosen with care
for people will hear them and be influenced by them for good or ill."
... ***Buddha***

Following my so-called misdemeanour on the bus, I had been confined to my bedroom with a bread and jam sandwich and a cup of orange juice. I lay there listening to Len's words ringing in my ears; *We don't need him here. Just get rid of him, he's a mistake!*

For some strange reason, my mind was reciting the alphabet song, over and over again, as I remained keen to master it; but the other half of me was planning my escape. "I must leave, I'm a mistake, I'm dirty," I thought, as his words ran through my head. I'd been planning to escape for some time now, but this latest episode made it all the more urgent.

Over several weeks I had accumulated what seemed in my childish mind to be lots of food; enough to last a lifetime! It was all hidden under the stairs, as I had spent considerable time incarcerated for my bad behaviour over the last few weeks. “I must to go, I have leave, I need to escape,” I thought to myself, but I needed something to carry my food in. This presented a big problem, for in my mind I was leaving forever, and I had no bag that was easy to carry on my journey.

Glancing down I saw Geoffrey had left a large round tin full of a big jigsaw. The tin had a soldier on it with a tall black hat that I had attempted to draw many times in the past. I couldn’t read what it said yet, but now as I recall it, I realise it was a very big Quality Street tin once full of brightly coloured toffees and chocolates, as Geoffrey loved sweets. I tipped all the pieces out into the shoe box that had contained my new school shoes, as I didn’t want to lose any of them. That was the one and only thing that ever made Geoffrey mad; arriving at the end of a jigsaw to find some pieces missing. I completely understood why, as to him he could never finish the puzzle and therefore could never know what the finished picture was actually like.

I planned my escape with military precision; I would wait until Len was asleep and silently creep down the stairs, fill the tin up with the food hidden under the stairs and make my escape through the back door; unlocking it with the key that was always hung on a hook beside it. It was going to be difficult as Paul slept in the bed next to me, and if he started crying, I would be dead in seconds. I patiently waited whilst they brought Paul up the stairs and tucked him in for the night. Margaret came over and muttered something that sounded like *sorry*, but I was hiding under the sheets, so I couldn’t hear properly.

“Come on it’s late, I’m tired!” I heard Len say, and the whole house shook as they prepared themselves for sleep. The toilet seemed to take hours to stop shouting like a waterfall, and the doors opened and closed as if the house was being invaded by aliens, but eventually the light switch clicked, and silence calmed the house. I knew that I could only move when I could hear Len snoring, as he always did, and was sure Margaret would not hear anything as she was well away from the door very near the furthest window. I waited patiently and tested my escape route by dropping my shoe on the floor; no one stirred not a sound. I was clear to move, there was no need to dress as I'd hidden under the sheets fully clothed hoping no-one would notice, and thankfully they hadn't. Carefully moving my legs to the edge of the bed, the springs creaked but still no one stirred not even Paul, as I slipped out of bed holding my shoes in my hand. I couldn't put them on yet as they would make a noise as I descended the staircase. Grabbing the empty tin, I turned the doorknob slowly and edged open the door with my heart thumping as if it was trying to escape from my chest. I started to sweat with anxiety as I pushed the door, knowing what would happen if Len woke up. After what seemed an age it opened fully, and I made my way to the top of the stairs, which were lit up that night by a full moon which seemed to be staring at me as I nervously placed my foot on the first tread. I knew how many steps there were as I had practised counting them many times with Margaret; twenty-three in all which included the rest bit in the middle. My mind was ringing with fear, 13, 14, 15, my heart was beating so loud I was sure they might be able to hear it. 16, 17, 18, I began to feel that I would never reach the bottom but clenched my teeth and carried on. 23, I was there and still no one had woken.

I tip-toed along the hall amazed at how bright the moon was as it shone through the window illuminating my passage to freedom. Suddenly the cupboard was in front of me and I carefully turned the brass slide to open the door. Putting my shoes down I quietly opened the tin before I slid into the pitch-black cupboard which I could navigate with my eyes closed. I could feel my escape food at the furthest point of the cupboard and was ready for my mental inventory to take place as I had often selected items in the dark, placing them in meticulous order for that reason. Three Wagon Wheels, two Mars bars, three packets of crisps, a packet of chocolate biscuits, two bottles of Tizer, three Kit-Kats and twenty sweets I had stolen from the box at

Christmas. I carefully placed the lid onto the rim and pressed it down, it clicked into place perfectly and I was ready to make my final escape.

Sliding backwards and sitting down with the moon light beaming through the window, I tied my laces as I had been taught; right over left make a loop and pull; I was ready. Cautiously I made my way to the door where I could see the latch key hanging limply on the hook and luckily it was positioned at my height and easily plucked. I inserted it into the lock and twisted it; a task that seemed to require immense strength to perform. I opened the door, unhooking my coat from the door peg as I did so, and stepped outside feeling very pleased with my efforts. I was free.

Clutching my life-saving tin, I opened the front gate and entered the big world and my uncertain journey. Hastily running down the road (or what approximated to running) I cut through the hedge to the main road as I had done many times before with Margaret. The streetlights had painted the roads with an orange and yellow hue which glistened in the moist air. We lived in Harrowgate Drive, Birstall and I had travelled down the main road many times in the past, so I knew exactly where I was going. Thinking back, it was quite a feat to have stored all the required knowledge for my escape; so I couldn't have been that stupid, could I? My mind was focused on freedom and I wasn't at all scared, but I was aware that a six-year-old child could well be picked up and so I chose the shaded paths all the time. Eventfully I reached the town which had taken what I perceived to be *days* to achieve and made my way to the London Road; which again I knew as it was where the dentist was. Something drew me to Victoria Park as I had spent some time with Geoffrey playing cricket, or perhaps it would be more accurate to say, trying to play, as he wasn't very good at it and I couldn't run! I could remember all the landmarks even though they were lit only by moonlight and finally found my way to the park where I sat down on a bench to rest.

The bench was back to back with another bench and I hadn't noticed a man sleeping on the other side, who suddenly emerged as if by magic. His clothes were very dirty, and he had a really long beard, but I didn't notice that he had been sleeping under newspaper and cardboard to keep him warm.

"Hello little boy what are you doing out so late?" he asked, not unkindly.

"I I'm just r-resting," I squeaked

"Where are you going?"

"H-home but I'm l-lost," I lied.

"What have you got in your tin?"

"My f-f-ood for the j-journey," I replied, without a thought to what I was saying.

"Can I see?" he asked, and I innocently opened the tin to show him what I had.

"Mmm that looks nice," he said, "I haven't eaten for ages can I share some with you?" I was scared to say yes, and equally scared to say no, so I just kept very quiet.

"Oh, go on don't be greedy!" the man exclaimed as his eyes bulged in his head drooling at the contents of my box.

My mind started to race, it was supposed to keep me going forever, the food in my box should have lasted for the rest of my life and here I was thinking about sharing it with him, as he did look very hungry. I paused and before I could say another word, he offered me some cardboard to sleep under which I thought was kind of him, as he obviously needed it to keep himself warm. In a blinding flash I offered him a biscuit and he gobbled it up so quickly it vanished as if he had performed a magic trick. He immediately seized my tin and consumed everything but a Mars Bar and a bottle of Tizer.

"There you are. I've saved you some!" he said, grinning as he handed me back the tin.

I was mortified; "How would I live without food, what would I do, where would I go?" I thought, and in my panic, I started to run up the road for some reason. I knew exactly where I was as Len had taken Margaret to Oadby several times, and I ran and ran as fast as the pain in my chest would allow, until my feet couldn't run anymore, and my lungs were bursting from the exertion. To my left there was a big gate that led to a farm building, and I instinctively opened it and staggered down the bumpy road. At the end there was a large sliding door with a smaller one built into it that was open, so I climbed through it to find mountains of egg cartons; the ones that held thirty eggs at a time. They were big, and I'd used something similar at school to make a playhouse, which is probably what made me decide to build a small shelter. I piled them together and climbed into the structure totally exhausted and was asleep within seconds.

I was woken suddenly by a loud *Cock-a-doodle-Doo*, right next to me. I opened my eyes to find a big bird staring at me with yellowy brown eyes and I could see he wasn't happy, as I'd invaded his home. Slightly intimidated I tried to shoo him away, as he looked as if he was ready for a fight, when at that moment a tall man slid back the door and walked over to me. "What are you doing hear my boy?" he shouted, "this is private property.

"I I'm l-lost," I managed to answer in my broken vocabulary.

"Where do you live?" he asked softly; then before I could say anything, he scooped me up and carried me along a bumpy road to his house. "Look what I've found Irene! He was sleeping in the barn," he said to his wife.

She smiled with a warmth that I'd never seen before and she picked me up. "My you are a big boy. What's your name?" she said in a soft kind voice, placing a comforting arm around me.

"D-David," I stammered.

"And where do you live?" she asked.

"H-Harrowgate Drive, B-Birstall," I answered, the words jumping out of my mouth by complete accident, and I immediately realised what I'd done.

"Where did you say?" she asked again, and I started to cry. The tears flowed down my face, but I said nothing more.

"Harrowgate Drive," she continued, "that's in Birstall isn't it? How did you get here?"

I didn't answer as my mind could think only of the terror of Len finding me, as I knew that by now Margaret would be panicking and calling the police. Irene sat me down and asked if I would like a drink and something to eat and by impulse I uttered "Y-yes p-please," and she set about cooking some breakfast.

"I I can't eat m-meat," I stuttered.

"No problem," she said with a smile, "do you eat eggs?"

"Y-yes th-thank you," I replied, and she carried on cooking.

I was starting to relax, in the warmth and kindness of the farm kitchen and looking up at her I asked, "C-can I stay here p-please?"

"Why would you want to do?" she asked, and not knowing how to answer, I kept quiet again. "I bet your mother will be very worried about you," she said.

Again, I kept silent and said nothing until she calmly came over to me and I started to cry again. "What's the matter, what's happened?"

she said with a kindness I had never experienced. “Why are you so scared, little one?” she asked me, but I couldn’t say anything as I was tongue tied and afraid.

It took a while, but she made a really nice breakfast, and sat by me whilst I consumed it. She tried again to coax some information from me, “Tell me what’s happened?” she said again, “why are you so sad?”

I looked up at her with tired eyes and a tear ran down my cheek, she smiled back at me and then turned to look away, trying to hide the one that was rolling down her own.

“Let’s see if we can help you, what do you think? Is that ok?” she asked.

Her husband had already rung the police and they arrived almost at the second she said she was going to help me. To my horror Len climbed out of the police car and two police officers followed after.

“I’m so sorry!” Len exclaimed. “He ran away last night, and we’ve been so worried about him. He’s adopted and he’s finding it very difficult to settle in with his new family,” he said, forgetting to tell them that I’d been with him since I was six weeks old.

I didn’t realise at the time, that anyone who had adopted a child was held in reverence, deemed to be upstanding members of society because they had been passed by the system that had held the country together. Len was smiling at me and came over making caring gestures, which to be honest scared me and I started to shake.

“You never know how an adopted child will turn out do you?” he declared as he looked around the room.

Irene looked at him and said, “Only if you adopt when they’re babies,” and I think she’d felt the truth even before he opened the door of the police car?

"Well thank you for your help," Len gushed, "I'll take him home now. Sorry to have caused you so much trouble." He was like a chameleon changing to suit the surroundings.

I was bundled into the police car and Len sat next to me with a very tight grip on my arm. Every time the police asked me a question, he tightened his grip in a silent signal which said, *don't you dare say anything*!

The police needed to report what had happened and I could see Len was determined to camouflage the truth. Looking up at his drawn angry face I could see that my worst fears were inevitable, and as every inch drew us nearer the house, I began to get more and more frightened.

One of the policeman turned around and asked, "Why did you run away from home, sonny?" and as I opened my mouth to answer, I could feel Len's grip tightening.

"I I d-don't know," I stuttered, and tears started to roll down my face again as the pain in my arm from Len's grip only added to my torment.

"How did you get to the farmhouse; its miles away?" was the next question, then, "did someone take you?"

"No, I w-walked," I managed to reply.

"What! All the way?" he said in amazement.

"Y-yes," I again stammered as Len clamped his hand around me even tighter. The policeman jotted down some notes and then turned his questions on Len.

"What time did you realise the lad was missing?" he asked him.

"I don't remember exactly, but it was around ten last night."

"Then why didn't you report it until seven this morning?" he said incredulously.

"Well! My wife and I walked the streets for some time thinking that he couldn't be far away," Len mumbled. "We were so worried that we spent longer than intended. But we called you as soon as we arrived back at the house."

"What did you do with your other son?" enquired the policeman.

"We called our next-door neighbour to keep an eye out while we searched for him," came the reply, and I knew he was lying because the house was in complete darkness when I escaped.

By this time, he was really hurting my arm.

"Ah you're h-hurting m-me," I screamed.

"S-stop h-hurting me," and the policeman looked around again, glancing suspiciously at Len.

"No I'm not! Stop telling lies!" barked Len. Then turning to the policeman, he whispered, "he's not my real son, he's adopted. You can never tell how they'll turn out can you?"

The policeman glared at Len and closed his book. "We'll have to make out a full report and will need to visit you to collect statements of *fact,*" he said, emphasising the word fact, "when would it be convenient."

"I'm at work for the rest of the day, so can you make it around six-thirty tonight?" said Len, and the policeman said they would.

All too quickly we drew up outside the house and as soon as the click sounded to release the door lock, Len opened it and literally threw me out of the car onto the pavement. "Thank you for your assistance," he said to the Policeman and he dragged me through the gates and into the house. Margaret was waiting in tears, "Where have you been?" she whimpered. "Why did you run away from home?"

"He s-said he w-wanted me to l-leave," I stammered.

"But he didn't mean it," she squeaked, as Len who was by now in a familiar rage, snapped, "I did no such thing!"

"You d-did you d-did," I managed to say, before he landed a heavy blow to my head which knocked me over and I fell to the floor.

"Get off him!" Margaret screamed; but Len didn't listen and dragged me into the lounge. "How dare you cause so much trouble," he snarled, and crashed another blow on my leg with frighteningly painful accuracy, and I started to scream. Len saw red and pulled me by the arms to haul me onto the settee, as Margaret not far behind him screamed, "Leave him alone!" but again Len was so mad that he just kept going.

"You did demand that he left home. Didn't you?" exclaimed Margaret trying to stand in front of me.

"Not you as well!" he snapped and pushed Margaret out of the way to get at me. He was acting very strange and it scared me as I'd never seen him quite so mad before. The hot teaspoons and scalding flannels, even being pushed down the stairs, were nothing compared to this and for some strange reason I began to feel guilty.

"I I'm s-sorry," I shouted out through the torrents of tears and mucus that had gathered under my nose. He picked me up and hurled me over the settee and I bounced on the carpet narrowly missing the hard wall.

"Leave him alone!" screamed Margaret again, "he's just a little boy. Stop this!"

I'd been thrown over the settee so many times in the past, that I'd learned how to make myself limp in order to counter his numerous attacks, but this was the first time that Margaret had witnessed the full force of his rage. Then, as if the wind had changed direction, Len changed, his anger tempered, and his face reverted back to a more tolerable semi-smile.

Margaret scooped me up and removed my shirt to discover that I was covered in bruises, both old and new. In one place my skin had blistered, and blood covered the wound, and she examined my leg to study a long black bruise beginning for form.

"How are we going to explain this at school?" she asked, "what have you done?"

"If he hadn't run away none of this would have happened," Len barked back at her.

She glared at him and I could sense a change in her opinion of him as she wound bandages around my arms and leg. "He can't go to school like this!" she said with a slight panic in her voice.

"Just tell them he fell down the stairs," said Len.

"Yes! He's often fallen down the stairs, hasn't he?" Margaret replied as realisation, disbelief and disgust dawn on. I watched as a range of expressions crossed her face and I began to realise she was trapped in no-man's land. On the one hand she was totally dependent upon Len as the bread winner, but now on the other hand she had been clearly alerted to and disgusted by what she'd just witnessed. His actions were beyond her comprehension. "I must go and fetch Paul from next door," she said, "so leave him alone and just go to work. Please!"

"This isn't my fault," growled Len as he put on his coat, and as he left the house my body instantly relaxed. The heat drained from by head, and my heart stopped thumping, the action of which had camouflaged the pain in my arms, and as the rhythm was restored I began to wince with pain that brought tears to my eyes once again.

Margaret returned with Paul, and I asked, "C-can I go to school p-please?"

"No I'm sorry you can't. Not until your bruises have gone away," she replied.

"B-but that w-will take ages," I pleaded, "I r-really want to d-do my ABC song."

"We'll see," she said, "let's try and get back to some sort of normality," and she took me upstairs to bed and tried to make me comfortable. I closed my eyes feeling suddenly very tired, but the pain prevented me from sleeping. Then I remembered the ABC song, "ABCDEFG, HIJKLMNOP, QR, STU, VWXYZ," I sang to Margaret, which seemed to take the pain away; and I wondered how Peter was doing without me.

Chapter Six

"Everyone has a photographic memory,
some just don't have the film"
... Steven Wright

Margaret informed the school that I'd fallen down the stairs, and everyone seemed to believe her, and although what she'd said was a cover up for Len, I never ever uttered a word against her. After that, I went to school every day and hid under a cloak of learning where I felt safe from the never-ending punishment that Len dished out on a daily basis.

I moved up from Mr Deacon's class to Mrs Scupholme's class, and on one occasion I can clearly remember writing a story that everyone considered very good. Mrs Scupholme pinned it on the wall and awarded five stars to me. At the end of the term I proudly returned home with my cardboard folder and presented it to Margaret, upon which, Len got hold of it and destroyed everything. On another occasion, I had spent hours carving out a plaster of Paris horse picture, which again was given a place on the wall with four stars; I wanted to give it to Margaret as a present, but Len declared it rubbish and smashed it into pieces.

My stuttering became worse, much worse as Len attacked me with ever-changing methods. Some began to be abusive and he always declared on each occasion *Now look what you've made me do!* usually after he'd insisted on washing me and stuck his finger up my bottom.

This book would be full up with his conduct and spiteful instincts, and the entire subject would become boring and needless. But over a five-year period, I drowned myself in schoolwork and books, expanding my knowledge and attaining very good grades.

I was almost eleven years old, and Mrs Scupholme had been preparing me for the 11-plus examinations, as she had taken me under her wing, trying I think to assist my speech impediment along the way? She was sometimes mesmerised with my intensity and dedication to work, and I think she fully understood that I had a funny brain that had adapted itself to survive under a dark cloak of learning. By this time, I had read dozens of books which made up hours of homework, but I don't think she had noticed my ability to write down almost word for word the contents of each book; just by reading it several times. I thought that my capabilities were perfectly normal.

The class were set to take what she called the 11-plus exam and she had given me a list of books to read, outlining the major areas that she expected to appear in the examination. I was transfixed with the prospects of passing the exam, and hid myself away in my bedroom, constantly reading and recording notes from the information that Mrs Scupholme had passed on to me. The closer I came to the examination day the more excited I was, even though Len did everything in his power to try and disrupt my efforts. Despite which, I was learning to be able to block him out, dry my tears and simply carried on.

I remember it was a Friday, and the following Monday was set to be exam day. That afternoon at school, everyone had been fretting and shivering with fear, all except for me. I don't think many had done their homework and they knew there was no more time to try and catch up. I on the other hand glowed like a light in a very dark room, which dislodged me still further the rest of the class, all except for Peter who had turned out to be a smelly but rather clever little boy.

I walked out of school with Paul who was in the class below me with Mr Deacon, and the smile on my face seemed to disturb him as he asked, "Are you okay?" I knew that I had carved a full understanding of what I had to do, and I had made up markers in my head to remember the pages in the books and walked along reciting them as the bus pulled up and I climbed aboard.

"Good evening David," called out the conductor; who by this time had clearly grown fond of me. He used to save sweets up and hand me one from time to time when no one was looking. "How are you this afternoon?" he asked me.

I looked at him and stammered, I I'm f-fine Frank, exams on M-Monday so I I'm a bit n-nervous." I wasn't nervous at all really, but for some reason I wanted to pretend that I was the same as everyone else.

"Don't worry my lad," replied Frank, "You'll be fine." Over the years Frank had listened to me in various states of mind, and I think he had a pretty good idea of what my home life was like. The bus set off and totally mesmerised with the unknown exams on Monday I recited what I'd read over and over again in my head. Everything that Mrs Scupholme had told me was emblazoned in my mind, and I became anxious that I might forget some part of it, and all would be lost. I was somehow comforted by the fact that Len couldn't break what was inside my head, and I'd developed a way of making him think that I was worried about the exams; which seemed to please him, as my failure would be his triumph.

Margaret as usual was waiting at the bus stop to walk us home and I could see her waving as we filed off the bus, and Paul greeted her with euphoric smiles. I on the other had was still embroiled in Monday's exam and with a serious face carried on repeating the pages in the books over and over again. I was so involved that I tripped and fell down the kerb as we crossed the road.

"Be careful," Margaret burst out with a semi shriek as I picked myself up and brushed the gravel from my jacket sleeves.

My leg was grazed but it didn't seem to matter as I continued to recite the pages in my head. We all arrived at the gate and Margaret opened it slowly, as the over tight spring tended to fight back and force it closed again. Not paying attention to the gate spring, I walked through still mesmerised with the pages I was reciting, and it flung back and slammed into my face with an almighty thud. Blood immediately began to pour from my nose, and I let out a scream which deafened the silence, and my efforts were thwarted as I fell to the floor in pain. Margaret pulled me up, producing a white handkerchief to catch the blood as she did so. "What on earth's wrong with you, are you drunk?" she shouted.

By this time, I was frantic as the tears mixed with blood from my nose dripped aimlessly onto what was once a clean white shirt. My eyes were streaming, and my nose was beginning to swell, but for some strange reason I was still going through the pages in my head; although by now they were becoming clouded by the pain from the gate's attack.

I felt disappointed and inwardly panicked that I would fail the exams on Monday, and that Len would delight in calling me stupid; demanding that I should be more like Paul. We made our way into the house through the back door and Margaret helped me up to sit on the draining board, where she started to bathe my nose, which by this time was becoming black and very swollen. "What a mess!" she said. "Why don't you be more careful?"

I looked at her intensely. “I’m s-sorry,” I said, the reply creeping out of my mouth, and I was a little surprised that the pain had eased my speech impediment.

Len appeared at the back door and glanced at me, immediately misreading the situation.

“What’s he been up to now?

“I hope you hit him hard?” he said with glee.

“By the looks of things, you did a good job. Why’s he always causing trouble?”

“It was that stupid spring on the gate that I asked you to fix weeks ago!” she snapped.

“Oh I see! It’s my fault is it?” he said, and he fell into his usual tirade of insults and embedded wishes to get rid of me again. After a string of insults he suddenly said, “Oh my God! I shouldn’t say that should I? He might run away and never come back!” sarcastically referring to my failed attempt to run away before.

“Wasn’t the last time good enough for you? It wasn’t his fault this time, it was an accident,” said Margaret in my defence. Even Paul spoke up and declared, “It was an accident Daddy, it really was,” but Len preferred to ignore his comments.

“Get him up the stairs out of my sight!” he snapped, and Margaret guided me up the stairs whispering softly, “I’m so sorry you don’t deserve this.”

My nose was really throbbing, and it became difficult to breath, and my mouth hung open gasping for air which made it very dry. “P-please may I have a drink?” I called out to Margaret, who by this time had gone downstairs. Len caught the request and thundered up the stairs, shouting “She’s not your servant you selfish little bastard, go and get it yourself!”

The word bastard became commonplace against me, yet at the time I had no idea what it meant; later to realise that Len intended to drown me in a tirade of insults designed to strengthen his case against me. Over the coming months he would sharpen his wit to make use of the fact that I was indeed illegitimate and do everything in his power to use my shady heritage against me. I spent the entire weekend in my bedroom, and I could hear Paul playing in the garden giggling and running around paying tennis with Len. I was not at all concerned though, as I much preferred the bedroom to the darkness of the cupboard under the stairs; where it would have been impossible to read my scrawled notes and scan thought the books that I knew were important.

Mrs Scupholme had told me that if I wanted to go to a *grammar*, I would need to work very quickly and accurately on each question; as I would only have a set time, which was in her view not long enough. I was so keen to prove that I could do it, and a part of me was hoping that Len might one day be proud of me.

Monday came, it was six thirty in the morning and I was ready for school; the plaster on my nose was still perfectly in place, and my nose though somewhat numb didn't hurt too much. "It's very early," Margaret called out, "what are you doing up at this time?"

I dared not answer as I knew Len would do everything in his power to make things difficult if he understood how important the exam was to me. I was sure that he didn't even know I was to take part in it; which was a huge plus, unless Margaret said something, but I almost knew she would keep it a secret. I sat down at the table with my customary bowl of cornflakes, which although no longer at eye level, I was still nevertheless careful not to make any mess. Shaking I picked up a cup of tea that Margaret had prepared in a blue melamine cup, fearful that Len might launch an attack from the side with a hot spoon. He sat stirring his tea menacingly and although it no longer hurt as much as it had when I was younger, if he caught me in an unguarded moment I might cry out in surprise. Ever vigilant, I hid my hands out of sight underneath the table, but this day however he abandon his assault in favour of grumbling about the plaster on my nose. "Don't you get saying I did that will you?" he growled at me.

"No, I w-won't. You w-weren't even their w-when it h-happened," I replied.

"Yes, that's right! We don't want any lies though. So, remember what I'm saying to you," he said.

And with that he rose from the table to put on his jacket, then he opened the door and was gone. My relief was immediate as the tension drained from me and the sunlight came back into the day again. Margaret smiled and calmly said that it was nearly time to go. I put on my school jacket, slipped my satchel over my shoulder, straightened my tie and opened the door. Paul was nowhere near as keen to move and made it quite clear that he wasn't looking forward to his day, but Margaret hurried him from the table, and we were on our way to the bus stop. I stood there mesmerised with the prospects of the exam and started frantically repeating line after line in my mind.

Where the time went was a mystery to me, as I missed the journey completely and eventually found myself in the exam room with each desk carefully spaced to stop anyone from copying. Mr Deacon, and Mrs Scupholme were walking up and down the spaces between the desks as we all sat there nervously waiting. Mr Deacon produced a big domed clock that was cream with a red dial, and very large numbers on it that could be seen from the back of the class. He had Mrs Scupholme carefully place the papers upside down on each desk and instructed us all not to turn them over until the signal was given. We had all been searched to make sure that we weren't cheating and given two sharp pencils each. I wanted to use my own, but I wasn't allowed.

Mr Deacon like a sergeant major stood up straight and announced, "Class! You may turn over your papers and start. NOW!" I picked up my pencil and turned over the paper, relieved to see that I already recognised some of the questions; also knowing that I was able to answer them properly. Tick, tick, tick, went the clock and the time dripped away. I could see the answers in my head when I closed my eyes and I wrote them carefully word for word on the paper. Tick, tick, tick, I was writing as quickly as possible, fearful that the time would run out before I had finished. I carefully went through each question again and realised that I had completed all of the paper. I was so pleased that I put my hand up to tell Mr Deacon that I had finished.

"B-be quiet D-David," demanded Mr Deacon never missing a chance to mimic my speech problem, which by now was considered perfectly normal to the class. I shrivelled up like a tortoise hiding in its shell. "Check your answers," he boomed. So, I pretended to check them although I was confident that the answers were all correct. After what seemed to be a lifetime, Mr Deacon in true military style announced that everyone should stop writing, and the room shivered as the click of pencils found their resting place in the grooves cut into the desks. The papers were collected, and we were all released into the playground for our customary small bottle of milk, and to play various games which I could only watch fearing breathing problems and unwanted attention.

It was almost a week later that I was called into the Headmistress's Office, and Mr Deacon and Mrs Scupholme were already sitting down when I arrived. Mr Deacon rose from his chair and looked straight into my face, demanding to know why I had been cheating. I stuttered to try and answer, but no words came out.

"How did you smuggle notes into the exam room?" he demanded. "Your answers are word for word the same as those in the books!"

I was puzzled and started to shiver with fright. "Speak up!" cried Mr Deacon, "answer me." But I just couldn't find any words, so I simply said nothing.

"You're obviously guilty, so you'll have to take the examination again," he said in response to my silence, and he marched me off to a room with only one desk in it. "Take of your clothes," he demanded; and my mind recorded fear as I unbuttoned my shirt and slipped down my trousers. I was just about to remove my underwear when he shouted, "That's enough, sit down, NOW!" I sat down, before which he searched me for hidden papers although where he expected to find anything still confuses me to this day.

"Right D-David," he smirked, reverting back to his fun. "Here is the exam paper, again, and two pencils. I'm going to start the clock and you will do the paper again."

I was so mixed up and totally confused that I started to weep. "Don't start that you b-baby," he snarled, and I set about the task at hand, feeling angry at what had happened, and still not really knowing why. I turned over the paper and my mind became focused as I shut out any exterior distractions. I had learned to hide in my work and that's just what I did then.

After what seemed to be a lifetime, the clock rang, "That's it!" declared Mr Deacon as he snatched the paper up to slip it into a cardboard folder, protecting it for its onward journey. I was allowed to put my shirt and trousers back on, and to be honest, sitting there without them hadn't cause me too much of a problem, as it was very hot and taking them off had assisted me to work more comfortably.

"Come with me," he said, marching me back to sit me down with the rest of my class, which was strange as Mrs Scupholme was my teacher. I was becoming concerned as he appeared to be very involved in accusing me of cheating and my worries became real when he told me to stand up as he addressed the class. "This is a cheat!" he said pointing at me, "which isn't fair to any of you."

"Cheats are dishonest liars, and they are not to be trusted," he carried on, and everyone apart from Peter started to giggle. I stood there frozen on the spot, shivering in what had become a huge marker in my passage through life. I had no idea what I'd done and had even less idea that I was able to remember things graphically in my brain, allowing me to record what I'd read word for word. I now know it to be a photographic memory.

The bell went, and I filed out of the door to make my way to the bus. Paul was waiting for me and I burst into tears, so much so, that even he appeared concerned as I had not mentioned or dared to mention what had happened. I knew that if Len ever got to hear about it I would be attacked from every angle, as it was precisely the ammunition he needed to affirm both my heritage and my character.

Several weeks later I was called in to the Head Mistress's office again and this time only Mrs Scupholme was sat there. "Hello David; how are you today," she said.

"I I'm fine th-thank you," I stammered, not quite sure why I had been called in.

"You like reading, don't you?" she said to me.

"Y-yes I d-do," I replied.

"What is your favourite book David?" she asked, and after a moments pause, I replied, "I l-like th-them all."

"What about this one?" she enquired showing me a book which I recognised immediately; it was The Little Drummer Boy. I knew the story about three Kings that had travelled to Bethlehem to bring gifts for the new-born baby Jesus, and that the little drummer boy came along as well. The little drummer boy was too poor to bring a present fit for the king, so instead, he played a song on his drum for the Jesus.

"Can you read this page for me?" she asked opening the book for me to read. By this time, I was beginning to relax as I knew the book, and even now I can recall that she opened the book at page twenty-seven. "Read it to me please," she said.

I began to read to her without a single stutter which always made me feel good, although I had no idea what was coming next. She then asked me to put the book down and write down what I had read. Thinking it was all perfectly normal I closed my eyes and wrote down each word, one by one, without even missing the punctuation marks. It didn't take very long as I had read the book many times before, and I handed the paper back for their scrutiny still not understanding what it was all about.

Mrs Scupholme read it out and compared my words to the words in the book. "I can see why we thought you'd been cheating," she said. "But you weren't, were you?"

"N-no" I said as my stammer returned, "b-but it d-doesn't m-matter. Did I p-pass the exam m-miss? I asked.

"Yes you did David, with good marks as well," she said kindly.

"Oh g-good," I exclaimed beaming all over my face. "W-what sc-school will I be g-going to?" She didn't answer but said they would be talking to my parents about a placement and handed me a paper in a large brown envelope, which I clung on to as if it was made of gold.

"David how long have you been able to remember words like this?" she asked me.

"F-for a long t-time Miss," I said.

"Can you remember numbers as well?" she asked.

"Y-yes I c-can," I replied; by which time I was feeling very important. So I asked them to write down some numbers and I would repeat them on paper without looking at them. Mrs Scupholme wrote down at least twenty-four random numbers and showed them to me. I looked at them and declared that I didn't need any more time to write them down. She handed me a writing book and I wrote each number down with ease, as I had played this game many times with myself whilst confined to my bedroom.

Mrs Scupholme smiled, “Well! You are a very gifted boy aren’t you!” she declared.

Her words bathed me in happiness, as all I had ever wanted was to be accepted as me. It wasn’t until that day that I began to realise who *me* really was. The bell rang, and I left the office to join my class who were already filing down the corridor. I was clutching my envelope with total pride and excitement at the prospect of handing it to Margaret; silent to the tirade of questions that were being fired at me.

As usual Paul stood there waiting for me, he had an air of expectancy as he’d heard that I’d been called in to the head’s office and quizzed me as to what it was all about. I said nothing and slipped away into my own personal success, which to me was only valuable if uncontaminated by adverse reactions. We boarded the bus for the journey home and as usual Margaret was waving as we drew up at the bus stop, we both rose and slid down the pole to land on the pavement with perfect precision. “Well did you both have a good day?” she enquired.

Unable to control himself Paul announced that I had been summoned to the headmistress’s office, but that I’d refused to tell him what for. “Well! Is that true David?” she said, sounding more than a little cross. “Y-yes,” I stammered.

“Well! What for?” she asked, but I didn’t want to tell her, so I pretended to stammer really badly as I didn’t want Len to find out. “Please tell me,” she said, “have you been in trouble again?” and I could hear weariness tinged with dread in her voice.

“N-no,” I replied.

“Then what was it?” she continued, intent on prying the information out of me. I had no idea how to explain what had happened and so I gave in and handed her the envelope.

“What’s this?” she asked.

I blurted out, “I p-passed th-the exam,” the answer shuddering uneasily from my mouth.

Paul’s demeanour changed immediately as in his mind I wasn’t supposed to be clever, “No you didn’t,” he declared. “He’s lying isn’t he mummy?” She slid open the envelope and quickly read the contents, and Paul being unable to wait a moment longer, tugged at her sleeve asking, “Well! What does it say mummy?”

“It says David’s passed his exam!” exclaimed Margaret.

“Oh!” sighed Paul with a dark frown on his face and he began sliding his feet along the loose gravel to make a scraping sound that always prompted attention from Margaret. I just knew that he couldn’t wait to tell Len, and that it would create huge problems which I desperately wanted to avoid. So I snatched the envelope from Margaret and held it tightly all the way home.

Sure enough as soon as Len appeared, Paul spouted out as predicted, that I had passed my exams and had hid the paper. “Where is it?” boomed Len.

I had hidden it under the stairs in my under-cupboard sweet store but didn’t want to tell him; Len glared at me and demanded to see the paper. Margaret looked confused as I could see she was wondering why I wasn’t proud of what I’d achieved. “He’s passed his exams with high marks Len,” she said.

“Oh! He’s been cheating again has he. Have you seen the paper?” he asked her, obviously thinking that if she hadn’t seen the paper then it must be a lie.

“Yes, but he’s hidden it away somewhere,” she said.

Len sharpened up his eyes and glared at me, “Where is it? Show me now,” he demanded, “go and get it or there will be trouble.”

I shivered with fear and without uttering a word, I crept out into the hallway and quietly slid into the stair cupboard, so they wouldn't know where I had hidden it. I was keen to guard my food supply which had accumulated considerably over several months and it was important that they didn't know my hiding place. I collected the envelope and hurried out into the open air and without a word I handed it to Len, shaking as I did so. He slid the paper out to read it. "This must be wrong!" he snapped, "have you been cheating again?"

I was so scared that I couldn't find any words to answer him, knowing that he was going to do something dreadful. I was right and watched as he predictably tore the paper into several pieces exclaiming that it couldn't be correct and that I must have been cheating.

Margaret looked on in disbelief, "Why did you do that Len? How could you be so cruel?" she said.

Len snapped back that it wasn't possible for a stupid idiot to get such high marks and I must have cheated. He glared at me again and I could see that he was about to explode; but before I could react, he grabbed me by the arm and landed the first blow to my head which felt like a brick. I fell to the floor and he kicked me hard; his anger consuming him as he did so. He was so out of control that he did it in front of Margaret which was something he didn't normally do. Margaret tried to drag him off but on seeing how dangerous it was she retreated.

"You cheating little bastard!" he shouted and continued to grab my leg. I kicked out and landed my foot to his leg, tripping him as I did so. "Did you see that? He's kicked me!" he shouted as he landed another blow to my body.

I began to feel dazed and totally resented the situation I had been forced into. It was all beyond my understanding, I had no idea what I'd done wrong or why he was hurting me. Something snapped inside me and I grabbed a long fire poker that was propped up against the wall. He backed off almost immediately and bellowed out, "He's going to attack me!"

I stood their poised to lash out with the poker when he dived for the telephone and dialled 999. "Hello, is that the police?" he whimpered with a completely prepared voice.

I was shaking with rage and advanced towards him. "I'm being attacked!" he called out down the telephone line. "Please! Come quickly," he bleated, and hurriedly gave out his name and address.

Putting the phone down he turned to me, "Right that's it! You've done it now. They're on their way," he said menacingly, his face twisting with every word.

I was strangely relieved that the police were being involved; believing that they would fully understand what had happened. I glanced out of the window as a white police car pulled up outside and two police officers climbed out; one of them a woman. The doorbell rang, and Len opened the door to land a tirade of frantic meaningless words at both of them.

"Calm down sir what's been going on?" said the policewoman; and getting no answer she looked across at Margaret, who was understandably speechless having difficulty getting to grips with the situation.

"Right sir, what is the problem?" the policewoman asked again, turning back to Len.

"He attacked me!" said Len.

"Who attacked you sir?" the policewoman asked.

"Him," said Len, pointing to me, and by now I was covered in red marks and several bruises.

"Who's he?" asked the policeman, who could see that his fellow officer was getting nowhere. Len posed and painfully admitted that I was his adopted son.

"What's his name?" asked the officer.

"David," replied Len as if controlled by an autocue.

The policeman turned to me and asked, "How old are you David?"

I stared at him still gripping the poker, "Eleven s-sir," I stammered.

"What's been going on David?"

"I I d-don't know," I said, uncomfortably, as I really didn't know what had caused any of it. I looked over at Margaret for support, but she was still shaking, and now had Paul clutching her hand for security, as he too was obviously very disturbed.

The policeman turned to back to Len, and said, "He's not a very big lad, is he?" and Len psychologically cowered as he went on to ask, "where did he get the bruises from Sir?"

Len paused to consider the question, then said, "He smashed himself at the wall! He was frantic, and I couldn't hold him back." And with that, Len started to wail as crocodile tears dripped down his face, "I've done my best! He's adopted, and I can't control him," he bleated.

"How long has he been with you Sir?" asked the policeman, flipping over another page in his notebook.

Margaret glanced up and squeaked, "Since he was six weeks old."

"Really! And you can't control him?" the policeman said in disbelief. The comment landed on Len's head like a boulder and I could see he felt compromised.

"Why are you holding that poker David?" the policeman asked me.

"T-to protect m-myself," I stammered.

The policeman looked at Len and calmly made it clear that he'd have to report the matter and that it was an offence to waste police time. "I suggest that you all calm down and stop this, as it isn't doing anyone any good. Is it?" he said.

Margaret was shaking, and Paul gripped her hand as if he would be set into a sea of terror should he let go and I was still clutching the poker for some reason.

"You won't need this will you David?" said the officer as has he gently retrieved it from my grip.

"N-no sir," I whimpered. "Th-thank you for c-coming to see m-me."

"That's ok David. You just calm down now. I've a feeling we'll see you again very soon?" he said and turning to the policewoman he ushered her towards the door.

As soon as the car pulled away Len flipped back to his terror campaign like the Chamaeleon that he was. "You little bastard!" he screamed. "What have you done?"

I was tired and completely worn out, my body still pumping with adrenalin and my heart began to pound again trying to escape from my chest. I was still getting pains from the tuberculosis, but the trips to Groby road were working and I was able to sustain much more movement, even running from time to time. Len still wasn't satisfied and started to set about Margaret. "Thank you for standing up for me! You're supposed to be on my side not his," he snapped at her.

He suddenly turned and advanced towards me trying grab my hand, and I immediately seized the poker again and pointed it at him.

"There you are! See, he's mad, violent and stupid," he shouted, but Margaret at last found her voice and shouted, "Leave him alone!"

"This is my house and I'll do whatever I want in it," snarled Len, snatching the poker from my hand and dragging me to the cupboard under the stairs. He opened the door and pushed me inside shouting as he did so, "Cool off in there, you little bastard," and the door closed to envelope me in darkness.

I sat on the blanket in the dark, feeling strangely relieved that I was temporarily free from his endless torment. The chemicals in my body had made me very hungry and I was so thirsty that my mouth was gluey and sore. I crawled to the end of the cupboard and reached for a biscuit, easily identifiable as they were all in order in readiness for my survival inventory. The Tizer bottle had grown in size as I had managed to steal a large one and no one had noticed; enough to last for at least six incarcerations I had calculated. It was very dark in the cupboard as Len had deliberately turned off the hall light, and I was almost entirely reliant on touch and smell. I was becoming good at navigating this dark world as I had practised many times in the past. I had begun to understand each part of my brain and identify the area that possessed the sensory information needed and was able to amplify it as I imagined a blind person would do. I had secretly played a private game many times as I sat in my cell, and I knew every smell and texture in the underworld cupboard, to the point of creating a second sight. I could feel the smoothness of the bottle, the coarseness of the cap, and I instinctively knew that undoing the cap would provide not only a hiss but a delightful aroma that enhanced the flavour of what was an ordinary boring drink. I turned the bottle top which instantly created a hiss; I was always careful not to shake it, as detrimental effects were always assured. The sweet smell of citrus surrounded me to provide an image in the darkness, a sight that was both unusual and unique, providing comfort but above all a release to the darkness and illumination in my brain.

After what seemed to be a lifetime; Margaret came to the cupboard and slid the brass lock to set me free. "Let him stay there all night," Len growled as he thundered up the stairs above me. Margaret was still shaking and whispered, "I'm so sorry darling."

"D-don't worry," I whispered, and in the light, I could see her face which was tired and drawn. "I'll be alright. I p-promise not to cause any m-more trouble," I said trying to give her hope, although in my heart I knew my situation was hopeless.

She forced a smile from her tear stained face and led me up the stairs. I momentarily panicked as I realised the bottle of Tizer was still on the blanket under the stairs, but luckily, she hadn't seen it. "I've left my hanky behind," I said, remembering that it too was under the stairs, making the perfect excuse for me to go back down and hide the bottle of Tizer. I crept back down the stairs, placed the bottle in its correct position and retrieved the handkerchief; clutching it as proof of my claim when I met Margaret at the top of the stairs again. Climbing into bed, I heard Paul stir and my body froze again, knowing that I would be attacked if he uttered a single word. But he didn't, and everything was fine.

As I lay there my mind wandered, "How did Paul get into bed?" I thought to myself. I hadn't heard a sound when he went up, which was strange as the staircase created acoustic thunder if anyone climbed the treads above me. I racked my brain but couldn't find any tangible information and concluded that I must have been so confused and scared that I'd blocked everything out except for the terrible situation. It was difficult to sleep that night as my head was still swimming with unanswered questions. The police officers had become part of a bad dream, as I started to block the painful reality of what Len had done. It was all very unreal, and I shivered at the thought of the day's events. Every joyous aspect of my examination results had vanished; the pride and effort had vaporised into nothing, becoming as unimportant as a precocious fly landing on one's nose without an invitation.

Morning came much too quickly, and I struggled to rise. My leg hurt, and my head was thumping as Len entered the room to assist Paul from his slumber. He stared at me with a hatred that I'd never seen before, untampered with synthetic influences. He stormed over and grabbed the leg of my bed turning the whole thing upside down, and I crashed to the floor with the bed frame narrowly missing my head. "Get out of bed you lazy bastard. Move!" he shouted.

I was still not fully awake, and my heart was pumping with the extra adrenaline and my head was aching with the attacks from the night before. I struggled from under the bed and he grabbed me again. It was always the same, my mind was so used to being told to go away, and that I was stupid, and I couldn't take it anymore. I started to scream uncontrollably which brought Margaret flying up the stairs. "What have you done now?" she screamed.

"Nothing! He just started to scream," he snarled, just as she entered the bedroom to see the bed upside down and the mattress twisted on the floor. "I'm not surprised! Are you?" she said looking directly at him.

He glared at her and stomped off down the stairs, protesting as he went. "That's it! Take his side why don't you? If it wasn't for you, I would have never agreed to adopt him in the first place," he shouted after her.

For some reason Len abandoned any further efforts to hurt me that morning, and when I entered the dining room he had already left for work. Margaret looked at me with caring eyes. "You don't deserve this she," whispered, "I'm so sorry. What have I done!"

I gently held her hand and smoothed it, "It's n-not your fault Mummy, you weren't to know w-what might happen," I said, and she kissed the top of my head. "You're too good to be with him but there's nothing I can do." She whispered, "If it wasn't for him, we would all starve." I had no idea what she meant as it hadn't occurred to me that

Len was paying for everything and that without his money she simply couldn't survive. I was later to realise that her statement and his control would be the bedrock of much worse things to come.

Chapter Seven

"A broken bone can heal,
but the wound a word opens can fester forever"
... Jessamyn West

I took my place at Loughborough Grammar school and the first day was frightening and very eventful, but I got through it. and buried myself in a routine of reading and learning as my ever-inquisitive mind was never satisfied.

I had been there for about year and I knew that Len resented every second because Paul had failed his exam and ended up in a school called a secondary modern. To be honest I found it challenging but very rewarding, with every step providing another steppingstone to a new adventure. on one occasion I was allowed to paint on the wall of the art room which I was told was a privilege. I was almost thirteen years old and my school reports were presented with volumes of applause, and on occasion resentment from my peers. I had found solace in work and freedom in success; which could cause what I had named the smart-arse syndrome.

At the end of each term a sinister game would unfold and be replayed time and again. At school everyone would congratulate me for doing well in each subject and hand me my school report which I would take home to give to Margaret. Margaret would leave it on the mantelpiece where Len would find it and destroy, further undermining my self-worth with verbal and physical attacks accusing me of being a cheat. I would then be incarcerated under the stairs, which by this time was becoming very cramped as I had grown a lot, and eventually I would be released and sent to my bedroom. It was a nasty vicious predicable circle of events.

On this particular day I had a report that presented first place in every subject, and I was dreading what would happen when I got home. It sounds stupid, but I had no idea what being first at anything was, as it all became muddled in a sea of confusion. I had long ago deserted the red double decker bus, as my journey to the Grammar school now took place on a swish coach, but still the eight-mile journey seemed to take for ever. That night I gingerly climbed off the coach clutching my report and slowly walked up the road with extreme trepidation. I opened the door to find Len already home as he was apparently unwell. "What's that in your hand" he snapped immediately upon seeing the envelope in my hand.

"It's my school report," I answered very slowly and precisely.

My teacher had recommended that I practised in front of a mirror to try and stop stuttering, and for weeks I had narcissistically stood in front of a mirror noting every movement of my mouth as the words were formed. I was still stuttering at times but nowhere near as much as before. "I suppose you think your clever?" he said as he snatched the envelope from my hand, and without even reading it he tore the entire document to shreds. "Been cheating again, have you?" he snarled.

An integral part of this sinister game of abuse, was that he would shout, and I was supposed to submit to his verbal abuse. This time I saw red and picking up a pot from on top of the kitchen table I threw it at him. It cracked him on the side of his head and it started to bleed. He completely lost control and produced a cricket bat from nowhere and whacked it over my head. Margaret was upstairs and didn't know what was happening until she came down to see me unconscious on the floor, knocked out by the blow.

He must have hit me again whilst I was out cold because he fractured my arm as well as my left leg along with the blow to my head. The simple fact is that I was all but dead and Margaret had already dialled 999 for an ambulance before I came around. The ambulance turned up as I was regaining consciousness, as did the police who had been also summoned by Margaret. The medics took one look at me and placed me on a stretcher to transport me to the hospital.

Len was busy presenting his bleeding head to the police, "I have a right to protect myself," he kept chanting.

Margaret was in tears unable to take in what had happened and I think was probably suicidal herself as she kept on repeating "I wish I was dead. What have I done?"

The ambulance transported me to the hospital very quickly with Margaret by my side. All I can remember are eyes looking down over me and kind caring hands applying something very cold to my head. I was rolled onto a trolley and pushed through two big plastic doors where immediately two doctors began shining lights into my eyes. I think Margaret had told them that I'd been hit on the head with a cricket bat, but I'm not sure they realised the true context of it, as they repeatedly asked how many runs I'd scored!

Some of the questions were obviously to see if my brain was working properly as one doctor held his fingers up and asked, "How many fingers can you see?" My head really ached, and I could feel a huge lump the size of a tennis ball on the side of it and they kept on asking me could I see them ok. They then rolled me on to another trolley and pushed me down a long corridor that reminded me of a rabbit warren, only it was littered with bright tubes that glared at me almost angry that I dared to be under them. The paint was very stained and seemed to extend the journey, as time stopped due to the never-ending upwards view of the domed ceiling. It reminded me of the ceiling upstairs on the double-decker bus that I had travelled on to school when I was younger, when one day I'd snuck up the stairs to sit on the very front seat to pretend that I was driving. The roof was creamy brown, and the condensation dripped in brown strands forming stalactites that aimlessly hung like slimy teeth waiting to consume innocent travellers.

My journey through the stained but brightly lit tunnel ended with a bump, as one of the wheels jammed up against a lift door and a smiling face looked down on me as I stared into space. "Are you alright David?" said one of the porters.

"Y-yes" I replied, wondering what was going to happen next as the lift door slid shut and the red buttons lit up at each level. One, two, *ding* and the door slid open and both people struggled to manoeuvre the trolley out of the confined space. "Whoops sorry!" one of them said as it banged on a badly dented metal rail that had obviously been an active collision point over many years.

This new corridor was less intimidating, and the ceiling was square not domed like the other one. They pushed me the final few yards to a very big door with a yellow and black sign with the words *Danger Radiation* emblazoned on it. The door opened, and I found myself in a strange place with tall machines and a large table that I was rolled onto and given a thing to prop my neck up with.

"Is that comfortable David?" asked a small lady with a very thick apron wrapped around her waist.

"Y-yes it's ok, b-but my head hurts," I said.

"Don't worry we'll soon sort that out for you. Now I need you to keep very still for me," she said, as she slid a large plate into a slot under my head and I froze as she went behind a glass shield.

"Hold your breath David," she called out and as the large glass eye clicked, I could feel some heat in the top of my head. The nurse did the same for my arm and my leg, which took what seemed ages and I was wheeled out of the room to be met by Margaret who had obviously been crying. "How do you feel?" she muttered.

"M-my head hurts, and I I feel a bit s-sick," I said, thinking that it was something to do with the X-Rays that had just been taken. I lay there for what seemed ages, as Margaret sat on a chair close to me and held my hand. Finally two more people came up to the trolley and smiled, "We're going to take you to have a cast put on your arm and leg David," they said as they guided the trolley back down the corridor to the lift and pressed the button.

The door swished open and they awkwardly attempted to manoeuvre the trolley into the space without bumping the metal strip this time. They pressed the buttons and the letters lit up, *ding* number one shone out and the door slid open again. I was wheeled into a room with curtains everywhere and they pushed the trolley into a space and closed them around me. A nurse opened the curtain and came in with a big white bowl and loads of bandages. The bowl was full of white liquid that bubbled and glugged as she placed it on the cupboard next to me. She wrapped the bandages around my leg first, and at every stage smoothed the white plaster into the absorbent material, until it was very thick and very warm. She then turned to my arm and repeated the same procedure, to produce a thick cumbersome plaster that was again hot and very heavy.

Margaret sat there in silence, managing the occasional whimper of "Are you OK?"

"Y-yes I'm f-fine," I murmured back and turned over feeling very tired. I had no idea what was going to happen next until a tall man with a beard swished the curtains back and asked Margaret what had happened. She burst into tears and told him everything.

"Well we can't let him stay there then. Not until we've had words with your husband, can we?" he exclaimed. "I'll have to arrange alternative accommodation until we can sort something out."

"He's still traveling to Groby Road hospital and he has an appointment tomorrow," squeaked out Margaret.

"What does he need to go there for?" asked the man who later identified himself as Mr Conrad-Dick. Margaret couldn't help herself and admitted that I had caught Tuberculosis from her husband when I was very young. "I thought he was adopted," said Mr Dick.

"Yes at six-weeks old," she answered, "and we were given him just as my husband was released from the sanatorium."

"What! Are you telling me that he was adopted into a family that was known to be infected with tuberculosis?" he cried out in horror.

"Yes I suppose I am," replied Margaret, "but we did inform the authorities that my husband was in hospital suffering from the disease."

Mr Dick went a strange grey colour and said, "But the system doesn't make these kinds of mistakes. He must have caught it somewhere else; school maybe? Well as I said I'll have to arrange a place for him to stay tonight until we can sort something out."

Margaret agreed, and the man left I presume to make some telephone calls. It wasn't long before he returned. "I've arranged some temporary accommodation at the Beechlands," he said. "Where we can also keep our eyes on his wounds."

Margaret burst into tears again as two more men slid the curtains back and wheeled me back down the corridor and out through the swishy doors. I was helped into the ambulance and Margaret sat beside me as it sped off to Beechlands, and I wondered what the place might be like. It was dusk by the time we arrived, and the trees shaded a very tall building that nestled in what appeared to be a peaceful place. A black man came to the door and introduced himself. "You're David, aren't you? We were expecting you," he said as I struggled up the steps and through the front door. There was a smell of unrest; a stagnant smell that scared me as I looked at the staircase that rose to several landings above, and I gripped Margaret's hand and cried out, "I don't want to stay here!"

"It's not for long," she whimpered. "I'll come and see you tomorrow with some fresh clothes." I was shaking with fear having no idea how I'd found myself in such a position. My head was aching, my leg hurt and all I could think of was sleep.

"I'll stay with you," she promised as I was led up the stairs to a small room with a slender bed and a brightly coloured eiderdown. Margaret pulled a chair up by the side of the bed and gripped my hand. "Try and sleep now. I won't leave; really I won't," she promised.

I can't remember anything else until I opened my eyes to the sunlight shining through the window and an empty chair by my bed. The window had been opened slightly to leave a gap at the bottom and I could feel the clean air floating into the room, and a very big lady came in. "W-where's Mum?" I cried.

"She's gone to collect some clean clothes for you," she said trying to reassure me.

I panicked, "She'd promised she wouldn't leave me!" I cried, and tears flooded down my face, just as Margaret appeared at the bedroom door with a case full of clothes. I glanced at her screaming through the tears, "You weren't here, you promised!"

She smiled and embarrassingly muttered that she'd been told to let me sleep and to fetch some clothes as I could be there for a few days. I could see she was nervous, and I half sensed that Len was downstairs, and fear paralysed my body. She held me close to her and whispered, "I have to go and sort this all out. I'll be back later on."

"P-please don't leave me here," I begged but she broke away and vanished.

The big lady helped me wash and dress, she was very nice and smiled a lot and led me down the stairs for breakfast. It was full of people much older than me, and they all looked surprised to see me stumble into the room. I sat down next to a girl called Deidre, who was shaking but managed a smile as she poured some tea into a mug for me. "Do you want some sugar?" she asked. "Uh n-no th-thank you," I nervously stuttered and she handed me the cup, blowing it to make sure it wasn't too hot, and I thought how kind she was.

The breakfast was good, much better than I had been used to, and I ate it without any fear of attacks from Len. We all filed out of the room to walk into the garden which was huge; there were wooden benches littered everywhere each with a brass plaque attached with four carefully measured screws. I sat down alone and cried and cried as if to let out the torrents of uncertainty that had almost drowned my mind in never ending pain. A whistle blew, and everyone filed into a wooden building which I hoped would be a school room. "School," I thought, and I panicked that my teacher would be wondering where I was as no one would have contacted him yet.

I walked through the glass doors to find a series of long tables set in two enormous lines, with dozens of chairs spaced equally across the entire length of the room. There were ladies that sat sewing and men that were just sat there doing nothing, and there were several people that were threading long sticks into wooden disks that had holes in them. I later found out that it was called basket weaving and that all the people there had problems; some more serious than others. But I had no idea that I was in a home for mentally disturbed and abused people.

I nervously selected a seat and the same tall girl that had made me a cup of tea at breakfast, immediately sat down beside me. “Hello, how did you hurt yourself?” she asked, and when I didn’t answer she went on to ask, “what’s your name?”

“D-David. What’s yours?” I replied, and she told me it was Deidre.

“Why are you in this place, did someone hurt you?” I asked her.

“Yes they did,” she replied.”

“Bet it was your father that hurt you,” I said instinctively, and she looked at me as if I had just performed a magic trick.

“Yes! How did you know that?” she burst out.

For some reason I retreated from the question and looked out of the window.

“How did you know that?” she demanded again this time showing signs of anger.

“I d-don’t know but it was m-mine that hurt me. So I just guessed you were the s-same,” I said.

Her face calmed, and she smiled, “How old are you then?” she asked.

“Thirteen, well nearly fourteen actually,” I replied.

“Did your father do that to you?” she asked pointing to my plaster casts.

“Y-yes, but I did throw a pot at him first though,” I said with a smile.

"Brave as well as smart," she replied.

"Well I probably deserved it," I said. "He doesn't want me there. I upset him and make him do things that he doesn't want to do."

My words hit her like a bullet, "Is that what he says to you?" she asked.

"Yes all the time," I answered.

She obviously wanted to talk, and I asked her how old she was, and she told me she was sixteen and very tired.

"What did your father do to you?" I innocently asked her.

She looked at me and snarled, "That's none of your business" and rose from the chair with tears in her eyes and stomped away.

I felt very guilty as I had no idea what I had said to upset her so much and I tried to follow her, but she simply ran away into the garden; running across the grass to the barbed wire perimeter. I could hear her screaming as she ran but impeded by my broken leg I couldn't run after her, and just sat down on a bench watching her run into the distance. I could see her bouncing her arms up and down on the fence screaming, but I had no idea what she was doing. Her tall frame fell to the ground and I was compelled to stagger to her as I just knew that she was hurt, and I somehow felt responsible. It seemed like hours before I reached her to find blood everywhere as she had slashed both her wrists on the barbed wire fence. I screamed out "HELP," as the blood gushed from her wrists and I pulled off my shirt to wrap it around her arms. By this time two men in white coats appeared from nowhere. "Help her," I screamed believing that it was me that had caused her to slash her wrists.

"We don't have to help anyone!" snarled one of the men. "Because nobody cares," taunted the other. His words hit me like a knife, and I started to shake with anger as Deidre lay limply on the grass.

"Help her you b-bastards! She's dying!" I screamed out. They picked her up between them, half dragging half carrying her up the steps into the building beyond. I never saw Deidre again after that day and no one could even guess where she had gone; but I knew in my heart that it wasn't good and that something terrible had happened to her.

Several days later I was sitting on a bench seat in the same garden when a man called Jim Brown came up to me and sat down. He had a funny lip and found it difficult to speak which I knew all about, so I was always careful to listen to him. "Hello David," he said, his words almost lost in the roof of his mouth.

"H-Hello Jim. What are you doing today?" I asked, which was my stock question to everyone as there wasn't much to do. I had been worried that Margaret hadn't visited me for several days and I was beginning to feel very nervous about it.

"Do you smoke?" he asked me.

"N-no," I replied.

"Well you should," he said pulling four pieces of very thin paper and some tobacco from his pocket. He carefully rolled the paper with tobacco inside it to construct a long tube, then wound a piece of cardboard into a roll and pushed it over one end, whilst he twisted the other making it look like a firework. He then lit it and sucked in the smoke which had a very peculiar smell, unlike any I had smelt before. "What's that Jim?" I asked.

"It's Turkish," he replied. "Do you want some?"

I was feeling angry about what had happened to Deidre and the fact I'd done nothing to try and help her, so I replied, "Yes ok." I took a very large puff and breathed in the smoke just as Jim instructed.

Within seconds I was coughing so badly I almost choked and then my head started to spin as if I had fallen into a river. I was so scared that I threw the cigarette on to the ground and Jim went mad. "Don't throw it away," he spluttered, "it belongs to me!"

By this time my head was in turmoil and I lifted myself up from the seat to walk across the grass. Every step took what seemed to be hours and I started to laugh uncontrollably. The two men in white coats suddenly appeared and walked towards me and I started to giggle. "What are you doing David?" called out one of them.

"I've been s-smoking with Jim," I replied and giggled even louder; when suddenly I was violently sick. They both came running towards me and I knew that I had done something dreadfully wrong.

"What have you been smoking?" said one of the white coats.

"A-a cigarette" I stammered, and I was sick again.

"Bugger Me! The little bastards been smoking pot. If this leaks out, we'll all lose our jobs. Where the hell did he get it from?" I could hear one of them say. "Get him into a fucking locked ward or we'll be in deep shit!" shouted the other.

They grabbed my arm dragged me across the grass, up the steps and into the building where they locked me in a small room. "Stay there you bastard," one of them hissed; and I could see the other making a call from the telephone in the entrance hall.

After some time, I heard the sound of an engine as a vehicle drew up in front of the building and my door was unlocked and the same two men marched me out to the back of a van; the gravel scraping under my feet as I clumsily walked across the driveway. It was a dark blue Comma van with bars in the back doors, which scared me as I was hauled into it and the doors locked shut, to prevent my escape. I became frantic and started to bang on the side of the van, as I could see the two men grinning as it pulled away.

Chapter Eight

"I believe the root of all evil is the abuse of power."
... Patricia Cornwell

I had no idea where I was being taken until the van pulled up outside a huge sinister looking building that seemed to go on forever. There were dozens of old people moving about slowly in the dimly lit grounds, with loads more white coats overseeing what looked to me to be a very bad place. It hadn't taken long to get there, so I presumed that it was close to the Beechlands and somehow connected. I was later to find out that it was a mental institution, but I didn't really know what one of those was until much later. I was literally dragged out of the van and led through a labyrinth of corridors to what could only be described as a cell. Every stitch of clothing was removed from my body and I was forced into a thin bed that rested only feet away from an old man who was grunting and wailing whilst farting as loud as he could. The room smelt vile and the atmosphere made worse by the black bars that blocked out the partial light of dusk. Laying naked in the narrow bed shivering with fright, I was still feeling the effects of the earlier cigarette. My blurred mind made it all seem like a bad nightmare from which I hoped I would wake in the morning. I heard the key twist as the door was firmly locked shut, drawing my eyes to the round window with wired glass in it, that shouted out *you're trapped!*

As I lay there in despair looking up, a light glowed in the ceiling, hanging there suspended it looked like a bat ready to feed on my blood and I started to scream. The old man in the bed next to me grunted and I had a feeling that he was not well; not well all. I was shivering and very vulnerable by this time, reduced to streams of tears amid my calls for help. I knew that I was in an impossible position as two more men in white coats peered through the round window and grinned as if they were enjoying it all. I was so tired as the effects of the cigarette wore off but the stench in the room was almost impossible to bear. I screamed still louder, but no one came, and as the night turned black the room became cold as did I with the bed presenting little or no warmth at all. In my mind I could feel myself slipping and yearned for my childhood innocence when I was able to escape to the security of my spaceship. My only means of escape now was sleep, as shivering I closed my eyes to block out the evil reality of the day's events.

Suddenly there was a violent growl as the old man in the bed next to me vomited so badly that it covered both me and the bed in a vile smelling liquid that clung to my skin like glue. The partial light in the roof illuminated the liquid and it appear to glisten, while the smell made it all but impossible to breath. It had all become a sinister story that few would even believe as I started to scream and bang the door to get out. The smell was so vile that my eyes watered, and my nose stung from breathing in the toxic air. Suddenly a man peered through the window in the door. "Go to sleep," he shouted … "Or we'll have to restrain you."

But still I screamed and screamed, somehow knowing that the old man was dead as he had stopped making any noise at all.

Looking back, it is hard to believe that human beings could treat a fourteen-year-old boy so badly, and I have no doubt that there will be some who will state that I had enlarged the facts, but it is all absolutely true. I can't remember when they finally unlocked the door; but I'm sure that they knew the old man was dead long before they did. They were just intent on teaching me a lesson for what I had done with the cigarette.

By the time they opened the door I was unable to speak at all as I had screamed so badly and for so long, that my vocal cords were damaged; something that has left me with a gruff voice to this very day. My entire body was shaking as I stood naked but for the soiled sheet I held around me whilst they carried the body out of the room. I later found out that the man was suffering from a disease called dropsy which causes inflammation of an artery or major organ such as the kidneys, liver, and heart; leading you to ultimately die from organ failure. It creates abnormal accumulation of fluids in the body which in his case had probably been waste products collecting in his lungs, which I guess was the reason he appeared to explode all over me.

I remained in the room alone until two ladies came into the room clutching a dressing gown which they insisted I put on, as they led me to a shower to wash off the congealed crusty mess that had formed on me overnight. I stood under the shower for a very long time trying to wash off the entire nightmare, but it wouldn't go away. One of the ladies came over to me with a towel and I embarrassingly grabbed it feeling shy at my forced physical exposure. She said that I had committed a crime by smoking the cigarette and that I would be dealt with accordingly at a later date, thrusting my clothes at me whilst imparting that information. I hurriedly dressed trying to answer but I was completely unable to communicate with her.

Mrs Oakley was a regular visitor to Beechlands and from time to time had sat with me talking about her family and the problems she had with her daughter Colleen. Mrs Oakley had always been kind and thoughtful becoming a sort of substitute for Margaret, as she spent several hours talking to me when Margaret didn't turn up to visit. I always put on a brave face to her but I'm sure that she realised I was very sad, hurting and possibly abused and needed motherly affection. She was a regular visitor to the Beechlands and gave the impression that she had volunteered to assist young people who found themselves in bad and disturbing positions; it turned out that she also visited the mental home and she came to see me. I think the visit was engineered by the staff knowing that I had met her before, but I was pleased to see a friendly face.

"What's been going on," she asked, "why are you here and not down the road?" I tried to speak but no words would come out not even a stutter. "What have they done to you? This just isn't right!" she exclaimed. "Tell me what happened?"

I couldn't talk as my throat hurt too much, but I eventually squeaked a few words out and slowly the entire episode unfolded. She was beside herself and stormed into a manager's office not far along the corridor, where I heard her screaming, "He's not fourteen yet! What are you thinking. He's not a mature person he's a teenager with teenager's problems?"

I could see the manager glaring at me from afar and I knew that they were not going to let me go as I had caused so much trouble by smoking the cigarette. Mrs Oakley came back and sat beside me on a grey plastic seat. "Listen to what I am saying," she insisted; "I've told them that you can't talk at all and that what you did won't be mentioned because you can't talk to anyone about. I've told them it's likely to be several weeks before you will be able to speak at all."

I managed to squeeze out some words, asking her why they were all so bothered about a cigarette; shivering as I did so. "They could all be sacked if it was found there were drugs on the premises," she told me, "especially the two at Beechlands who brought you up here."

It was a startling thought; I was being tortured to save their jobs. They were scared that I might speak to the wrong person and the whole matter would blow the place apart and they would lose their licence.

"I've told them that you're not going to say anything because you can't, and that I am perfectly prepared to let you come and stay with me," she said.

It was obvious that they would go to any lengths to hide what had happened, and I was guessing that without Mrs Oakley's help I may well be locked up there forever. Mrs Oakley collected my things and I think she signed a release form, which surprised me as I knew that Len was still responsible for me, as I was not yet twenty-one. I was still shaking when she led me out of the door to wait for the taxi which would drive us to her home in Harlaxton Street on the outskirts of the town. I didn't realise how close I'd come to being committed; as I've since found out that such action was very common at that time and teenagers did go missing.

The simple fact was that my night in a cell with a dead body whose medical condition covered me in grime and having been stripped naked for some reason; which to this day continues to elude me. Can only be described as a punishment which reduced me to a quivering wreck and as a consequence, I was desperate to leave the place as quickly as possible and probably would have gone with anyone.

As the taxi crunched along the driveway, I could see the grounds of the mental institution were lit up with an array of lights, so bright it would have been impossible not to detect anyone in the huge expanse of land. My attention was drawn to a large man stumbling around in his night clothes, wailing and screaming as he attempted to escape. He was closely followed by several men in white coats, who were brandishing what looked like a thick light brown jacket with leather straps protruding from it in every direction. They too were charging around clearly engaged in an important pursuit. Waiting for the taxi I was able to absorb the full extent of what I can only describe as a truly frightening and evil place. The entire building looked as though it had been designed by a rabbit, with long domed passageways connecting a labyrinth of what can only be described as cells. Every cell had a thick generic light-brown door with a number-plate screwed to it and a sinister round window set with wires forged in the glass, I guess to prevent the inhabitant from hurting themselves. The windows were always barred and painted black, each cell had a scary light fused to the roof, glowing tirelessly to give a never-ending diffused view of the incarcerated victim inside when the men in white coats chose to peer through the window at them. There was not a single place where a half-dressed person wasn't staggering around moaning and groaning in their often stained nightclothes. As I'd sat waiting for the taxi a man came up to me and exposed himself not feet away from where I was sitting.

Throughout the twenty minute or so journey, I couldn't help thinking about what I had witnessed at the Beechlands as it was very clear that the entire establishment was being run by sadists. My mind went over and over the days that I'd spent at the home, and to the many sights I had witnessed, but I chose to say nothing for fear of reprisal.

I remembered the first day after I was taken to the Beechlands, I was led into a very dark office and introduced to a foreign man whose name was Dr Patel, who sat there perfectly blended into his surroundings making it difficult to see him behind his desk. I hadn't realised up until then why he had asked me so many weird questions. I was almost fourteen years old and his first question was to ask how my sex life was? I had found it both embarrassing and difficult to answer as up until then my life had been consumed in school work only. I had pushed the question to the back of my mind but now as we drove away, I remembered that he laboured the point over and over again. I had refused to answer; covering up my response with a bad stammer. He then asked if I had ever been abused, and I had nervously stammered *n-no*, fearing reprisal from Len if I dared to say anything. He went on to give me detailed descriptions of the acts that could have taken place, all the time asking if they had happened to me. He even said the abuser would be likely to blame me for what had taken place, which I knew to be true. I was in his office for at least thirty minutes and the more time that went by the more uncomfortable I became. I could see he was enjoying the interview and that he was aware his questions were making me feel very uncomfortable.

I left the office without a chaperone and on that particular day chose to wander around the building like a cat marking its territory on a temporary basis. Walking along one of the corridors, I could hear a very strange sound; like high voltage electricity escaping from a charging unit. It sounded like the equipment Len had used many times to start his car and hearing a noise that seemed familiar to me I wandered in search of it. I located the door where the noise was coming from and peered through the window to see there was a girl laying on a couch with nothing on but her underwear. There was a strange strap over her head with an array of wires connected to it and every time the system surged, she would rise from the couch whilst her onlookers stared at her convulsing body. Seeing the perverted looks on their faces I was both horrified and scared and ran off as quickly as I could. What I had witnessed was frankly terrifying and I didn't want it to happen to me. I remembered making my way up to my room, my head filled with disturbing thoughts as what I had seen bothered me, leaving countless unanswered questions. After that I had regularly roamed the building in search of answers, seeing many disturbing sights as I did so. I remembered seeing the girl on the couch walking around the next day as if she was on another planet, complaining that she was sore; but I never dared ask where.

My mind was racing as I mentally went through the many sights that I had witnessed during the few weeks I had spent there. They belonged to a sinister horror story, and I found it difficult to record them in my mind for fear of reprisal. I had dared to tell a man in a white coat called Terry, what Dr Patel had said, but I was called a liar and a cheat.

Despite my attempted warnings Dr Patel was found guilty of abusing old people in a home he had set up in South Devon decades later. I wondered how many people I could have saved from his evil if only I had been stronger.

Suddenly the taxi pulled up and my thoughts were diverted as Mrs Oakley cried out, "David we're here!" and I peered out of the window to see a strange looking house. It stood out from the others in the road, lit by the streetlights which enhanced its coloured bricks creating a mosaic in a sea of otherwise generic buildings.

There was a tall man standing at the front door. "Hello David, I've heard all about you," he called out, "my name's Keith." He was smiling gently, and I immediately warmed to his calming manner. "Come in, please; you're very welcome," he said to me and I knew he meant it.

"Alice close the door on your way in," he called out behind him as he led me through to the front room.

I sat there with very much the same thoughts as my first day at school. *School! School!* I thought as it suddenly it dawned on me that the school wouldn't know where I was, and I panicked, *they won't know where I am!* I tried to tell them, but my voice was virtually destroyed by this time, but in the end, I managed to screech out, "W-what about my school," and I burst into tears.

I must have wailed for at least an hour unloading all the pain from my head, and Keith looked at me in horror of what must have happened to cause such a serious breakdown. "What the hell have they done to him?" he exclaimed, "how can someone so young be in such a bad state."

I started to shake; the visual markings of my nightmare were staring me in the face, and I was having real trouble coping with the horrendous pictures in my brain. I have since understood that such a reaction could be compared to a soldier having returned from a war zone, which today would be called Post-Traumatic Stress Disorder [PTSD]. I felt as if I was falling to pieces and my brain was screaming at me in an attempt to add reality to the entire nightmare. I was so scared and so frightened that I hadn't noticed I was wetting myself, and the plaster cast on my leg began to burn like a raging fire with the fluid that was trickling down my leg.

"Get it off get it off. Please get it off," I screamed, but it came out as faint whisper.

Keith came over with a tear trickling down his cheek not really knowing what I needed to abandon. "Get what off David? What do you want to get off you?" he asked; thinking that I was having some sort of mental or drug induced hallucination. I later found out that his daughter had been a serious drug addict and that he was well versed in such behaviour. He thought I was referring to a mind induced monster that had infected my brain.

"The p-plaster! Its b-burning me," I croaked, pulling at it.

"I can't take that off or you might end up with a twisted leg," he calmly responded.

"No p-please g-get it off," I pleaded, struggling to force any sound from my mouth at all. Looking back I'm not sure if I was trying to relieve myself from Len's torture as the plaster cast was a permanent marker to his actions. I started to feel very nauseous and in a desperate bid begged for a bowl to be sick in. Keith went to the kitchen and produced a large pot bowl accompanied by a green towel and I was violently sick. "I'm so sorry," I said waiting for him to be angry, but Keith looked at me with caring eyes. "It doesn't matter my lad," he said, "don't worry about it, it's not a problem."

By this time my plaster cast was burning so badly and creating so much pain, that I began to claw at it and the sharp corners scraped my hand to make it bleed. "I n-need to get it off," I painfully whispered, "It's h-hurting me."

Alice Oakley came over and sat down beside me, "Don't worry I'll take you to the hospital tomorrow," she said.

"N-no no I must have it off now! P-please!" I said, but although I mouthed the words, no sound came out and my reply failed to fill the room.

By this time Keith who obviously had experience of such situations, went into the kitchen and returned brandishing a large pair of heavy-duty cutters that looked as though they were capable of chopping through anything. "These will do it. Do you want me to cut it off?" he said, expecting me to say no.

"Y-yes please," I whispered, and he reluctantly started to chop away the plaster. "I'm not sure I should be doing this but it's your leg," he said, and with that the plaster burst at the seams and spilled out an obnoxious sweaty smell.

I was still screaming in silence but the relief to know that it would be off me very soon had a calming effect and my body began to relax with each slice of the plaster bandages falling to the floor. Eventually the last piece fell to reveal a smelly shrivelled up leg that looked as though it was badly infected with an unknown disease. My mind immediately turned to the dead body that had exploded all over me the night before. "Oh my god!" I whispered. "It got into my leg as well!"

"What did?" barked Keith.

"The glue the glue," I said.

"What glue?"

"The dead b-body the old man," I croaked, and Keith looked at his wife shaking his head as he asked her what I meant.

"You don't want to know," she replied, "just leave it alone and I'll tell you later."

After what seemed to be a lifetime my leg was cool and the pictures in my head, though still very real, were fading slightly.

"Would you like to take a bath?" Alice asked me.

"Yes please," I said, and she ran to the stairs to run one.

For some strange reason the cast on my arm had become very lose and it was itching like mad. I could move it up and down easily and were it not for the bit that ran over my hand I was sure that it would slip right off as it wasn't very long. "Can I t-take this off as well p-please," I croaked.

"Not a good idea," sparked Keith who by this time was starting to feel uncomfortable with what he had done to my leg plaster.

Alice led me up the stairs which were decorated with a brightly coloured carpet with green leaves and a chase of woven farm animals that lined the outer edge. Each rung had a bar that was neatly clamped across the width of the carpet, finished off with a band of glossy white paint at either side. She opened the door and I slowly moved into a steam filled room insisting that I bolted the door behind me. I slowly undressed and put my hand into what I had expected to be very hot water. Surprisingly it was comfortable, and I slid in with euphoric ecstasy, feeling safe for the first time in ages, but still plagued with a minefield of terrible pictures in my head.

Swishing about in the water in this new-found freedom I completely forgot about the plaster on my arm, forgetting I shouldn't get it wet. The itching was easing, and I had an uncontrollable desire to slip it off as soon as it had softened enough to do so. I'm guessing now that my bones were cracked and not broken, but at the time and after due consideration I believed that my arm would be fine as the pain had subsided several days ago. I was so very keen to get rid of Len from my mind and discharging the plaster cast would clearly achieve that for me. I lay back closing my eyes and slipped my head beneath the water as the never-ending pictures flooded in again. I witnessed again the blood from Deidre's wrists and the man in the white coat grinning whilst admitting that he didn't have to help any of us *because nobody cared: because we were no-one!* My mind felt like a roundabout with moulded horses moving up and down on golden twisted poles, and I could hear the organ music playing louder and louder as the views changed with each rotation. The music achieved fever pitch and my head felt like it would burst, and I began to get angry; so angry that my body shook with rage. "Stop!" I shouted at the voice in my head. I needed to calm down, and to divert my attention I slipped the cast from my wrist achieving a strong note of freedom.

My head was banging as I stared at my arm which was surprisingly intact considering I'd been told it was cracked in two places. It wasn't shrivelled and there were only faint traces of bruising that were fighting to stay black, having now taken on a burnt yellow colour whilst I was healing. I moved my wrist with extreme caution thinking that it would hurt and whilst some pain twisted around my wrist it was much less than I had expected. In any event I felt liberated; I felt free from the hell that had contaminated my life since I dared to come home with my examination results.

My lungs filled with air and I started to cry uncontrollably, the pain dripped from my heart like the tears of a wailing baby; so lost, so lonely and so scared. Suddenly there was a knock at the door. "David are you ok?" It was Alice who had been listening at the door concerned at what she had witnessed at the mental home. "Y-yes," I whispered. "I'm f-fine.

"Do you want anything to eat you must be hungry?" she said and surprisingly I realised I was starving. "Y-yes please," I whispered my reply.

"Well, get your clothes on and come downstairs," she called out through the closed door, "I want you to meet my daughter."

I climbed out of the bath and by now my hands were shrivelled and looked spooky, so I waved them about whilst perfecting a ghost sound with my broken voice. "Stop playing around it's late," she called out, but I could hear a refreshing giggle in her words which made me feel strangely calm.

I was never very thorough at drying myself as it was always a speedy procedure to avoid Len's attacks. I swished the towel around and slipped my clothes back on which fought to slide over my body because I wasn't properly dried. Nevertheless, for the first time in a very long time I felt that I was in a place that was relatively safe. I cautiously opened the door and slid down the stairs to open a second door that led to the lounge. Peering in whilst at the same time hiding behind the door, I slowly made myself visible, seeing a young girl with short cropped hair that had been dyed a frightening colour.

"Hello David," she smiled, "I'm Colleen good to meet you."

I cautiously walked over to her to shake her hand.

"Come here, give us a hug," she said smiling

At that moment something clicked in my brain telling me that I had at long last found a place where I was safe; but how wrong could I have been!

CHAPTER NINE

"An insincere and evil friend is more to be feared than a wild beast; a wild beast may wound your body, but an evil friend will wound your mind"
... Buddha

I had been at Alice Oakley's house for almost a week, and my voice though beginning to get slightly better was still very croaky. Keith Oakley was a school caretaker and worked nights; so he was usually asleep when I was awake. I liked him and missed his kind comments and looked forward to him being at home at the weekend, which was tomorrow. He was a very kind man so different from Len, and on the occasions that I'd spoken to him I could feel he was someone that genuinely cared. It was plain that his son Christopher meant a lot to him and that both he and his son were overpowered by the two dominating women in the household; namely Alice and Colleen.

I'd been told that Colleen had a serious drug problem and was uncontrollable, spending most of her time out at parties. The word drug didn't mean that much to me as my only brush with them was when I was introduced to marijuana by Jim Brown, the devastating effects of which had brought me to where I was. I had no idea there were other perils out there that the younger generation had locked on to, for what they termed kicks. Colleen would return home almost every night at gone three in the morning, and make loud noises banging doors and clanging plates as she prepared her regular early morning feasts. I was still not sleeping very well and would often rise and go downstairs to meet her, curious to see what would happen as Colleen was always talking very fast and couldn't stop moving even when she was sitting down. I now realise her behaviour was due to effects of the drugs she was taking.

It was Friday night and like clockwork I'd gone to bed early, and Alice had made a cup of Horlicks to help me sleep better. I was finding it difficult to stop shaking and my speech had become much worse. Alice spent her time talking to me as often as she could, always insisting that I try to calm down, and on that particular day I had mentioned school and how desperate I was to go back there. I had spent several nights waking up dripping wet with sweat and shaking uncontrollably, which was alarming for all concerned. I had also started to shake with fear if I was presented with anything that vaguely reminded me of my past nightmare. For some strange reason I felt most secure when tucked up in my room on my own, as I'd found some books to read which were identical to the ones I was given to read at school. On this particular night, Colleen obviously determined to wake everyone up in the house, had invited some friends back who were adding extra pandemonium to the equation. Suddenly there was a huge crash that sounded like broken glass which instantly shocked my already shattered nervous system into action. I jumped up dripping with sweat, almost paralysed and shaking with fear as I climbed out of bed. There was music playing and I could hear Colleen laughing uncontrollably as I gingerly crept down the stairs to open the door. It creaked and groaned as I did so; and peering through I could see two girls and an equal number of boys lying on the floor completely naked. I froze and started to shiver again, my thoughts reverting back to the dying old man and my own forced nudity at the mental home. They were all performing on the floor and I instantly found myself staring as I'd heard what goes on between the sexes but never actually witnessed it. My staring was totally misunderstood, and several comments came floating through the air accusing me of perverted behaviour, but I was shocked and not at all stimulated with what I had witnessed. My life to date had never contemplated relationships at all; as I naturally composed Len and Margaret into that equation which rendered them toxic. I could feel my face getting red and the heat rising further in my body. "Have you got a hard on you dirty little bastard," shouted out one of the boys.

"You didn't tell me you had a pervert up the stairs Colleen," shouted the other as they gyrated up and down on the carpet.

"What's he doing here? Go away you fucking little pervert," the first one called out again.

I froze even more not knowing what to do. Colleen slid herself from under her partner and came over to me, her pupils so large and black they almost consumed the real colour of her eyes. It hadn't occurred to me that she was still naked until she grabbed my hand and pushed it on to her body. "Go on Colleen give him a free one why don't you?" shouted one of them.

By then I was shaking so violently I began to feel the bile rising from my stomach. "L-let m-me go," I pleaded, and she released her grip on me. I ran to the kitchen with Colleen trailing along behind me and was violently sick. I could hear Alice moving about above, followed by the thud of feet as she came down the stairs two at a time. "What the hell's going on?" she snapped as she surveyed the scene.

"Colleen get some clothes, on what on earth do you think you're doing?" she screeched as she saw her standing there still naked.

My head was thumping and my heart pounding as I turned around with tears flooding down my face. "Sit down David," she said, then turning to the others she bellowed, "you lot! OUT!" and they all clothed themselves and retreated in astonishingly quick time.

I'm not sure what she said to me, but I know it involved several hours of speech that I really didn't either understand or was too tired to take any notice of, and as the sun rose taking the night stars so far away, the brightness of another new day appeared at the window.

That morning Alice paid very keen attention to me, as if concerned about what had happened that night, and when Keith twisted the Yale lock on the front door marking the end of his nightshift, she was careful not to mention any word of what had happened. His face was drawn, and I could see he realised something had gone wrong, but he was simply too tired to pursue it and staggered off to his bed. I felt very guilty about what had happened, and the word 'pervert' kept on ringing in my head. Once again, I had no idea what I'd done wrong, but the effects were permanently burned in my head and again I had an uncontrollable urge to escape. This was to become a common thread throughout my early life.

"What's the matter David," whispered Alice as she smoothed down my hair.

"I d-don't know b-but I w-want to leave now," I told her.

"Oh I see!" she snapped, "that's the thanks I get is it?" and I felt mentally stagnant as she pushed me away.

"I I'm sorry A-Alice," I said; as *sorry* was always my reflex answer.

"Let's just forget it," she whispered as she turned back with a smile. "It's alright now, everything will be ok."

The front doorbell rang disturbing the silence, and to my horror as Alice opened the door, I could see Len stood there with a grey and stubborn face, demanding to take me away. At that point I hadn't even considered Len, let alone the fact that he would try and take me away from Alice and Keith.

"I know he's here," he shouted, "you've no right to keep him here he's my responsibility. Why did you remove him from the home?"

Alice glared back at him. "You sick bastard!" she shouted, "have you any idea what happened to him?"

"It's got nothing to do with you," he snarled. "He's our son. You need to mind you own business."

At that moment Margaret appeared behind him, asking if she could come in for a moment. Alice agreed as long as Len stayed outside. "Where is he? I want to see him," said Margaret.

I had taken up my defence behind the settee and I was lying flat on the floor shivering and shaking at the prospects of another excommunication. I think she must have sensed me hiding there as she suddenly peered over the back to see me. "Oh there you are! What happened are you alright?" she asked as though everything was normal.

It was clear that no one at the hospital had uttered a word about what happened, most probably because they were trying to protect themselves fearing reprisal. I suspect that even if Margaret had been given the truth, she would never have believed it, so both Alice and I kept perfectly silent and said nothing.

"Get your things please. You're coming home with me," she said in a matter of fact tone, and as I looked at her the fear in me drained my face of all emotional recognition, feeling only an impending and grey fear.

"Wh-why didn't y-you come and s-see me?" I croaked.

"I had to sort something out. I needed to speak to your Father and he's sorry for what he did to you," she said, but her words were pointless, and her reasoning totally flawed.

"How could Len ever be sorry and why would she lie to me so badly?" I thought, as the many unanswered questions stormed through my head.

"Come on! Get your things David, you're coming with me," she demanded in a very authoritarian manner, when suddenly Keith appeared from nowhere.

"Who's this?" he asked looking from Margaret to Alice and then to me. "Do you mind being quiet please?" he added.

Alice spluttered out that this was my mother, and Keith knowing what had really happened immediately took up a defensive position.

"He's not going back with you until I've got to the bottom of this. You've no idea what has happened, have you?" he barked at Margaret.

By this time Len who had been isolated at the front door, burst in and attempted to snatch me up from behind the settee where I was still prostrate and shaking. "It's alright you can stop the show now!" he snarled, "and you can stop your lies. We're all going home." But as he said it something in his voice told me that Len was feeling threatened. He was obviously keen to protect his own position, not wanting the truth to come out about why I was in the Beechlands in the first place. Although how he thought everyone didn't know, still puzzles me to this day. All I can assume is that his domineering and tyrannical behaviour placed him in his own protective capsule shielded from the reality of what he did.

"David do you want to go with them?" barked Keith.

"N-no," I stuttered.

“Then you aren’t going until I find out what’s going on!” he said.

Margaret let out a shriek again. “I want him to come home,” she demanded, but Keith became even more determined that I stayed put.

“Who placed him at the home in the first place?” he asked, and Margaret turned around just as Len was about to answer for her.

“Mr Conrad-Dick,” they both spouted at the same time.

“Very appropriate name!” he exclaimed with a wry smile. “Does he know what’s been going on?”

“What has been going on?” Len asked, “I was told he’d run away.”

“Oh were you,” said Keith. “Well, you were told wrong. From what I understand that’s not at all what happened. I’ll tell what *is* going to happen though.

“You’ll give me Mr Conrad-Dick’s number and I’ll call him. He can visit David; and if he thinks it’s appropriate, he can then come back to you,” he said, making it clear there would be no compromise.

Len glared at Keith, “You’ve no right to do that,” he spluttered, but Keith was having none of it. “You didn’t see the state of the Lad when he arrived here. Were it not for my wife, he’d have been in real trouble; all through no fault of his own,” he said.

Len started to rant that I was his responsibility until I was twenty-one and that Keith had no right to interfere with the law, but eventually after what seemed a never-ending debate they finally left, promising to return the following day.

Because I’d been crouched on the floor for so long, both my arm and my leg were really hurting me. Alice realised I was in pain and noticed my arm was swelling and led me to the cold-water tap. She turned it on and ran cool water over my wrist, “This is what you get from taking the plaster off too early," she grumped. And whilst I knew she was probably right I didn't care because something told me deep down that I'd need my full faculties in the near future.

The day was very long, and Keith spent much of the time in bed asleep, but eventually he came down the stairs for something to eat. Alice had spent the day talking to me about Len and Margaret; warning me with tedious regularity that what they were doing was wrong and that it would all end in more trouble. I really wanted to return to school and I knew that I needed to catch the school bus from home because it came nowhere near Harlaxton street. I was transfixed with going back to school and the prospect of learning again. Keith slid behind the dining table and started to consume some freshly cut sandwiches Alice had prepared in readiness for him. "I'll be working tonight," he said. "I have a classroom to fit out for Monday."

Alice smiled, "Oh that's disappointing, you should have some time off. You work too hard," she said.

"Someone's got to earn the money!" snapped Keith, who was obviously tired from his broken sleep.

"Point taken," said Alice and she turned on the television.

It's strange the things we remember, and I clearly recall that Dixon of Doc Green came on the TV, and I was struck by the storyline in which he was dealing with a runaway boy who was mistreated by his family. Keith lay back in the chair and stretched out his legs, "I'll be gone all night, but it won't happen too often," he said. We all sat watching the programme, and after an hour or so he rose and went up the stairs to get changed into his overalls. From what I could see Keith was a very keen craftsman capable of fashioning anything from wood, as the house was littered with all manner of things he'd built into the surroundings. He came down the stairs and kissed Alice on the cheek, Colleen was still sleeping as she was virtually nocturnal, and Christopher was upstairs getting ready to go out.

"See you tomorrow," he said, then shouted up the stairs, "Colleen! you be good; no problems please!" There was no sound from her, not even a grunted reply as he closed the front door and went off to work. I hadn't noticed that Alice had become very affectionate towards me as I sat on the floor by her chair. She was obsessed with smoothing my hair and kissing my forehead, but I took it to be a caring gesture and nothing else. The night ticked on and Colleen and Christopher prepared themselves for their Saturday night adventures whilst Alice sat almost mesmerised at my position on the floor beside her. "Do you want a drink?" she asked. "Yes please," I answered.

"We're on our own tonight," she said with a strange smile. I thought nothing of it and simply rested on the settee, which was something I'd never been able to do, and before I knew it, it was eleven-thirty and I was feeling very tired. Christopher was on a sleepover and Colleen was due back sometime in the coming month. I got up and went upstairs to brush my teeth, and as I came out of the bathroom to go to bed, Alice appeared on the landing.

"I'll bring you up a drink in a bit," she said.

"Ok," I insolently replied and closed the bedroom door.

It wasn't long before I heard Alice climbing the stairs and I sat up in the bed to prop myself up with a pillow as I didn't want to spill my drink. The door opened slowly and as I looked over, Alice stood there stark naked with a cup of Horlicks in her hand. My mind went into turmoil and I literally lost control of my thoughts. My head exploded, and my eyes stung at what I saw in the doorway grinning at me. She walked over and attempted to pull back the bed clothes, but I lashed out grabbing the lamp that had stood majestically by the bed. The shade ripped open and the bulb disintegrated into a million pieces as I attacked her with it. Anger ran through me like a white water rapid, struggling to find an exit for the water pressure needed to carve its way to freedom. I pushed her through the door and banged it shut in her face, locking the door. "You dirty bastard! How could you?" I shouted at her through the closed door. "Why me? What's wrong with the world?"

I can't remember getting dressed but I do remember packing my suitcase. I had so few possessions, but with each one I placed into the case I was a step closer to escaping from yet another nightmare. I opened the window which was difficult as it was made of metal and very stiff; but eventually I was able to open it and climb out onto the windowsill where I hoped to lower myself down to the ground, but it was too high. I have no idea how I climbed back inside again, but I did and stripped the bed to tie the sheets together securing one end to the bed leg that was jammed against the wall. I grabbed hold of the tied sheets and gently lowered myself to the ground where Alice was waiting with a broom.

"Where are you going," she whispered, being careful not to disturb the neighbours nearby. I on the other hand had no respect for privacy just the strong desire to escape from her. I grabbed the broom from her hand and whacked her with it and she fell to the floor. Yet again, I had no idea what was going on, but I did know that what I was doing would land me in huge trouble, as I was slowly learning just how evil people really were. She picked herself up bleating, "I'm sorry I'm sorry," but just looking at her revolted me. I picked up my case and opened the front gate.

"Don't follow me just leave me alone," I screamed as I staggered off; the pain in my leg aggravated by my descent from the window.

"Come back," bleated a frail voice. "Please come back, I'm so sorry!"

But I just kept on walking.

Chapter Ten

"A true friend encourages us, comforts us,
supports us like a big easy chair,
offering us a safe refuge from the world"
... H. Jackson Brown, Jr.

The night was cold and my clothes thin as I had not prepared for such an occasion. The streetlights pierced my eyes with a yellow and orange tinge and the damp in the air glistened as I gulped in another mouthful of air. All I could think about was escaping but I had no idea where to escape to. Harlaxton Street was on the other side of Leicester, which meant that to get to Birstall would take hours if I walked. I made my way to the clock tower, which was a familiar landmark, as I'd often seen it when I had travelled to Groby Road hospital with Margaret, and I knew there was taxi rank there. As I reached the clock tower, I could see the illuminated signs of 'ABC Taxis' along a long line of cars and I walked up to one of the drivers and spluttered, "Please s-sir I n-need to get to Birstall and I don't h-have any m-money."

I painfully went on to explain that my dad would pay, and to my astonishment the driver agreed to take me there. His name was Sid; I knew this as I'd heard one of the other drivers call out to him.

"What's your name?" he asked.

"D-David" I stammered, and he then wanted to know how old I was. I stuttered out "F-fourteen," and he leaned across to open the passenger door.

"Do you want to sit in the front?" he asked, and I nodded for ease and climbed in to sit beside him.

"What are you doing out this late you should be in bed by now?" he said, and as he started the car a message came through over the radio telling him to pick a passenger up from somewhere called the LMS.

"Wh-where is the LMS?" I stammered.

"It's the railway station but I can't take the fare coz I'm taking you home," he fired in a broad Leicester accent. He picked up his radio and told the controller he had a fare to Birstall and off we went, along the Melton Road, past brightly lit shops that were enhanced by the orange street lights. I began to get really nervous as I didn't want to go back to Len and Margaret, but I was trapped in my lie and sat there shivering in total uncertainty. It wasn't long before we were turning in to Harrogate drive and Sid spoke, bringing me out of my thoughts.

"Which one is it?" he asked, and I pointed to the house. He pulled the car up to the kerb and climbed out of the car with me, obviously focused on getting his money. My heart was almost jumping out of my chest as I knocked on the front door and Len appeared to darken it.

"I've brought your son back home," Sid rumbled, "and I need the fare."

"He's not my son!" snarled Len as he glared at me with a hatred that was all too familiar and slammed the door closed. I heard Margaret asking who was at the door, but Len gave no answer and I gingerly walked away back down the pathway with Sid.

"OK David. Let's have it. What's going on?" he said.

I burst into tears and tried to explain but there was so much to say that I couldn't say anything. I couldn't bring myself to tell him what had happened as I knew he probably wouldn't believe me anyway.

"Well what do we do now?" Sid barked.

"I'm r-really sorry!" came my stammering response, "I didn't lie to you, he really is my father," I said. "But he hates me."

"Do you have anywhere else to go?" Sid asked.

I looked up like an injured dog and whimpered, "No I don't!"

"Well we're buggered, then aren't we?"

My mind suddenly turned to school where I buried myself in books learning as much as I could. At school I had earned the respect of several of the teachers through my hard work and one in particular was my art teacher who was called Gethin. He had often helped me, spending time listening me in an attempt to understand the reasons for my odd ways and sporadic depressions. He was the one person who knew what had been going on; I knew he would help and more importantly I knew exactly where he lived.

"I-I do have a p-place to go," I stammered. "It's in Loughborough."

"You'll get me the sack!" said Sid, as he picked up his radio again and reported in to say that his car had a puncture and he needed to change the tyre. "You'd better be right this time!" he snapped as we sped off down the road and on to Loughborough. Sid was very quiet as he drove the eight miles to Gethin's house.

"Do you think your friend will be able to pay me?" he finally said.

"Yes," I replied, "I-I'm sure he will."

My art teacher wasn't married and lived in a small terraced house in the centre of the town. I knew where it was as I had often gone there after school for extra lessons, as he was very clever, and I was keen to learn as much as I could from him. As we sped along the road I had no idea what time it was, but the dark of night was gone and I could see the first signs of dawn breaking. A message came over the radio again and Sid answered. A voice asked if he was going yet and he answered, "Yes I'm rolling. I'll be back on the rank in ten minutes."

"I'm sorry David I'm afraid I'll have to drop you here," he said. "I have to get back to the rank or they'll sack me."

"I understand," I spluttered, "Sorry to have been so much trouble to you. What about the money?"

"The trip's on me. It's my present," he said, as he opened the door to let me out. "You take care now," he called after me, and his tyres squealed as he drove off into the distance.

I knew exactly where I was and with great relief calculated that my teachers house was only just down the road. I didn't have a watch, but I heard a town clock striking one-two-three-four-five-six, it stopped, and I realised that the entire night had vanished. I turned the corner into the road and started to panic. All the houses were joined together, and I couldn't remember the number. I walked up and down, passing every house looking for clues as I went. Suddenly a window appeared with a poster for an art festival and I just knew it was his house. I dropped my case and lifted the brass ring on the door which echoed as I frantically beat the plate. My teacher appeared in front of me and I broke down into uncontrollable sobbing.

"Where have you been?" he enquired in his broad Welsh dialect. "You are supposed to be seriously ill. You had better come in and sit down."

He took me into his front room, and I sat down on the sofa and looked around to see I was surrounded by books on every wall, the room lit only by a single window that broke the pattern of the spines.

"Where have you been?" he said again, and I began to stutter and splutter. "No! Calm down, remember what I taught you. Look into your imaginary mirror and watch the way the words are formed, s-l-o-w-l-y."

His calming manner washed over me and I instinctively knew I had made the right decision coming here. I looked into the mirror in my mind, to slowly start a re-run of what had happened to me and why I hadn't been to school. It seemed to take hours to explain as some of the horrors were already filed away in a place where they couldn't hurt me anymore. Gethin was horrified.

"Are you sure that you're not enhancing this?" he said.

I looked at him and shivered. "Why would I do that?"

"Yes you are right," he said as he lit a Tom Thumb cigar and blew a Christmas smell into the room. "Well what are we going to do I wonder? I need to speak to the authorities. And you my lad need to be at school," he said, and his rich Welsh accent and short clipped sentences made me somehow feel secure.

I knew that speaking to the authorities would not do any good as Mr Conrad-Dick had already signalled a reluctance to accept that the system had made a terrible mistake. I also knew that as far as the law was concerned Len was my guardian until I reached the age of twenty-one. I don't know why, but every time I spoke to Gethin I felt a strange confidence and my brain seemed to function with total reasoning and complete clarity. I guess it was my quest for learning and my complete respect for him that caused it to happen. Nevertheless, I felt that speaking to the authorities would only land me back in exactly the same place, with much more serious consequences. I calmly explained to Gethin what might happen and why; he puffed on his cigar and nodded his head, "You are right," he said solemnly, "So what am I supposed to do?"

I took a deep breath and stared at him. "Can I stay here for a while? I'll work very hard and I won't let you down."

"But if I do that the authorities would definitely come down on me. I might even lose my job!" he exclaimed. I knew exactly what he meant and stared at the window as tears distorted the vision in my eyes. He sat down next to me. "We need to think about this," he grunted. "We could all sink. And your father is clearly not a very nice person."

I was so tired that I hadn't noticed my eyes were closing, and my head was swaying forward in a desperate bid to sleep. I can't remember anything else until the clock on the mantelpiece began to chime and I opened my eyes to see Gethin standing there with a cup of tea. "I've been thinking," he said.

"If you stay here, you cannot tell anyone about it until I have perfected the authority to help you."

He always used big words and I always felt impressed, saving each one in my mind for future reference.

"Do you understand what I am saying?"

"Y-yes I think s-so," I stammered.

"You my boy need to slow down and talk properly. Or you won't get anywhere, because no one will understand what you are saying," he said, and his words struck me like a chisel, carving the meaning into my mind like a cartouche in a Pharaoh's tomb. It inspired me to take another deep breath and place another solution before him for his consideration.

"I could only stay here when I'm at school because its close and I won't have to travel. In the holidays I could look after myself and not stay here at all," I said, not only pleased with my idea but doubly pleased by the fact I'd said the whole thing without stuttering.

"You will have to get permission though, or I could be in a lot of trouble," he sparked.

"I think Margaret would agree,"

"Why do you think that?" he asked, and I told him how Margaret had started to support me, apologising for the position she had placed me in.

With that, Gethin sat down in front of his gold and cream Smith Corona typewriter and started to compose a document. I had no idea why, but I assumed it was something to do with Margaret. He made a call to one of his friends and I couldn't help listening as he used a string of fancy words, the meaning of which translated to, *will you allow your son to live here for a while.* I hadn't noticed midday looming up, but as it was Sunday, I was thinking it would be possible to talk to Margaret once I knew what needed to be said.

Gethin sat down and calmly muttered, "Now look. You can stay here for just a few days until we can sort something out. But only a few days mind. Do you understand?"

I gulped with excitement then tempering my exhilaration I said, "Yes," very slowly with great verbal precision. Gethin grinned understanding the effort it had taken for me not to stammer.

It turned out that I didn't need to speak to Margaret, and I have no idea what happened, but she ended up signing a paper agreeing to let me stay whilst things were sorted. In my heart, I knew that she would have been uncertain about the situation, thinking it unsustainable and certainly un-sortable. I sat there gazing at the books that sat on the shelves all around the small front room, longing to pick one up and read it. Feeling clever and more than a little cocky in this new found sanctuary, I sparked up, “Gethin! How long did it take to build the Giza Pyramids?”

“Shelf four, book seven, chapter five. Read it! Then you won’t have to ask so many stupid questions, will you?” came the reply.

It wasn’t long before I was able to properly navigate the bookshelves deliberately constructing questions that were aimed at my analytical behaviour.

Margaret had given Gethin my school clothes, and I had taken time to iron them using a very old but functional iron with total precision. I was keen to look properly dressed as I had been instructed not to mention where I was staying or who I was staying with. My solution was to mimic Margaret’s meticulous nature, which would give the impression that I was still living at home. There wasn’t a day that went by when Gethin didn’t remind me that it was a temporary arrangement, and that at some point I would have to return to Len. I had been there for a week and just returned from school when the front door shattered the silence.

Gethin wasn’t back yet and so I instinctively went to open the door and to my horror both Len and Margaret were stood there. Margaret wore a caring but frightened face and Len was frozen in a transient time warp standing there with his dark coat looking like one of Hitler’s storm troopers.

“Hello David, are you ok?” squeaked Margaret.

I took a really big breath before speaking, then accurately replied, “I’m fine thank you,” in an attempt to demonstrate the effects of my freedom.

“That’s good what have you been doing?” she asked.

I took another deep breath and confidently stated, "I've been working very hard at school."

Len looked disappointed that I wasn't broken and that my vocabulary had improved in such a short time.

"We want you to come home now. We've been talking to Mr Dick and he thinks is a good idea, as we need to be a family again," he said.

I shivered in my soul, but somehow knew I would have to return. Almost on cue Gethin came up the street and through the door, introducing himself in his most officious manner.

"I presume you are David's parents," he said, having seen Margaret only once before.

"Yes that's correct," Len replied in an attempt to bolster his position.

"And why are you here?" Gethin asked them.

"We've spoken to Mr Dick and he thinks it would be a good idea for David to return home," explained Margaret.

"Yes I can see that makes logical sense, as when all said and done you are both still responsible for him," said Gethin and my heart sank. I knew I would have to climb into Len's car, and I shivered at the prospect of the next nightmare that was likely to take place. Gethin invited them both in and beckoned them to sit for a moment.

"Let me make this very clear," he sternly affirmed. "I know what has been going on. And you need to know that I believe your son, completely.

"If he comes back to you, please be assured that he has a place with me if anything goes wrong again. I also want to make it equally clear, that he's not a cheat; but actually, a particularly clever chap. Who you have moulded into an immature individual, who relies upon schoolwork to preserve his sanity."

Len almost shrivelled up and I could see that he felt vulnerable as the truth was finally out, and it was clear that Mr Dick had placed them into a fairly uncomfortable position as I had never seen Len look so subdued before. However, my instincts told me that Len was my enemy and just looking at him struck fear into my heart, as it was he and he alone that had punished me, thrown me away, and devastated every part of my existence. I stared at him without realising that I was clutching the poker that normally hung by Gethin's fireplace. My breathing became unexplainably erratic as I stood up in rage not really having any control over my actions. Gethin became aware of my pending frame and intervened grabbing the poker from my hand.

"If you do that. You will be in more trouble than you could possibly imagine! So, *don't* do it," he growled warningly.

Len immediately boosted by his words, chirped up, "You see how violent he is, I told you Margaret." Gethin glared at them both

"What the hell do you expect?" he said raising his voice. "You have no idea what he has been through. Grow up the pair of you?"

I have no idea how or why, but I agreed to go back with them on the condition that I could return if I found it impossible to cope and I ran up the stairs to collect my things. Returning I bid Gethin goodbye, running over to hug him, but he pulled away.

As I climbed into the car; Margaret smiled and said, "It's good to have you back," having not once asked where my plaster casts were. Seemingly she had forgotten that I'd almost had my skull smashed in with a cricket bat and that she had failed to visit me in hospital, despite promising several times that she would.

Looking back, I find it strange that the adoption society didn't assign anyone to monitor the situation, and that Mr Dick a probation officer, took no action to make sure that no one was hurt again. The simple fact is that due to the war, the entire country refused to believe that their system could get things so wrong. They had to believe in the system because if they didn't it would render the entire conflict pointless. Such atrocities as those I'd experienced at the mental home were comparable to those of the Nazis, and this country and the system they'd fought for wouldn't allow things like that to happen; would it?

Chapter Eleven

"I fear not the man who has practiced 10,000 kicks once, but I fear the man who has practised one kick 10,000 times"
*... **Bruce Lee***

Len seemed unusually quiet on the way back, and I knew he'd retaliate at some point, I just didn't know when. I started to locate weapons in my mind ready to store them in strategic places around the house, when I suddenly realised that Paul wasn't with them.

"Where's Paul?" I asked.

"He's with my mother," chirped Margaret as we pulled into the driveway.

I was really scared as I climbed the stairs and entered my bedroom, it was like being in a time warp but much more confusing. In my mind I could see the bed upturned as I'd seen so many times in the past, and I hated the bathroom being so close as it was the place where so much abuse had taken place. Gethin had made it very clear that what I'd been through wasn't my fault and had seemed to understand what I'd been through, but as I stood there all the memories came back and I was lost in a torrent of thoughts that far outweighed anything we had ever talked about.

Margaret knocked on the door and asked if she could come in, which I thought was strange as Len had always taken the view that it was his house and I'd never been afforded any privacy before. I was instantly suspicious and taking a deep breath I answered, "Yes but not Len." She opened the door and slowly walked in displaying what I perceived to be a suspicious smile on her face. I took another deep breath and started to speak slowly; not wanting to let Gethin's teaching down, as I knew I had to stop my broken speech. He had told me it was a marker of the torture Len had inflicted on me over the years. There was a burning hatred in my heart that consumed every part of me, and I knew I couldn't stay there for long; equally realising that the system would need a good and a just reason to allow my departure. My actions could easily be translated into uncontrollable behaviour and I would be dealt with by torrents of injustice, dealt out by people who were both privileged, and naive to anything that didn't fit into their individual protected worlds. Gethin had made it very clear that some of my actions could be very easily be misread and as a consequence the system would find a box to slot me in, not really caring if the box was appropriate as long as it protected those that started the chain of mistakes that had ruined my childhood to date.

Margaret looked at me and was just about to say, "I'm sorry" when I politely interrupted her and taking a very deep breath I calmly continued.

"Please don't say you're sorry. It doesn't mean anything, as I know you are neither distressed nor sympathetic to what has happened. Nor do I believe that you have the foggiest idea of what I have just been through."

I felt proud of my flowing speech and the fact that I had quoted almost word for word what Gethin had told me in the many hours he had bathed my mind back to some kind of normality.

"H-Have you any idea w-what they put me through?" I stammered, slipping back with anger and forgetting to take a deep breath. She looked at me and advanced to give be a hug, but I retreated.

"Don't. Please don't," I whispered as I didn't want to give Len any excuse to set about me.

"What's the matter? Why are you so cold with me?" she muttered.

I took another very deep breath and concentrated on my reflection in the mental mirror secure in my mind.

"You say you're sorry, but you don't seem to regret Len's actions towards me, and you must know he doesn't feel any remorse." I said. "Are you saying sorry for him?"

I was in full flow and continued, "The simple fact is he did mean to do it and he'll do it again if he gets the chance. If he was a proper person, he would be at the door being sorry and trying to put it right. But I can't see him, can you? Or have I gone blind?"

I silently sighed with delight having again remembered what Gethin had given me in preparation for what I was later to learn was his master plan. Margaret smiled and opened the door to retreat, and I could see that Len had been listening at the door to everything I had said. I started to sweat, and my heart raced, as I braced myself for him to burst in and start attacking me in what he believed to be an acceptable way. Margaret looked at him and calmly asked what he was doing there, but he said nothing and simply moved away from the door.

I was shocked, *what's happened, why isn't he throwing me around?* I thought and as the questions stormed through my mind, I grabbed a paperweight that sat on the bedside table, with the obvious intent of hitting him with it. Then thinking of what Gethin would have said to me, I loosened my grip and placed it back on the table; gazing at the three-dimensional butterfly as I did so, and it seemed to calm my mind and cool my brain. The door closed, and I could hear their two sets of feet going down the stairs. I wasn't ready to go to bed yet and I didn't want to be downstairs with them, so I selected a book and sat on the bed reading it.

I had been reading a book called *The Magic Mirror of MC Escher* before the cricket bat attack, and the book reminded me of my own magic mirror that would one day help me to speak properly. I picked it up and calmly selected the page that had been bookmarked, casting my mind back to pick up the flow and read on. It was a really good book full of mathematical problems with lots of visual illusions which were essentially magic tricks that mesmerised me. As I started to turn the pages, I became lost in the wonder of it, completely forgetting my fear of where I was forced to sleep that night. I read with frantic speed, aware that the book was shielding my fear, and that any break in the flow would cause me to panic and shake. It wasn't until now that I realised just how badly I'd been affected. It was only when the drops fell on the pages and distorted the print, that I realised I was sitting reading with tears streaming down my face. I grabbed a tissue and mopped the pages, but the tears just kept on flowing and I became scared to close the book for fear of a complete collapse. I had no idea why I was falling apart as I hadn't really considered the enormity of what had happened; failing to associate or connect the terrors Len had inflicted on me from the age of three and quite probably before.

I think Gethin knew I was close to cracking up and had devised a plan to save the situation; hoping that I had enough energy to fight the mental stress that had been evident in my actions since I joined his class. My mind cried out for help with a deafeningly silent scream as shaking uncontrollably I could see a clear picture of Alice Oakley standing at the bedroom door naked; and I felt stupid that I hadn't understood the devious nature of the human race. I was a loan animal in a cruel jungle surrounded by human predators, many of which had engineered my entire life to become a living hell.

I suddenly panicked realising I hadn't been to the Groby Road Hospital for several weeks now. I could still remember how painful my breathing had been before I started going there and I didn't want to visit that same state of pain again. Like a giant spring I closed the book having moved the marker to the correct page and sprang from the bed. "Mum!" I screamed, "What about the hospital? I haven't been, and I don't want to get ill again."

She came to the bottom of the stairs and called up to me, "We'll sort it out tomorrow. Don't worry."

"But I have to go to school tomorrow,' I shouted down to her, "I don't want to miss my lessons."

And each time I spoke I made sure I took a large gulp of air so that my speech was unbroken.

"We'll sort it out don't worry!" she said again, and Len appeared behind her with a glare as he directed his apparent anger at me.

"What are you saying?" he grunted, "are you blaming me for your trips to the hospital?"

"N-no!" I squeaked. Then remembering the deep breath again. "I just don't want to be ill and miss school."

I was shivering, and the familiar heat was rising in my body and fearing an attack I returned to the bedroom and closed the door. Margaret came running up the stairs and knocked, "Can I come in?" and this time she entered without a response to her question.

"Don't worry about the hospital, you're much better now and I think they're going to cut the visits down anyway," she said.

"But I don't want the pains to come back again." I responded with astonishing precision.

"They won't but you'll need to run, and exercise more. Perhaps we could find you a bike to ride," she said.

"What! One like Paul's?" I chirped.

He'd not long ago taken possession of a brand-new Raleigh bike that I admit had made me feel very envious.

"We'll see," she whispered and closed the door again. "It's time for bed soon, you have to be up early in the morning."

I could hear Len grumbling downstairs as I stood at the door.

"I'm not buying him a bike," he snapped. "Who does he think he is?"

"It's not your problem. I'll find one for him," she snapped back at him.

"Huh! How are you going to afford that?" he barked.

"I'll ask my mother," she shouted back at him.

"Oh I see! Your rich family again is it?' Len snarled, "he doesn't deserve one."

My mind clicked into overdrive as I contemplated the injustice of what had just been said. I hadn't given one single thought to a bike, yet here I was in the middle of what had become a flow of insulting comments against me.

"I don't want a bloody bike, what are you going on about!" I screamed and slammed the door shut.

I was sure Len would return with an axe as I'd dared to slam the door, but nothing happened. It was quite late, and I looked out of the window to see the sky had darkened and night had closed in exposing millions of stars supported by a large mottled moon that sat there like a giant eye looking down on me. I opened the window to breath in the air staring at the sparkling sky that seemed to give me a hidden form of security and protection from the endless fears that fogged and clogged my brain. There was a chill in the air that was camouflaged by the angle of the window, and I reached out beyond it to catch the cool breeze, mesmerised by the vast array of stars that were placed with such precision; obviously calculated long before time began.

I'd always been keen on trying to understand the planets and Gethin had spent several hours discussing them with me. He'd impressed on my brain that the milky way was a galaxy so big it was outside even his understanding and produced a saucer asking a profound question that should have been easy to answer, but I'd failed.

"If this is the size of our solar system. Then by comparison, how large is the milky way?" he'd asked.

I remembered contemplating his question, thinking really hard trying to imagine that a saucer represented the size of all the planets in our solar system; thinking that the milky way couldn't be that much bigger. Now, staring at the vast night sky I was reminded of his astonishing and questionable answer.

"Well?" he'd said, "answer please?"

"Might be that bookshelf," I'd muttered pointing to the vast array of books covering the wall of the room.

"No. Bigger,"

"Err, England then."

"No! Even bigger," he said smugly.

To my astonishment it turned out, that it was the entire earth that represented the size of the milky way if the solar system were the size of a saucer.

As I sat there now remembering the lesson with Gethin, my head was thinking we were logically so insignificant, and it was impossible to digest the information without gasping. I stared at the night sky to snatch a final glimpse which helped me to relax before I slid the curtains closed, and still puzzled by Len's actions, I undressed and climbed into bed.

There was an almost silent knock on the door; "Darling," whispered Margaret. "Would you like a drink?" In those days it was unheard of to go to bed without a milky drink, and Horlicks was the brand of choice to provide us with a good night's sleep. "Yes please" I answered as she entered, already clutching a tray with three drinks, each with regimented spoons placed on the saucers all at precisely the same angle.

"Thank you, Mum," I said, and as I removed a cup from the tray, she leaned over to kiss me on the forehead. Something collapsed inside me, I just wanted to be safe and so I held out my arms and gripped her as tight as I could, and she melted into floods of tears.

"I'm so sorry," she said and sat down by the bed. "Do you need to talk? I'm ready to listen if you do."

"No it's ok, I'm very tired," I replied, but in truth I had no idea what I could speak to her about. My mind was clogged with unanswered questions, but no one could answer them except for Gethin.

As Margaret closed the door, clicking the light switch off as she did so; thin shreds of light filtered in through the curtains creating an eerie image of the old man who had died next to me at the Beechlands. I started panicking again as I remembered the sticky shiny grime spewing over me as he breathed his last hacking breath. I turned over, but it was no use the fear rose in me and I started to sweat so much that the pillow was sodden and my pyjamas felt like I'd wet them. I was determined not to make a sound, as I just knew Len would intervene and accuse me of all manner of things; incontinence being one of them. Grabbing a towel that was draped over the bedroom chair, I mopped up the deluge that had engulfed me, not understanding what I was experiencing. As I've said before, it didn't dawn on me until years later that I was suffering a form of post-traumatic stress disorder; although in those days it wasn't a term that was used, and the condition certainly wasn't understood in the way it is today. I opened the curtains and hung my head out of the window to try and cool off, making a loud creaking noise as I did so, and I heard Len shouting out to Margaret, "If you don't shut him up I will," but I was so wet nothing else seemed to matter.

The temperature had dropped considerably, and the night air bathed my face to relieve the burning that was almost melting me. My heart had started to pump again, my head was thumping, and I could feel my eyes burning and stinging as I desperately tried to correct the dire situation. I'm not sure how long it took but eventually I dried off and slid back into bed between the damp uncomfortable sheets; laying the towel on top of them to try and mop up some of the residue. Despite my best efforts I was obviously making a noise, because Len banged on the door shouting, "Shut up you bastard, I'm trying to sleep."

Disappointed that my efforts to be quiet had been in vain, I turned over and tried to sleep; relieved that at least Len hadn't attacked me but at the same time I was bitterly aware there was no lock on the door and my silence was essential if his perverted ways were to be avoided.

Morning came with Len deliberately trying to make a noise as he clattered in and out of the bathroom. He possessed little or no consideration for others and didn't mind the thundering sound as he passed water in the toilet. Most polite people would have tried to muffle the sound by aiming at the side of the bowl, but not him who worked on the simple principal of take aim and fire. Knowing he was trying to get even for my disturbing him the night before, I pulled the pillow over my head to muffle the sound. But in my attempt to block him out I'd completely forgotten he was prone to attacking me if I didn't rise at his designated time. He burst into the bedroom and pulled back the bed clothes to expose me to the cold air.

"Get up you lazy bastard," he snarled at me and stormed back out again.

My instinct was to say nothing, and I got up. At the very least I was thankful the bed was still the right way up and I wasn't fighting for my life again. My arm was hurting like hell and the pain in my leg was nothing short of crippling, with sharp pulses shooting up and down. It seemed like years ago when Keith had relieved me of the plaster on my leg and I had slipped the one off my arm whilst I was in the bath at Mrs Oakley's house; and I was beginning to wish that I hadn't. Gethin had demonstrated that I needed to exercise my limbs, making it very clear he believed I'd done the right thing. He said that plaster casts restricted movement and damaged the tissue; something I still believe to this day. I was comforted by his teachings and was equally willing to sit on the bed manipulating my bones as he had instructed. I was just setting about my exercises when Len broke into the bedroom again and glared at me.

"What are you doing you bloody ponce," he growled taking care to stay well out of Margaret's hearing, "you need to get ready for school."

He clearly had no remorse over what he'd done to me with the cricket bat, the damage and effects of which were erased from his mind. His own injuries from the missile I'd thrown had completely healed without a trace and I felt a deep sense of resentment and total injustice at his evil wrongdoings. Nevertheless, I carried on without further attack and entered the bathroom to wash myself after the severe sweating episode the previous night. I had remembered to hang up my school clothes the night before, and Margaret had prepared a clean white shirt to accompany them, carefully draping my tie around the collar ready for me to tie the Windsor knot which I had perfected some time ago.

In the week I'd spent with Gethin he'd insisted that I did everything myself, which I was delighted and privileged to do, as independence represented a freedom where I no longer relied upon anyone and it felt good. I called down to Margaret and asked if I could polish my shoes. "I'll do them," she chirped but I immediately responded, that I'd rather do it myself, which caused Len to immediately spring into action. "Oh I see! Your mother's efforts aren't good enough for you now?" he shouted up to me, and as he slipped his coat on, I could see the effortless hatred in his eyes, and I knew he would never change.

My leg was hurting as I slowly crept down the stairs, wincing and groaning at every step, and Margaret finally noticed I no longer had the plaster casts on and in a shocked voice asked who had removed them. I didn't want to trouble her and told her it was one of the doctors at the Beechlands.

"Bit soon wasn't it?" she exclaimed.

"Yes," I said, declining to tell her the real story; and as I sit here writing this book, I think back to how different this story would be if I hadn't removed them. For one thing I would never have scaled the window of Mrs Oakley's house on my improvised ladder.

I sat at the table and consumed my customary bowl of cornflakes, and Margaret prepared my favourite scrambled eggs. I felt strangely sorry for Margaret as I knew that if it was in her power to change what had happened she would.

"I have to go and collect Paul today," she said as she placed the eggs in front of me, "he's already missed a day at school."

"Ok," I squeaked back at her as my voice was still hoarse and prone to infection. I tucked into the food and the sudden unexpected heat made me start to cough, bringing a concerned and horrified look to Margaret's face. "I love you mum," I said, and she smiled back as if I'd just lit the brightest warmest fire in her heart and I knew then that she was just as much a victim as I was. I finished breakfast and put on my blazer ready to go off to school.

"I'll be back quite late, so I'll leave some sandwiches in the box for you," she said.

"Ok," I croaked and slid open the door to walk painfully down the road to catch the school bus.

Like clockwork the coach drew up to the pickup point with timed precision, the doors slid open and I parked my school cap on top of my head, as it was against school rules not to wear it on the bus. What made it even more difficult was that the cap had a cord with a tassel attached to it which made it even more difficult to balance on the back of my head. I slowly moved up the bus to the back seat to receive volumes of applause. I had no idea why, but the entire bus appeared pleased to see me back again. The applause was a shock, and I felt almost honoured; I wondered if Gethin had said something to his colleagues, but at the same time I knew he wouldn't have given away any of the gruesome facts. However, they all seemed to be aware that I'd been through a bad time and deemed my return was worthy of applause. My friend Tony was sat at the back as usual.

"Hi, David, how the hell are you? We've missed your smiling face, what's been happening are you ok?"

I took a deep breath and responded, "I'm fine thank you."

"Christ! What happened to the stuttering? Is that what you've been up to?" he said in amazement, and as I was keen to cloak the truth I said, "Yes I've been having speech and elocution lessons."

"Where's the limp come from?" he asked, having not missed a thing as I stumbled up the bus.

"Don't know it's just a bit stiff, I fell of my bike and bruised it," I said.

I could see he knew more than I was telling him, so I simply sat down and affirmed that I didn't want to talk about it, but I was very keen to ask them what I missed at school. Tony smiled, "You're right. Sorry nothing to do with me but if you need an ear then I'm your boy," he said with a grin.

I have no idea where the day went as it was four-thirty before I knew it. Gethin had been very careful to avoid me, except in English where he had collaborated with Mr Griffin who asked me to read a poem out loud to the class. I performed it perfectly without even one break in my speech and the entire form celebrated with applause as my impediment was all but gone, and with it my confidence dramatically increased. I am delighted to tell you that thanks to Gethin's efforts I have been able on occasion to address several hundred people at various rallies and meetings in later life. It was he and he alone that battled with me and released me from my broken speech and uncertain future.

The bus was slightly late that day and several people had given up and called their parents to come and collect them. I on the other hand had no one to call, and as such, sat on my bag reading a book awaiting its arrival. Eventually it did arrive, and I filed onto the bus with the rest of my patient friends. For some strange reason I'd forgotten to put my cap on, and a prefect stomped up to inform me that he'd report me if I didn't put it on. I couldn't see much point in the cap, and waiting for the bus, combined with the pain in my leg had made me irritable. I snapped back at him and he took my name to report it to Mr Modrell the deputy head, the next morning. I retrieved my cap and placed it on my head, but the prefect would have none of it and still intended to report me the next morning. Immediately feeling uncomfortable with my actions and regretting the way I had snapped; I went up to the prefect to apologise. "I'm really sorry Roger. Not feeling very well and I shouldn't have snapped."

Roger was adamant and refreshed his commitment to reporting me the next day. I didn't want to let Gethin down, so glaring at him I said, "Oh I see, you're going to threaten me now, are you?"

"I'm only doing my duty," he said, and his words glued themselves in my brain. I started to shake with rage, managing to stop only when I considered the effects of such actions, all thanks to Gethin and his never-ending bounty of information.

The bus pulled up at the usual place and the door slid open, Roger was still growling but wished me a pleasant night and I returned the comment. I slung my bag over my shoulder balancing my cap on the back of my head and sauntered up the road to cut through the hedge and was soon outside the house opening the gate to squeeze past Len's car. I was dreading being alone with him as I knew that Margaret was going to be late. I quietly opened the door and carefully removed my shoes before I went up the stairs to hang up my clothes. Len was in the kitchen glaring at me, his face twisted and determined to comment upon my arrival.

"What are you doing here? Why don't you just bugger off?" he grunted, confident that there was no one around to hear what was going on.

I kept on seeing Margaret's face shredded with pain and confusion; uncertainty ground into her kind generous face. I gripped my teeth together, said nothing, and simply walked past him to get to the bottom of the stairs. On the way I saw the cricket bat that he'd used to crush my skull and instinctively picked it up fearing another attack. He must have been watching my every move as he loomed up behind me and demanded to know why I'd picked it up.

I knew exactly why I had picked it up, and momentarily forgetting to check my stammer, I answered, "I I w-was going to put it away for you."

He glared at me again, "No you weren't you little bastard. You were going to attack me with it, weren't you?"

I bit my tongue again and slowly climbed the stairs in complete silence. He thundered up to me shouting and swearing, "You bastard you won't beat me. I'll get the better of you." I still said nothing and kept on walking with the bat firmly gripped in my hand.

"Why don't you just bugger off and leave us all alone?" he shouted which was baffling as it wasn't twenty-four hours ago that he'd stood at Gethin's door whilst Margaret begged me to come home.

By this time, I was alight with anger as he followed me up the stairs. "Go away," I pleaded, "please leave me alone," but he continued to advance towards me. I was starting to shake, and the heat was rising in my body again. My head was screaming out for answers but there were none; just confusion pain and heartache. Still gripping the bat, I turned and held it in the air. I could see him crashing it down on my head and felt totally broken when I remembered what had happened; reminded that his actions were all because I'd done well at school. My mind was in rage and my heart thumping out of my chest.

"Put that down you bastard," he screamed, "or I'll ring the police again."

His words cut me like a knife and ricochet back to Gethin's prolific words; *Don't do anything rash*, he'd said. *Keep your temper under control even if it feels impossible. You will win through, but the system is strong and full of people who would not benefit from exposing what has really happened since you were adopted.* But I was so angry that I swung the bat around and smashed the bedroom door.

"That's it you mad bastard," screamed Len. "You're out of here."

I shivered with fear at what I'd done but, in my mind, there was a complete blank as if nothing had happened. Len was watching as the emotions played across my face and looked delighted with the result.

"I'm not a bastard," I screamed out at him.

"Yes you are!" he snapped. "You were the product of a prostitute who didn't even know who your father was!"

"How do you know that?" I said, realising that the strain on my vocal cords was beginning to show again.

He sneered and said, "I met your slut mother and you come from shit. You're nothing but a failure from start to finish, a cheat and a liar."

By this time, I was starting to realise what he was up to, trying to provoke me into actions that would be seen in a bad light by the system. A system that would naturally support him, the upstanding perfect person that had freely offered to adopt an unwanted child. I realised that I'd fallen into his trap again by smashing the door, and that his interpretation of what happened would be miles away from the truth. I tried to stop shaking, which was very difficult, then I opened the broken door and went into my room to lie down on the bed. To my astonishment he turned around and went downstairs, but I knew my position was shaky and the smashed door was about to become the centre of his devious plan. I lay on the bed hoping that Margaret would return and understand what had really happened, but I also knew deep down that she was just as trapped as me and I was about to be kicked out again. I consoled myself with what Gethin had said and closed my eyes.

Suddenly I heard the kitchen door open as a car pulled away. Paul's familiar chatter filled the air and I could hear Len informing

Margaret that I'd deliberately smashed the door to my bedroom. Within seconds my bedroom door opened, and Margaret entered the room.

"Why have you smashed the door?" she snapped at me. "What happened?"

Her words were accompanied by a spontaneous glance at the cricket bat propped up against the bed.

"Why's that in your bedroom? What's been going on?"

I had no idea what to say. My mind was littered with possible consequences and I knew that Len would contradict whatever I said, so I simply kept quiet.

"David what happened, why have you smashed the bedroom door?" she asked for a second time.

Realising I'd have to respond sooner or later I searched for an answer, but as I did so I could hear Len's breath behind the door and knew I was a prime target for his hatred again. Nevertheless, taking a deep inspired breath I slowly recorded the truth to her, reporting everything second by second, with extreme accuracy.

Len came bursting in. "You liar!" he screamed. "You hit it with the bat deliberately!"

Margaret looked at him wearily, clearly bored with the evasion of the truth. "Why did he need to pick up the cricket bat in the first place?' she asked.

"He was going to put it away as it was still propped up in the hallway," Len answered.

I knew I was going to be tangled up in a torrent of thoughts and feelings, because what Len had said was precisely what I'd told him and therefore the truth.

My mind span into confusion as it dawned on me the real reason I'd picked it up was to defend myself. I was also aware that the bat had sparked in me a deep resentment of what had happened; not dissimilar to a man visiting a crash site where his family had been badly hurt. I was lost; my speech paralysed with a sea of thoughts and I knew that whatever I said would be re-written to Len's version of the truth. I turned over to face the window feeling very guilty that I'd likely let Gethin down. I was in an impossible position as my anger had caused me to distort the reasons for my actions; just as Gethin had predicted. Len stood triumphantly demanding a response.

"Is that the truth, did you tell me you were putting it away?" he questioned me.

"Y-yes" I stammered.

"Oh please! Cut the acting, I thought you d-didn't s-stutter anymore," jibed Len.

I was devastated, frustrated and completely lost; unable to react, but equally knowing exactly what the truth was. My thoughts turned to Mr Dick who had asked me if I'd ever been molested by Len? I remembered how I'd innocently told him the truth, only to receive a barrage of excuses about how the system would never place a young child into that position, which hurled me into total confusion. I began to feel that I was a liar and there must be something wrong with me. Len had groomed me with his favourite phrase, *Now look what you made me do!* and I stumbled around the possibility that it could have been all my fault.

Margaret squeezed by the window to stand beside my bed and turned my head to face her. "Don't worry, we will sort this all out," she said. But in my heart, I knew it was all wishful thinking, I was on a collision course with Len and I knew that he would never rest until I was gone.

Once again, I was tearing my head apart trying to find a solution to what was a totally impossible problem. My head was aching, and my leg was shooting pains up and down whilst planting a permanent dull ache in my back that made it very uncomfortable to keep still. All had become almost silent again, apart from Paul laughing and giggling as Len chased him up the stairs to bed. I was exhausted and yearned to close my eyes, yet the light shone through my eyelids illuminating strange shapes that drifted across my frustrated sight. I was mesmerised at the array of shapes and lay there in anticipation of the next graphical display. Paul by now had his own room for what Len had suggested was his *protection against my violent behaviour.* I heard the sound of the light switch being turned off and the door to Paul's room being closed and I listened out to hear Len descend the stairs before heaving a sigh of relief. I was almost unconscious when I realised my own bedroom light was still on and I slid out of bed to take off my clothes and prepare to sleep. I nervously opened the bedroom door which now creaked loudly since my attack with the cricket bat and pulled the cord to turn on the bathroom light. Running some water into the basin I selected a flannel to douse myself all over in the hope of removing the days grime.

Since Gethin had determined the importance of cleaning my teeth, I pulled my brush from the rack and pressed a measured amount of white paste onto the brush. In only a week I had become obsessed with the cleaning process and spent perhaps longer that I should have, scrubbing them to what I hoped was perfection. Len came thundering up the stairs and burst open the door. "Be quiet," he shouted destroying the silence with his own voice. "You'll wake Paul up. Get to bed you bastard," he whispered so that Margaret couldn't hear, and he pushed me into the bedroom with toothpaste still running down my cheeks.

Luckily a towel was still draped over the chair, and carefully removing the white foam from my face, I finished undressing and climbed into bed. My head hit the pillow and I was out like a light until morning appeared as if by magic and I slowly opened my eyes to another day.

Keen to get out of the house as soon as possible, fearing an overflow from the night before, I quietly rose and opened the door wandering to the bathroom in a daze. It seemed like only seconds since I'd been cleaning my teeth the night before.

Margaret came running up the stairs and shouted, "Are you ok?"

"Yes, I'm fine," I replied, thinking that I was soon to be facing Len around the breakfast table again.

"Your father has already gone to work," she said, and my mind was bathed with total relief. "He had to go and purchase some hardboard to repair the door," she went on and I felt strangely guilty at being the culprit of his errand.

"Sorry," I said in a subdued but meaningful way.

"It wasn't your fault. I know what happened," she replied.

"How do you know?" I croaked, as my voice started to rebel again at the straining of the new day. Margaret paused for a moment and came up to me and smoothed my hair.

"Because you told me, and I believed every word," she whispered.

It was perhaps the best breakfast that I'd ever had at that house, even Paul was nice, and Margaret seemed to enjoy every second of the newly found harmony. Finishing breakfast, I slipped my coat on, kissed her cheek and set off down the road to the bus stop.

Arriving at school I couldn't wait to tell Gethin what I'd done and why, as I feared I may have placed him into an awkward position. I knew where he parked his car, so I waited for him to arrive, sitting down on my bag as I did so. After a few moments, Gethin drove up, and I rose running to him. In my desperation to tell him what had happened, my words glued up and I stammered worse than I had ever done before.

"What the devil has happened to you?" he cried, "Have you lost your mirror what's happened to you? D-e-e-p breath."

I could see that he wasn't comfortable with my presence but still found time for me to sit in his car. "Deep breath, now what is wrong, what's happened?" he asked.

I took a deep breath and slowly started to unwind the seconds of the night before.

"Well you can't stay there. It bloody dangerous! Why the hell did he want you to go back?" he exclaimed. Then after a few moments he calmly grinned, and said "Come on, school. It's learning time now," and I followed him up the steps and through the main door.

The day flew by much too quickly and all too soon I found myself climbing aboard the coach for the homeward journey. Nevertheless, it was a good journey as Tony cracked jokes and the whole bus enjoyed the humour, with some buckling up with uncontrollable laughter. Suddenly it was my stop and my heart slipped a beat as I reluctantly waited for the door to slide open. Glancing at the hedge I aimed at the gap and sprang through to take the shortcut, having no idea why I should want to speed up my arrival. Nearing the front gate of the house with its neat and tidy garden I had an impending sense that something was wrong.

As I slipped past Len's car to the back door, I was confronted by a huge cardboard box with the Kellogg's logo on the side. It was the large outer packing case used to house dozens of smaller boxes of cornflakes, like the one that sat on our breakfast table each morning; and it was parked directly outside the back door. I peered in to see that it was packed full of clothes; my clothes.

The back door was closed and as I peered through the reeded glass I could see Margaret had been crying and that Len had bolted the door. "Bugger off," he shouted glaring back at me through the striped window.

"I warned you what would happen if you caused any more trouble. And don't think you're going back to Gethin's. I've already spoken to him."

I was speechless as my mind raced around in circles that made me feel dizzy, there were so many unanswered questions and I could see that Len had deliberately visited Gethin's home to protect his position with Margaret. My heart shivered, *how could he be so evil*, I silently screamed and taking a deep breath I went to respond but no words would come out.

Staring at the Kellogg's packing carton which was easily five feet high and stuffed with everything I possessed, my eyes were drawn to the Beatles album that Margaret had bought me the week before. It was the appropriately named Help album and it was tucked in at the top of the box. I will always remember the pure white sleeve with John, Paul, George and Ringo posing in athletic positions across the front cover. I was almost grateful that they'd packed it, despite the fact I had nothing to play it on. On the rare occasions I'd played it I'd been allowed to use Len's Danset Major which I had taken as a huge privilege. I was consumed in ridiculous thoughts and just stared at the box with utter amazement. My head was in turmoil, but it was impossible to cry or show any emotion at all, and so I just sat there dazed and shivering.

I have no I idea how much time slipped by but finding some coppers in my pocket that Margaret had given me for the tuck shop at school, I decided to get up and go to the telephone box. For some strange reason the further I walked down the road away from Len, the more emotional I became, and when I reached my destination I was in floods of tears unable to focus on the dialling disk. Eventually I picked up the telephone, inserted the money and dialled the number which I had indelibly recorded in my mind. The phone rang, and Gethin answered. I remember having trouble pressing button *A* as it was stiff but managed it in the end.

"G-Gethin," I stammered, and he sternly told me to slow down and speak properly. I took a deep breath and slowly started to unreal what had happened.

"What is your number?" he demanded, but someone had unscrewed the middle and the paper disk with the number on it wasn't there, so I couldn't provide him with the information.

"Ok," he said, "if the phone goes, dial my number and ask the operator to reverse the charge. This stops now!" he growled. "Enough is enough."

Gethin clearly new nothing of what had happened and Len keen to torture me at every opportunity had made up a story just to cause terror, inferring that he'd spoken to Gethin and that I wouldn't be able to return to him. The bleeps went, and my money fell into the box beneath. I panicked but remembered what Gethin had instructed and dialled 100 for the operator and a kind voice answered, "Number please."

I stuttered, "I I need a r-reverse ch-charge number please." I gave her the number with ease as it only had four digits. I heard a voice ask Gethin if he would accept the charge and I was back in contact again. Determined to be strong I listened as Gethin told me that he wanted me to return to my box of possessions and wait there, as he was coming over to pick me up.

"You do not deserve this. It is totally disgraceful," he barked; his speech always precise even when angry, his Welsh accent lengthening the vowel sounds.

Putting the phone down I pushed open the door which was heavy, and spring loaded. I slid through the gap not realising it had started to rain. The journey back seemed to take hours as I simply didn't want to return, but once there I opened the gate to find the box all but saturated and the Help album had gone. Len was behind the door again and I could hear Margaret wailing in tears.

Disappointed and angry I screamed out, "Where is my record?"

"It's not yours it's ours," came back Len's reply.

I tempered my anger as I knew Gethin would be arriving and Len would have to explain what my clothes were doing in a saturated box. Like the box I was also getting very wet, so I took shelter under the front porch; sitting down as I waited for Gethin to arrive. As I sat there my mind drifted as if to provide an escape from what was going on.

I raced back to my fourth birthday when Margaret had brought me a Dinky Toy crane; it had an orange body and a yellow crane with a winder on it and a huge hook to lift all manner of things including knives, forks and spoons. I was so proud of my toy and had been playing with it for hours when Len had revolted and accusing me of stealing the cutlery, he seized the crane, took it to his garage and smashed it up with a hammer.

I am guessing that the Help album was yet another act of sickness that was beginning to erode on me as a person and I knew I just had to escape.

CHAPTER TWELVE

"It is the supreme art of the teacher to awaken joy in creative expression and knowledge"
... Albert Einstein

The rain began to get really heavy but no one not even Margaret came out to cover up the box. I hadn't really given any accurate thought to the fact that everything I owned was in the there, and that my life would be thrown into visual havoc if I had nothing to wear. But I was somehow comforted by the fact that I'd tested Gethin's iron and proved that I was capable of producing a presentable effect. Gethin drew up in front of the house and immediately saw the saturated box by the door. He climbed out of his car, walked straight up and peered into the box then violently banged on the door.

"What the hell is going on?" he snapped, "You evil bastards. This is as close to torture as your ever going to get."

Len unlocked the door to be met with Gethin's fuming outraged anger.

"Don't say anything, not a word! Do you understand?" he went on and Len retreated.

Margaret came to the door weeping and wailing that she never wanted this to happen.

"Well it has, hasn't it?" Gethin said to her. "And as usual the lad has done nothing to deserve it. What makes it worse, is that you *chose* to look after him; no one *made* you do it, did they?

"You need to leave him he's a mad man!" he said, pointedly.

Margaret froze as Paul tugged on her shoulder to close the door.

"Mum come back in," he insisted, "you can't change anything."

By this time, I was standing by Gethin peering into the box as the rain had drowned everything.

"I'm taking him with me and if you come anywhere near again, I will report you to the authorities," he snapped.

The rain had eased off and had nearly stopped as I looked into the box which had all but collapsed and my clothes were falling out.

"Do you have any plastic bags?" barked Gethin at Margaret who was still standing behind the door. "Or would you prefer that he just wore his underwear from now on?"

Margaret opened the door clutching several large plastic bags and handed them to Gethin.

"Thank you," he said "It's about time someone displayed some sense. We'll be gone as soon as I can get his clothes into the car."

Len was very quiet, and I began to worry what he was up to as he was prone to jumping out with surprise attacks and I was scared that he was planning a move on Gethin. I looked at Gethin and he smiled, "We'll have you out of here soon," he said. "Won't be long now."

Some of the clothes from the middle of the box were quite dry as I stuffed them into on one of the bags, but others were saturated and difficult to handle as I loaded them on to the back of the seat of Gethin's car.

"I'm sorry Gethin," I said.

"What for? You've done nothing wrong," he answered. "Nothing at all, so what have you to be sorry for?"

There was something in me that felt uncomfortable as I realised that Gethin was the innocent bystander.

"Are you sure you don't mind Gethin. I had no idea this was going to happen. I shouldn't drag you into it, it hasn't anything to do with you really," I squeaked as my voice had changed again suffering from the effects of past terrors.

He looked at me again and smiled, "Tell me about it when we get home," he said. "It *is* something to do with me now. I've made it so. Now just shut up and finish moving this stuff into the car."

It was surprising how much Len had managed to pack into the box, and he had lined it with shoes and socks at the bottom making it very heavy. It would have busted for sure if I'd tried to move it, which was obviously his intention. I piled the last bag into the car and feeling very damp I climbed in and sat in the passenger seat to wait for Gethin. I could hear him shouting at Len, "I don't know what you think you're doing? You adopted him, no one forced you, did they?" he repeated. "This is wrong!"

Len sprang out from behind the safety of the front door; "You have no idea what he's like! He's violent and stupid and lies about everything," he shouted out.

"I can see that he was with me for a week, until you turned up begging him to come back to you," said Gethin. "*You* are the liar. *You* are violent. And from what I can see, *you* are certainly stupid as well!" he said emphasising the word you, each time he said it.

Len fell back as if he'd been shot with the truth and sank it to a tirade of self-pity, calling Margaret to come and listen but she didn't appear. He slid back into the house as Gethin walked back down the path, opened the door, started the engine and we were off.

It didn't take long at all to reach his home but all the way I'd felt strangely quiet, lost in a never-ending stream of thought. I was desperately searching for answers in what had become an epiphany; a sudden realization that I was not wanted and that my position was totally predictable, yet no one wanted to listen save tarnishing the system that had allowed Len's tirade of torment and disease.

As we pulled up outside the house, it had completely stopped raining and the dusk had illuminated the horizon marking the end of yet another day. "Well come on my lad, it's time we put all this rubbish behind us," he chirped. "Move your clothes out of the car and put the wet ones into this basket please." I was tired but not with exhaustion and immediately sprang into action.

"Your hell is over!" he pronounced. "I won't let his happen to you again."

I looked up took a deep breath and answered, "You know that he's still legally responsible for me and that I have to be twenty-one before that changes?"

"Yes I know," said Gethin. "We'll just have to deal with that when we get there." But I just knew deep down in my heart that it wasn't over yet and that it wouldn't be the last time my life would be dislodged by Len's actions. It took me ages to unload the car and I knew that Gethin wanted me to understand that every bagful was a statement of freedom; preferring that I did it all alone, and he was right. As I entered my room, which had been mine for a week before, I carefully folded each dry item with complete precision and placed it into the already open drawers, each action giving me a strange and dramatic feeling of belonging.

I had finished the task when Gethin produced a cup of Darjeeling tea; I didn't want to insult him as I secretly didn't like the taste and so I sipped it slowly remembering to turn my head away if the smoky taste made me shiver. We sat for a while until, producing a pair of his own pyjamas, he handed them to me laughing as he did so. "You'll have to climb in and hide in these, as yours are all drenched," he said.

The night air was cold as it blew in through the sash windows which had been left slightly open to fill my room with clean fresh air. I undressed and climbed into Gethin's pyjamas which were so big I had to turn the legs up several times and the sleeves were even worse. Opening the door to go to the bathroom, I could smell the aroma of Tom Thumb cigars wafting up the stairs. I had a very quick wash and cleaned my teeth as surprisingly my toothbrush had been in the box in a proper bag with toothpaste slid in by the side, there was even a bar of soap. I suspected that Margaret, trying to repair the damage with her cleansing feelings, had slipped them in without Len seeing them.

I stepped down the stairs one by one following the aroma of Gethin's lighted cigar. "Can I sit for a minute?" I asked faultlessly. Remembering to take a deep breath before I attempted to say anything.

"Yes of course," he calmly answered. "What do you want to talk about?"

"You know," I whispered. "I'm worried about the problems that are almost certain to happen if I stay here. Len doesn't want me to do well and I don't want to let you down."

He looked at me puffing on his cigar and calmly answered, "I know. It will get worse before it gets better and I am likely to come under fire, so not a word until I can sort this out."

"But why are you doing this for me?" I asked.

"Well; you're smart, you listen, you have a hunger to learn, you are a brilliant artist, and you are a fighter. To be honest you remind me of me," he said smiling as the words left his mouth.

I had no idea how to answer and so I just rose up from the chair climbed the stairs and jumped into bed. The entire episode seemed like it was lost in my mind, all I could think about was Monday when I would go back to school, and I ticked off all the problems that could or were likely to happen. Saturday morning came, and the sunlight peered through the heavy curtains that clung to the wooden rods above the window. I was startled, somehow forgetting that I was no longer at Len's house. My head was thumping, and I was sweating under the heavy sheets that felt like they were crushing me.

I climbed out of bed and went over to the window which was still slightly open letting cold air in through the gap. Lifting the window still higher I peered out to breath in some clean air and my head suddenly became engaged in what had happened the night before. I hadn't had the time to really consider the facts, as it all happened so quickly. So many questions looming in my head came rushing back, like flaming arrows that set fire to the anger in my mind. Piece by piece I put my feelings in to place like a giant jigsaw puzzle, to expose what I considered to be the facts, and my deep intention to protect Gethin. It was an horrendous picture as all the pieces served to illuminate the many areas that I'd chosen to hide for so long. Looking back I must have been suffering from a sort of shell shock again as I began to re-model the events in my mind, every aspect left the need for answers but there were none just a darkened frameless sepia picture with nothing to read or explain.

I felt like screaming as loud as I could but my respect for Gethin prevented me from doing so. Glancing at the clock staring at me from the bedside table, I noted the time, six-thirty which was very early and verging on inconsiderate seeing as it was the weekend. Respect alone forced me back into bed and I retrieved a book that I'd started several days ago before Len had chosen to invade me again.

I sat there turning the pages of the book not really reading as my head was still trying to correct the injustice of it all. My vision was blurred with the tears that fought to escape from my brain. It had all become too much and I started to wail, holding my breath to avoid waking Gethin. I was reeling in pain as I realised that the end of one set of trouble was just the beginning of another. I had contaminated Gethin's tranquil life with uncertainty and doubt at how the system would react, if they realised I was living in his house. Slowly the heat began to rise in my body and the pain flowed into me like a flash flood that had broken the banks of an angry white-water river.

I glanced at the clock again, it was still only seven-thirty and time was dripping by more slowly that I would have liked. Suddenly the door opened, and Gethin walked in and I realised I'd been so lost in thought I hadn't even heard him get up. "Good morning are you ready for the new day my boy? New challenges, new learning and that sort of thing?" he said cheerily. I think he'd heard me silently weeping and he could now see without doubt that I had, but he chose to ignore what he knew were the inevitable consequences of the nights edification.

"I don't want you to be bothered about *me*," he calmly announced.

"I am big enough and ugly enough to sort this all out. In fact we need to *both* sort it out *together*," he said.

I was lost in a sea of transcriptions, reminded that this was all about opinions, and that most people were aware of only their own positions, which was why Len had been able to cause so much havoc over the years.

Gethin on the other hand was bucking the system and appeared to have no regard for his own position, much less the inevitable problems that would emanate from his innocent involvement in my life.

His retro behaviour made me feel important and his words built up my confidence to take on the day, but I was tied to a see-saw that disallowed my weight to make any difference to the outcome; all I had was my thirst for learning and Gethin was the oasis that offered those dreams to me.

I felt guilty to the point of being greedy as I knew that my stay with Gethin would be a lot longer than before, yet something inside me hammered out the inevitability that Len would appear in the darkness again and intentionally interrupt or even destroy my efforts and in doing so ruin Gethin's as well.

The rest of the weekend went without incident and I was kept busy trying to dry the clothes that were salvageable and washing the others that weren't. I remember thinking that Margaret would be proud of my efforts, but I wasn't doing it for her, I was doing it for Gethin in order to maintain the pretence of still being at home. By the end of Sunday, the entire contents of the box were neatly packed away and I felt rather pleased with myself as I sat in the front room with Gethin surrounded by hundreds of books that I couldn't wait to read. We'd chatted on and off and talked through how things were going to work, and it was quite late when he said, "Come on now we need to be early in the morning, best get off to bed now. And remember, the same rules apply as before until I can sort this out properly."

I knew exactly what rules he was referring to and I mentally ticked off each point as I went up the stairs to sleep. Part of me was looking forward to going to school but the other half was nervous at the prospect of slipped words that could be innocently manipulated by interested parties who were bound to ask searching questions.

Monday morning came, it was six-thirty and I'd woken early as I was keen to get to school where I could bury myself in books and learning. I planned to walk to school in an effort to further protect Gethin and I wasn't entirely sure how long it would take me. Rising I made my way to the bathroom and carefully maintained my hygiene with detailed precision. I had this new-found desire to make sure that my outward appearance added credit to my stay with Gethin, even if I couldn't actually tell anyone.

I finished and went downstairs to enjoy my breakfast of toast and marmalade more than I had done for years. With no glares, no insults and no attacks, just the polite meaningful conversation in which I felt a newly found importance that was so strange it made me shiver with excitement.

"Right then my boy we need to make a move," said Gethin, and like clockwork I adjusted my tie, placed my cap on my head in exactly the right position and opened the front door to leave.

"Where are you going?" Gethin asked.

"I'm going to walk, it's not far," I said.

"Far enough!" exclaimed Gethin. "Jump in the car."

I smiled and looked him straight in the eyes, "I have to protect you! As well you know," I said, and I closed the door and set off on what did turn out to be much further than I thought.

School was somehow more intense now, I found myself focusing on every tiny detail, nothing escaped my attention. If there was a question to be answered I was always the first to put my hand up and answering correctly was quite simply a new-found pleasure that I somehow pinned in Gethin's lapel. The last lesson of the day was art and I knew I'd be working with Gethin which would test my clarity and stealth and strengthen my resolve to protect the man who I wished was my father. Gethin barely paid me any attention, yet my efforts were intense, and I felt as though my skills were enhanced. For some reason I was more focused and much more determined than ever before. I remember him saying, "My little geniuses are about to paint history!" as we mapped a mural on a large part of the classroom wall.

Before long the day came to an abrupt end and the school buzzer buzzed, chairs screeched as they were hurriedly put under the desks and the noise of unimportant chatter filled the air. I was very hungry as I hadn't taken any food with me and the school dinners left much to be desired as most of it was meat; with few options for what was then seen as a fussy eater. I didn't have any money and I didn't want to sponge off Gethin, and in my mind, I had already planned to find a job.

As everyone left to go home, I turned in the opposite direction in search of my own financial independence. There was a fairground that had set up its caravans and rides just down the road from the school, so I sauntered into the gate and banged on a caravan door. Looking back, I have no idea why it was that particular caravan that I chose to knock on, and to this day I can't help thinking that someone was looking down on me that day, as it turned out to be another huge turning point in my life. Any other door and my life could have been very different, in much the same way as knocking on Gethin's door some weeks before.

A huge man appeared in the small doorway, looking more like a giant that a man, looking down on me with terrifying eyes. I gulped and looked up him, "Err I need a job please. I'll do anything at all, anything!" I spluttered.

His voice boomed out, "Jane, come here for a minute," and out came a dark-haired lady who I presumed was his wife, who smiled and said hello. I was not in any way narcissistic; in fact, I was very naïve for my age. I hadn't really noticed my long dark curly hair and sallow skin but obviously Jane did.

"The lad here wants a job," he said to her.

"We could do with a pretty boy round here," she said immediately.

"What do you want me to do?" I asked.

"How would you like to the take money on the Waltzer?" said Jane.

"Wow yes," I responded. "Can I really? That sounds great."

I was so excited that I forgot to ask how much they would pay me, but I bounced off having been told to come back the following night. I didn't say a word to Gethin about the fairground when I got to his house, and when he asked me where I'd been, I looked at him and grinned, "It's a surprise," I said, "tell you on Saturday."

"What are you up too?" he said looking slightly suspicious.

"It's all good and I promise nothing bad," I said, as I'd already planned to pay my way or even buy a present for him to show my appreciation. I had visions of earning several hundred pounds a week thinking that I'd be able to support him, and yet I hadn't the foggiest idea how much I was going to earn. I went to bed that night with a smile on my face and a look of triumph signalled what I hoped would be a new life.

Because Gethin didn't like televisions at all, my time was spent reading books and I soon learned to ask the appropriate questions on the books that interested me most. "Gethin," I would ask, "what is the big bang theory?"

He would look at me and always started off by reeling off the wall number, followed by the shelf number, book number and chapter; with a final, "Read it."

CHAPTER THIRTEEN

"The will to win, the desire to succeed, the urge to reach your full potential... these are the keys that will unlock the door to personal excellence"
... Confucius

Life began to get much better and I even started to enjoy eating which was a huge step forward, as until now I had viewed food as an outdated habit that involved tormenting force and at times outright hatred. I rose each morning with gleaming eyes almost intoxicated with the coming day as I was also earning money; nowhere near as much as I'd thought but nevertheless a small income. I was earning the princely sum of ten pounds per week which was paid to me as a percentage of what I took from the clients on the ride. The job was simple, all I had to do was to stand on the boards, chewing gum, looking cool and spin the girls around as fast as I could. They would all scream on the verge of being sick, wobble and smile at me as they got off the ride, but always come back for more. I remember counting one group returning nine times in one night and was told by Jane that my takings were higher than anyone else's in the ride gang.

I think that my love of music started on the Waltzer; that, and looking cool, which Jane had helped me to perfect as part of my financial training. I had realised that I was not a stupid idiot but seemingly a desirable young teenager with a lot to offer and I enjoyed the day by day growth of my new stable life. As each day passed, I didn't give Len or Margaret a single thought as I had buried their memory deep in my mind, knowing that it would always be there but that it was definitely possible to hide it away in the dark.

There were times when I had to pinch myself, as life was fun, and I didn't want it to stop. Every day I would go to school and work as hard as I could, and afterwards, for a short time work on the rides looking as cool as I could. Jane had grown fond of me and her giant husband had also made me feel as though I mattered.

I was riding the Waltzer on what I knew would be the last Saturday before the fair closed for the season and knew I would be helping to pack things up at the end. Part of me was sad that I was going to need another job, but the music was really loud that night and I made the most of it, messing around dancing as the Waltzer sped up to thrill the riders who were mostly girls. I was miming Elvis Presley, singing 'It's now or never' and doing that lip thing, when Jane shouted and waved me over. I used to like showing off by jumping off the ride at full speed and landing by the entrance area without falling down the steps. To be honest it was all an optical illusion as it was the speed that helped me do it, but weeks of training had honed the act to almost perfection without breaking any bones. I landed inches away from Jane who was screaming with delight at my high-speed act. "How do you do that!" she screamed. Then looking more serious she said, "I want to talk to you, Dave."

She called out to Keith my second and told him to carry on without me for a while. This meant he had to start the ride up, and then leave the centre control box to take the money, and then go back to control the ride before stopping it again, so he wasn't best pleased.

Jane led me to her caravan which was like an Aladdin's cave sprinkled with every piece of finely painted porcelain imaginable, all inlaid with gold-leaf and jewels. The caravan was always spotless with a sweet smell of perfume that had a definite calming effect on everyone who visited her.

"Sit down Dave," she said, having long ago abbreviated my name.

"Yes, what do you want," I asked nervously.

"Don't worry, it's all good," she said. "I wanted to know if you'd like to come on the wagon with us for the winter?"

"What wagon?" I asked as I had no idea what the wagon was.

"We sell pots and porcelain pieces from the back of our lorry and I know you were made to entice the clients to buy them," she said. "I've even had riders refuse to get on our rides unless you were there, so the job would be a walk in the park to you."

She had no idea that not long ago I couldn't speak a word without stuttering, and I wasn't going to tell her. In my mind I wondered how I'd respond to the groups of people I would have to speak to without the music there to drown out my voice.

I looked, at her, then putting on a pretend swagger, I answered, "How much?" pretending I was part of a film set and compelled to look tough, and she started to laugh.

"You see! A born actor that's what you are Dave," she joked. "Jake and I have grown very fond of you, you're a very important person to have around."

I looked at her as she went on, "We both love you being around. Well, we both love you, that's what I'm trying to say," she said. "You're like a son to me and Jake, that's the fact of it," and I looked away trying to hide my tears.

"Don't look away, be happy," she cried. "Well! what's the answer? Will you come and work with us every Saturday?

"We'd pick you up and drop you off again," she said as I still hadn't answered.

I turned around drying my eyed and said, "Yes of course I will Jane, when do I start?"

"Next week, but you'll have to be up early. It takes a long time to set the lorry up."

"What time would that be," I asked.

"Around five-thirty in the morning," she answered.

"That's fine," I said with a nod, not having given Gethin a single thought until then.

I was just about to tell her that I lived with my teacher when I froze, *My God* I thought, I nearly told her, and I'm not allowed; what the hell was I thinking. Jane looked at me with outstretched arms, "You've had a tough time, haven't you? I can feel it," she said. "One day I hope you'll tell us all about it. I sense you've a lot of hurt inside you."

I responded by walking to hold her outstretched hands tightly and kissed her on the forehead as shows of affection were still difficult for me. "Thank you for being so kind." I whispered. "I don't deserve it."

She looked at me and sighed, "One day you'll realise just how valuable you are. Now bugger off back to the ride," she laughed sensing how uncomfortable I felt.

I opened the door of the caravan to let in the bright lights and penetrating music of the fairground and walked slowly over to the ride again to find Keith had cranked it up to Mach-1 and everyone was screaming. I whistled at him, but he didn't hear me, so I stood at the side of the boards and with perfect timing jumped onto the moving platform and made my way to the first spinner which was full of screaming women. The entire ride had seen what I had done and as it slowed there wasn't a person that wasn't clapping with amazement. Even Keith came out of the control box and shouted, "How the hell did you do that? It was at Mach-1 you idiot! You could have killed yourself!"

I stood up straight secretly thinking, "Not bad for a person that couldn't play football or walk without hurting," and I grinned at the realisation of just how lucky I was. "Len 0:1 David," I thought to myself.

That night it was quite late before I turned the key and let myself in the front door, to find Gethin sitting in his favourite chair reading. "Hello are you ok? Where have you been it's late?" he asked.

I'd just been paid and had bought some cigars from the nearby corner shop; the owner had seen me run errands for Gethin several times and assuming they were for him, he sold them to me even though I wasn't old enough. "I've brought you a present," I said, and pulled out two boxes of Tom Thumb cigars.

He smiled asking, "What have you been doing?" as he surveyed the bruises on my arms which were an inevitable result of spinning the Waltzers.

"I've been working at the fair," I answered. "Yes, I know! I had a walk earlier on down by there and saw you. I was pleased to see you so happy," he said.

I'd been paid more than I should have as Jane had given me a pretend bonus, and as I sat down and looked at Gethin he glanced back with a look of respect in his eyes.

"I want to pay you some rent every week. Because I just need to," I said to him.

"I thought the job was only temporary," sparked Gethin.

"Well they want me to work on the lorry at weekends, selling porcelain. I'll have to be up on a Saturday at half-five in the morning if that's ok?" I replied in rather a hurry, and he smiled at me with such contentment it was almost soothing.

"My oh my! How quickly things change," he said. "Welcome to the real world. The one that should have been yours from the start." I stared at him and slipped all of the money into his hand. "That's too much!" he cried out in surprise.

"No," I responded, "It's not nearly enough, but thank you for everything."

"What are you reading Gethin?" I asked, changing the subject. "Anything interesting"

"Yes," he answered "Drawing Lessons from the Great Masters. There are a hundred Great Drawings that have been analysed. You should read it."

"I think the expression is, *it's very cool* as you would say." And he grinned at his little joke. "It's good to have you here and it's not at all one sided. I greatly enjoy your presence as well," he said.

Then he stopped for a moment and took a deep breath, before saying, "Len and Margaret turned up again this evening. They accused me of breaking the law. As it is they who remain responsible for you and not me." My heart stopped, and I couldn't help swearing.

"F-Fuck me" I stammered, "Why don't they just leave me alone?"

"Well! You will have to face it at some point, and that point isn't far away. They could legally order me to release you to their custody. I have absolutely no claim on you and I'm expecting allegations to come flying about, so you need to prepare yourself for more problems."

"Thank you for telling me," I whispered. "It's good to be respected and treated like a proper person. You're ten times the person Len will ever be."

I needed to break the feeling of impending fear, so I pondered for a while before asking the question, "Gethin where do the words *Take nothing but a staff*, come from?"

He looked at me and said, "You know very well where it comes from! You are just trying to block this rubbish out of your mind. You tell me; as I saw you reading the bible several days ago."

I took a deep breath and recited to him word for word. "Take nothing but a staff and if you come to a town or village where they won't listen to you, kick the dust from your feet; for Sodom and Gomorrah will fare better on the day of judgement than they"

I looked up and whispered "I wonder if Len would listen? I know that Margaret would."

"I fear that you are a shining light in a very dark world, and that your motives are right, but your target is wrong," he replied

"Well, I'll do what I think then, because if he won't listen, I could kick the dust from my feet couldn't I?"

"Yes indeed you could, but Len is suffering from his own brand of hell, which appears to be linked to his own childhood. So I wouldn't hold out too much hope," came back Gethin's reply, and he sat back and stared at me for what seemed like hours. "Before you make any decisions you will tell me, won't you?" he said.

"Yes! Without a doubt, I don't want to go back there again," I answered immediately.

"And I have to protect you," he said, "It's obvious that they bother you or you wouldn't have come looking for me."

"Right then!" said Gethin, changing the subject. "Time for bed my lad. We have a big day tomorrow and I don't want to miss a second."

I stood up and opened the door ready to climb up the stairs, I paused and looked back at him knowing he wouldn't appreciate a hug even though I was dying to give him one.

"Good night son," he called out, which was at least a clue to his affections.

Chapter Fourteen

"There is nothing impossible to him who will try."
... Alexander the Great

I had smoothed my way at school by working very hard, and on the Friday my teacher Mr Griffin had privately congratulated me on my efforts. It was always good to achieve such heights, as one day I hoped Gethin could take all the credit for what I'd done. I went to bed early that night, excited about the next day when I'd see Jake and Jane and start my new job. Despite the excitement I slept especially well, probably aided by the deep satisfaction at Mr Griffin's comments.

Before long, it was five o'clock in the morning and I rose out of bed bleary eyed and only half conscious. It was to be my first day selling china and I'd read all about Capo Di Monte fine porcelain figures; although I suspected that Jane's were probably made in China as she had loads of them stacked up in the lorry.

I rushed around readying myself for the days adventure and like clockwork a grunting lorry pulled up outside the door and hissed like an angry snake as the brakes were applied. I peered out of the window and could see Jane equally bleary waving by the lorry. Jake her giant husband was revving the lorry up to make sure that everyone knew he was there. I loved his arrogance and was keen to grow to his height, as no one argued with Jake, not ever.

I didn't want to wake Gethin although I was sure Jake had already achieved that, and quickly scribbled a note and left it in the kitchen table. 'Dear Gethin, I'm off on my adventure. Hope you have a good day. Love David.' I was just about to open the door when something inside me screamed out, "You can't put love, he's a man." So I ran back to cross it out but somehow, I just couldn't so I left it as it was.

By this time Jake was hitting the horn as well as revving the engine and hissing the brakes so I guessed he was cross as I ran outside. "Come on its five-thirty we need to get going," he grumbled

I climbed in the lorry and sat in the middle, Jane grinned, and Jake smiled, "Right then son let's go and have some fun," he said.

We drove all the way to Leicester and parked up with loads of other lorries and Jake started to set out the back of the lorry. It looked like a big stage, with cups, saucers, tea sets and endless porcelain figures, all set out on coloured sheets to make them look more expensive.

He stood up on the back of the lorry and called over to a passing woman, "Now then my dear! Are you interested in a bargain?" smiling as he thrust a shiny figure into her sight.

"How much do you think this is worth? A lot of money eh?" he called out.

I could see her face as she stopped to look at the figure, followed by several other women who were curious. "Well how much do you think its worth?" he continued.

By this time there were at least fifteen women there and one of them piped up, “Ten pounds.”

“It’s a *Capper Diamonty* isn’t it?” another said, struggling and failing miserably to pronounce the word correctly.

“Yes, it is!” said Jake, egging them on. “With a certificate of authenticity and a beautiful box to take it home in.” I was getting excited as I watched, and just knew that I could do this, and so did Jane.

Jake carried on, “I’m not gonna ask you for ten pounds,” he called out. “Not even nine, or eight, or even seven. This is a genuine figure, so how much d’you want to pay for it?”

“A fiver,” someone shouted.

“Ok five it is,” he shouted back. Then suddenly, he stopped as if unsure of himself. “…No! I’ve changed my mind,” he said, and everyone held their breath, uncertain at what was coming next.

“I’m feeling especially kind today. You can have two for a tenner!” he shouted out, and everyone started to clap. At least seven people purchased fourteen figures in total, which was really cool, and I just wanted to have a go.

Jake climbed down and immediate grunted, “It’s your turn now *pretty boy*,” and I climbed up on to the stage. I’ve no idea how I did it or where the words came from, but Jake had given me the price he needed to make on each item and dozens of women were drawn to the stage. “I have some bargains here!” I shouted with my gruff voice and I could hear them chuckling.

“What a sexy voice,” one of them called out. “Who’s that?” said another, “Not seen him before,” came yet another, as they all gathered around to see what came next. I smiled and knelt down to try and reach the level of my audience and pinning a huge smile on my face, I pointed at it saying, "Come on now ladies! I need to see *your* smiles as well."

I could see they were liking it and I gained confidence. "Show me your purses!" I said grinning as I did so. "Come on! You haven't shown me your purses yet! Don't be shy."

Soon, everyone was waving their purses in the air, so I picked up a basket of cups and saucers. "Oh, I've made a mistake!" I said, "This is the only one I remembered to bring and it's your favourite colour isn't it?"

By this time there were at least thirty people, mostly women, standing around waving their purses. "I'm gonna make you happy," I called over to one of the women, "What's your name? Bet it's something Posh."

"Jessica," she replied.

"Well!... I told you it was posh," I said to the crowd as I turned around to pick up a figure. "Jessica! I've just found a figure of you in this box; It's so beautiful" I said, winking as I moved around the stage.

"Mistake, …I've just found the tea sets, but I only have three left. How much do you want to pay for them?" I asked as I closed the box and labelled it for Jessica.

"This set's normally thirty pounds, but I want you to smile and remember the deal that I'm about to shock you with. "You can have the complete set for..."

"Twenty pounds," piped up someone, interrupting me.

"No darling," I chuckled, "My name isn't Dick Turpin its Dave. I have three of them left and you can have them for fifteen."

I looked around and there were three women fighting over who would have last one. I went into the back of the van, and re-appeared like Houdini, shouting "I've some great news I just found three more. But after that, that's it no more left!"

I spent the entire day working the crowds, loving every moment and I sold every single pot and figure in the van. I heard Jane say, "Didn't I tell you? The kid's a bloody natural," as she offered her hand to stop me from falling off the lorry.

I was starving hungry and my voice hurt a lot as I'd forgotten to slurp the glass of water on the side, whilst I was shouting. "Come on you two we need to eat," said Jane and she led us to the café over the road. "We won't need to lock the lorry," she grinned, "There isn't anything left."

I was still buzzing with adrenalin when we arrived back outside Gethin's house. Jake applied the brakes with a deafening hiss, and I climbed out almost too tired to walk. Jane hugged me, and Jake smiled. "You're a strange kid," he said. "Where do you get your guts from?"

I smiled back at them and said, "You're both very important to me."

Jane smoothed my hair and whispered, "I always wanted a son and now I've got one; see you soon," and she kissed me on the cheek.

Jake looked over the steering wheel and grinned, "You're a great kid and a good friend; we're both very lucky to have found you."

"No I'm the lucky," one I squeaked. "You're both everything I could have ever dreamed of, I am proud of you," I said as I staggered to the front door.

The lorry revved up and Jane called out, "See you next week," as they pulled away. Suddenly there was a screech and a hiss of brakes and Jane jumped out and came running up to me, "This is yours, we almost forgot," she cried, and thrust thirty pounds into my hand.

I didn't know how much she'd given me and just looked at her as she hugged me again. "Go on in, you look knackered," she whispered, and I twisted the key and went inside.

Gethin was sat in his favourite chair and looked up, to ask if I'd had a good time?

"Yes I did. Great but I'm very tired," I said.

I paused for a moment as he looked very serious; my heart thumped as I was sure Len and Margaret had been bothering him again. "You do know that they are fairground people, don't you?" he said, "And that they can sometimes break the law."

I looked at him and smiled, "You really do care about me don't you? Yes! I am aware that they're *pikeys* and they live in a caravan. But they've treated me very well," I said. "And I made thirty pounds today." I didn't like the word pikeys, but I wanted him to know that I was well aware of his derogatory term for them.

"Bloody hell!" he sighed. "You'll soon be earning more than me!"

I split the money in half and pushed fifteen pounds into his jacket pocket. I knew he wanted to talk but I'd been up since five and I was falling asleep on my feet. To be honest I felt awkward; somehow disloyal. Gethin had taken so many risks, and even now Len was stalking him; whilst I was off on adventures that clearly made him feel uncomfortable. I walked back from the door and gently asked if he wanted to talk as he had been on his own all day?

"Solitude is the key to knowing oneself," he muttered, "And you my boy, are very tired. Go to bed," he said, as he pointed to the door.

I looked at him still feeling guilty and turned to face the door, "I don't have to work again till next week. It's not every night like the fairground, so I can spend more time learning and reading."

I literally staggered up the stairs, washed and dried myself and fell asleep in seconds. I didn't hear a sound, not even when Gethin came up the stairs; and the night vanished to start yet another exciting day. It was Sunday and I lay in bed listening to the distant chimes of church bells; there was something slightly unnerving about the sound of church bells, I'm not sure why but there was. Maybe it's the call to attention that I didn't like, or the fact that Henry the VIII had generated hatred between the Catholics and Protestants for a variety of reasons that I had been told to keep quiet about. I was amazed that it was he who had caused the troubles in Ireland towards the end of the Hundred Years' War, but although I was keen to make my point Gethin had advised me that this was, "A delicate area in which many people had lost their heads." I chose to relent and save my comments for a more appropriate time and as I such secretly hid my views, in a labyrinth designed to locate the facts at my leisure.

I knew that Gethin was Church of England but to be honest I had no idea what I was; even though it seemed to be expected that I was C of E. I crawled out of bed still listening to the damn bells that simply wouldn't go away, "I'd better be careful not to say anything," I thought, or I might upset Gethin.

As I made my way to the bathroom with the intention of having a bath, I called down to Gethin who was already up, "Can I have a bath please?"

A voice came back, "Good idea; you're beginning to stink a bit!" but I could hear the chuckle in his voice, so I paid no heed.

I ran the bath and sank into it slowly, but despite the soothing warmth I shivered as I remembered the scalding baths that Len had subjected me to as a small boy and thought of how far I'd come. From the warmth of this newly experienced luxury, I noted that the day outside was cold as a cool draft billowed through a gap in the sash window. It seemed to be hours before I slid out to dry myself and make my way downstairs. Gethin was already preparing breakfast despite the fact that we had agreed to do our own.

"I thought we were going to do our own," I snapped, ever keen to express my new found independence.

"Well I've changed my mind, we're friends, aren't we? Apart from which I like you being around." I was stopped in my tracks, my mind racing with pleasure at his caring words. My life had changed so much in just a few short months, and I had become a confident focused teenager with dreams and inspirations, all forged by Gethin's efforts.

I walked over to him, "No kissing or hugging, let's just get on with enjoying ourselves please," he said, with a caring smile, obviously reading my intentions. "You really are a determined talented lad," he muttered, "something you should be very proud of."

We sat down around the kitchen table and I tucked in to scrambled eggs and toast whilst Gethin feasted on a full English breakfast. I was mesmerised and slightly uncomfortable at the site of the sausages regimentally lined up on his plate; still suffering from a fear of the smell of meat. But the day promised to be perfect and I was proud to be sat with a friend, who in such a short time had proven his dedication to my complicated cause. He was reading the Times Newspaper, grumbling at every turn of the pages of what he considered were, "The writings of mindless morons," and I secretly grinned.

I didn't want to spoil the moment, but I was desperate to discuss what I considered to be very important matters. Believing that my future was set to be in Gethin's care, I understood how important it was to protect him from the senseless problems that Len was almost bound to inflict, especially if he realised that I had fallen on my feet. I sat up straight and glibly stated, "I've worked out what to do in the summer holidays."

“Well out with it,” barked Gethin. “What have you planned? Have you decided to travel with the Pikeys or join a Circus? Pray tell me oh mighty one!”

I gulped as I could see that the subject was uncomfortable for him, “No not at all, I’m just trying to protect you from the wrath of Len,” I said, “As he’s my problem not yours.

“I’ve been reading the laws concerning adoption,” I rambled on, “They’re very complex and above all, binding, until I reach the age of twenty-one. I’ve a feeling that Margaret will soon apply pressure to him, and they’ll appear one day to accuse you of all manner of breaches of the law. If I’m not around in the holidays it will make things much easier for you,” I said, barely stopping to take a breath.

“I agree upon reflection you are right! But you still haven’t told me about you plans,” he said.

I took a deep breath and slowly explained in a back to front manner what my master plan was. “You consider me to be a *cool* artist, don’t you?” I said.

“Quite!” he answered. “Talented is perhaps a better word.”

“And you think I’m sensible for my age, right?” I continued.

“Debatable,” he snapped with a grin on his face. “You’re very headstrong,” he added, clearly realising that I was after as many yes’s as possible before I presented my plan.

“It’s not a good idea for me to be living here in the summer holiday is it?” I said to him.

“That’s my problem, but I take your point,” he muttered, slurping down a mouthful of tea. “So what’s the plan then. Out with it!?”

I took a deep breath, "I've been reading all about Cornwall; there's a place called Newquay where all the artists go and another one called St Ives.

They're both littered with shops all wanting to buy paintings and drawings and there's an inner harbour where people hang pictures up and holiday makers buy them,"

I sped up with excitement. "There's also stuff called caricatures, and artists' charge ten shillings for each sketch depending on the size. Whilst I was at the fair, in my tea-break I drew some to try it out. I only asked for half a crown, but everyone thought they were great; which was strange because I really made some of them look silly."

I rose from the chair having consumed all of my breakfast and ran up the stairs to fetch several drawings that I'd slipped under the bed as samples; anticipating a detailed explanation of my plan. Banging down the stairs clutching two charcoal drawings I presented both to Gethin.

"What do you think? Ten bob each for these! Money for old rope," I declared.

He smiled, "Well how are you going to get down there?" he enquired.

I knew that he wasn't keen on Jake and Jane so taking another deep breath I said, "I I'll walk, w-well th-thumb lifts," as my stammer exposed the white lie I was telling.

"What you really mean, is that your friends are traveling to Cornwall and have offered you a lift. Right?" he said, having seen right through me. My face coloured up and I looked at him feeling very guilty at what I'd just done.

"Lies are untruths with intent to deceive," he snapped. "They also smell of disrespect."

"Well you don't like them, do you?" I said sullenly.

"Oh no! That is not what I said. If you think back. I advised you to be *careful,* did I not?" he said, keen to correct my mistake.

By now the guilt was oozing out of me as I stared straight into his face as he puffed on his cigar. "I'm really sorry, please forgive me. I'll never do that again."

"I know you won't, you might be headstrong, but you learn very quickly," he said, and I smiled with relief. "Not so fast! I haven't forgiven you yet!" he said and then relented, "Oh go on then but don't do it again."

Every Saturday I sold pots, and each time accumulated more money; although I suspected that the amounts were not commensurate with my efforts, as Jane had started referring to others that I was her son.

I worked so hard at school for Gethin having now read and re-read around a hundred books. Gethin had declared me a speed reader with a sponge like brain whatever that meant.

I had achieved first position in virtually every subject at school, apart from Domestic Science and Sport, and Gethin had pinned my report on the wall declaring, "We should **both** be proud of that my boy!"

Chapter Fifteen

"It is better to bind your children to you by a feeling of respect and by gentleness than by fear"
... ***Quote unknown***

It was Saturday morning, the first one since school had shut down for the summer holidays, when there was a knock on the door. "I'll go," I shouted and opened the door with wide eyes looking forward to the coming day, as Jake was driving me to Cornwall and a new adventure was about to begin.

I froze as if I had just been struck with a lightning bolt as I saw Len stood there, with Margaret who had obviously been crying standing just behind him. I could see Paul sitting in the back seat of Len's green Hillman Minx estate car parked in the street. I have no idea why, but everything came flooding back and I instinctively backed away from the door to collect the poker from the lounge. I hadn't said a word and Gethin was still upstairs when I returned to the front door shaking with rage. My whole body shook, and I started to sweat; something I had been free of for several months.

"What do you want?" I growled glaring at Len with unbridled hate.

"You're still my responsibility," he said, speaking in the soft tones of a badly performed Shakespearian act.

"No I'm not! I'm my responsibility, go away!" I snapped.

Margaret started to weep, and I could see she wasn't happy; nor had she been for a very long time I suspected. Keen to be kind to her I loosened my grip on the poker and said, "Hello Mum are you OK?"

She looked back wearily, her eyes pleading with me, "Come home. Please come home you belong there," she said.

I looked over at Paul who seemed limp with his snail-paced brain, and called out, "Hello Paul, you ok?" but he didn't answer. He wasn't the brightest of boys and I guess he felt deflated at his inappropriate presence and not being the centre of attention.

I had almost dismissed Len as invisible, when he barked, "See I told you, he's still violent, but you wouldn't listen," instantly bringing him back into focus.

"This isn't violence," Margaret said in a whisper as Gethin appeared at the door.

"What the hell do you want?" he snapped. "I thought I told you never to come here again."

"He's our responsibility," replied Len in a muffled voice.

"You should have considered that long ago, shouldn't you? But you preferred to torture him instead. Please go away," he said, and I never ceased to marvel at how he maintained an air a social politeness in such situations.

"We have a right to see him," snapped Len again.

"Well that rather depends on whether he wants to see you. Doesn't it?" returned Gethin, and again I noted how he cleverly outfoxed Len, ending his response with an awkward question that he wouldn't be able to answer; another observation I would store up for future reference.

"He's doing fine as you can see," Gethin went on, "I've dried all his cloths and I exchanged your cardboard box for a wardrobe."

The quick tongue in cheek jibe hit home with the desired result, and Len turned around to leave. "Come on Margaret, we're not wanted here," he said grabbing her arm to escort her back to the car.

Gethin could see the pain etched on Margaret's face, and with a smile directed at her he said, "Please come in Margaret. Would you like a cup of tea?"

Len froze in his tracks as Gethin made it very clear that the invitation was hers and hers alone. "Yes please," she whimpered gratefully as she walked over to the front door.

"Come in, sit down please," Gethin said kindly, and I could see that he'd hatched a plan and I was interested to know what he was up to. Margaret sat down, and I instinctively sat down beside her. She looked at me with adoring eyes and softly enquired, "How are you, you look very well?"

I paused for a moment as my next answer could easily destroy her status as what I believed to be a caring person. "I'm d-doing fine, but I m-miss you," I said, the stammer relaying a signal that only Gethin recognised as a necessary white lie.

"Then why didn't you call me? You could have called me," she said.

I paused again to think, as she was quite right, I could have called her, but I didn't. "Uh! I guess it was for the same reason that you didn't visit me in the Beechlands!" I snapped, instantly regretting the cruelty of my remark.

"Sorry mum, I shouldn't have said that. It was selfish and I'm sorry, you're right I should call you each week just to tell you how I'm getting on," I said, as I realised the effect it had on her clearly broken and unhappy life.

"I really am very sorry. You have a right to be angry," I said again, as the reason I hadn't called dawned on me. The real reason was that I was having a ball, and she and Len were clearly unimportant to me and quite frankly a threat to my health. In short, I needed to forget in order to survive.

I wanted to ask why she kept on turning up but didn't want to hurt her feelings anymore, so I relaxed my grip on her hand a said softly, "I can call you every week from now on. Can we make a special time; just for us?"

She looked up and smiled. "Yes please that would be lovely, and it would make me very happy."

"Right then, that is exactly what I will do," I said, just as Gethin came in with the tea.

"I hope you don't mind but I only have Darjeeling, is that ok?" he chirped.

Margaret took a sip and stared at me, "My god! You have grown up; do you drink this as well?" she asked.

"Yes of course," I said, managing to reply without a stammer but knowing that Gethin had logged yet another essential lie.

"It's good to see you again," I whispered and put my arms around her neck in a fond and caring embrace. She not surprisingly responded with torrents of tears, something that was all too familiar to me, an unwanted memory I associated my time with her and her husband.

I was keen for her to leave now, as I knew that Jake was likely to turn up at the front door, his lorry painted with the names and telephone numbers that would be ideal for Len's evil antics. She however, just wanted to talk and talk, but luckily Gethin came to my rescue.

"We can't leave your family out there for much longer, it's not very fair is it?" he said, and I immediately recognised his first *essential lie*, and I smiled as he collected the cups on his willow patterned tray, ready to transport them back to the kitchen.

Margaret rose, still staring at me lovingly, "Promise you'll call me," she said.

"Yes. Of course I will," I replied, as Gethin mentally cut another notch in my *essential lie* tally.

However, the simple fact was that although I cared about Margaret, I had no idea why I hadn't thought to call her. I felt like a cad as she was no more and no less trapped in a situation that was clearly not being repaired in my absence; which made a mockery of Len's theories that were neither accurate nor constructive.

Margaret walked through the front door to be by met by Len who had been polishing yet another Shakespearian act. With a flourish, he helped her into the car, like a limousine driver ushering in an important passenger; something I'd never seen him do before, and quite frankly had no wish to see again. I was inwardly pleased at his departure and hugely relieved that I hadn't done anything stupid.

Gethin looked at me and commented, "You were first class, my boy. But I think you lost by two points," he said, referring to our *essential lies* tally. I was pleased at that score and for the first time in my life felt a deep sense of belonging. I looked at him again, "No kissing or hugging," he said. "Just go and get ready, you're on your way to Cornwall. Is everything packed?"

It wasn't long before Jake turned up, the van hissing and roaring whilst bellowing out black smoke. He had his caravan tied to the back of the lorry and shouted, "Come on Dave! We need to join the convoy."

Clutching my case, I looked at Gethin, "You won't think it's soppy if I call you? It's essential to me," I said. He frowned and shook my hand and I ran off to the waiting van, "Be careful," he called after me, "and remember what I have taught you." Jake revved up and we roared off to Cornwall in a frantic hurry.

It was a long way to Cornwall, and it turned out to be much further than I'd realised. We joined the convoy of brightly coloured wagons, the biggest and most powerful was the Dodgem Cars set which I had often helped set up. Once we'd left Leicester, we made our way to a three-lane road which looked pretty new to me and sped along, but very soon the entire convoy was beating a path through winding roads and tall hedgerows over which our passage was only made possible by the elevated position in the wagon. "Christ," I grumbled, "We've been driving for hours."

Jane looked at me and put her arm around my neck, "There-there, does my pretty boy want to stop for a drink," she teased.

"Yes please, that's a good idea," I said, but Jake was having none of it.

"Sod off," he snapped, "We haven't got the time" and he just kept on driving. "We have to be all set up for tomorrow, so we'll be working all night," he said, "there's a flask in the back there, full of coffee," and Jane reached over to sort through the bags that were stored in the sleeping area.

"Got it, do you want a cup darling?" she finally said after much searching.

"No thanks," Jake roared.

"I wasn't asking you, I was asking my *pretty boy* here," said Jane, and we all giggled as she poured out three cups of hot coffee into the yellow cups. "Christ he's right though!" she grumbled. "We've been driving for hours."

It was about three-thirty in the morning when we pulled into a really big field, just up the hill from Perranporth. It was almost opposite the sea I later found out, but that night the dark sky served to shield any clue that it was there. I was really tired but keen to start work as I knew everything was a timed rush, and that no set-up, meant no money. Jake climbed out of the lorry as three other men started up a huge generator that lit up the night sky. "Right then you two," he said, "Time for work," and knowing exactly what to do I sauntered over to the Waltzer wagon to help unpack it.

I was always amazed at how many pieces were needed to build the Waltzer, but as the boards came off the wagon I knew exactly where they all fitted. The lads were debating which bit went where, as someone had forgotten to number the parts. I stepped in and essentially took over to give everyone a hint, showing them why we didn't need the numbers. "Look guys," I said pointing as I did so, "each board is a different colour, so just follow the colours instead of the numbers"

Jane looked over at us and I could hear her shout out, "Here we go! *Pretty boy* to the rescue again," chuckling away to herself.

It was hard work, but in the end, everything was built and tested, as there were strict safety rules and specific tests to run before it was safe for clients to ride on it. I staggered back to the lorry and sat on the front seat, just in time to see the sunlight breaking over the horizon, illuminating the golden sands that had previously been hidden. The light blue sea was almost flat, devoid of even the smallest ripple, sparkled in the sunlight with an almost hypnotic pleasure as I slowly closed my eyes and fell asleep where I sat.

I was woken up by Jane, where I found myself tucked up in the caravan with my pyjamas on. "Hope you didn't mind," she said. "Jake carried you in and I put your pyjamas on."

"Really," I gulped as I glanced over at Jake who looked to be developing a decidedly red face. "She's only joking, but she did comment that you weren't just a pretty boy but a big boy as well," he said with a grin and a wink. I'm not sure who was telling the truth, but it didn't matter as I really felt as though they were my family in every way, even if Gethin wasn't too keen.

The food that Jane cooked that morning was sensational; I think that flavours are enhanced by your environment, and today felt good. I had broken my fear of eating, as long as I didn't have to sit before a white table cloth, but in all honesty, I preferred to eat alone. However I was fully aware of the message that would give, so I braved my affliction for their sakes.

I'd promised Jane I would work for the first week, but I was fairly sure they wanted me to follow them from site to site, and I hadn't plucked up the courage to tell her about my plans to go to Newquay. I knew that they were moving on to several other sites further afield, so I needed to plan exactly what I was doing and when, before I told her. I wasn't in the least bit scared about staying on my own as I hadn't even considered the possible problems I might have to face. The only thing I was nervous about was breaking the news to Jane.

The fair started at two in the afternoon, not like Loughborough which was at night time, and I was keen to go and explore the area and finalise my plans. Jake had a motor bike which he strapped to the back of the lorry, it was a 250 Greaves Trial-bike which I'd often wanted to learn to ride and it would be great for exploring.

"Err, Jake do you think you might be able to… no it's ok, it doesn't matter," I started to ask but changed my mind.

"What doesn't matter? He said.

"It's ok it doesn't matter," I said again.

"Yes it does, and the answer's yes," he said, "but be careful."

"Yes what?" I said as I scratched my head.

"Yes, I'll teach you to ride my bike," he sniggered.

"What! Really?" I shouted out in delight.

"Yes. Really!" he grinned.

"How did you know what I was going to ask?" I said.

"I don't miss a thing; ask Jane," he said, and I looked over to see her grinning at the other end of the caravan.

The next morning and every morning after that; like clockwork Jake would dig me out of bed and sit me on his bike. He prepared a really good track for me to practice on, which required me to use several gears and maintain perfect balance, thereby giving me all the skills I needed. By the end of the week I was riding really well and enjoying every minute of it, he was a great teacher and now I wanted to go out on the road. I'd told him that I was nearly sixteen and I'm sure he knew I was lying, but he didn't seem to care as long as I was smiling, and Jane was really like a doting mother full of pride at every move I made.

He finally agreed and didn't seem to care that I didn't have a licence, so I just got on and rode it off down the road, as in those days helmets weren't compulsory. I was tall, and he'd taught me how to ride well, so as long as I didn't do anything stupid, I believed I would be fine and so did Jake, who had zero respect for the Law. My first call was to Newquay just a few miles down the road; it took my breath away especially when I viewed the inner harbour, where I'd planned to hang my pictures. For some reason it was always important to do everything myself, not because I was ungrateful, but Len had ground me down into thinking that I would never be good enough.

I rode all around Newquay and it was everything I'd hoped it would be, and I was filled with excitement as I made my way back to the fairground. But in the back of my mind I knew I couldn't postpone telling Jane any longer. It was now urgent to tell them my plans.

When I arrived back, Jane told me they were moving to the next site in four days, to somewhere called Penzance and this news reinforced the *urgent tag* I'd place on my duty to inform them of my plans. I was nervous that afternoon as I rode the Walzer, knowing that quite soon I would miss the music, the lights and the security of my traveling home, but I just had to try and drag my dreams to reality. Gethin was always telling me that if I couldn't prove to myself what was possible; then nothing would be possible at all.

One of the difficult things to battle with on a fair ground is the long nights, as sometimes the music played, and the screams persisted until way gone midnight. The only time I had to speak to Jake and Jane was in the mornings, as things were always relaxed then, and I had a better chance of explaining why I was person I was, and I planned to do it the next morning.

That night we really cleaned up, the takings went through the roof as some girls were coming back eleven or twelve times; Jane was convinced it was *pretty boy cool* that did it, but the takings were definitely up, so I didn't really care. I crawled into bed that night with my ears drumming and my eyes suffering from the strobing lights, that at times had a hypnotic effect.

I woke up early to see Jake's face. "What no bike this morning?" he grunted disappointedly.

"No, I want to talk to you both," I said, and when Jane looked over at me, I could see she knew what was coming.

We sat around the table and talked and talked, I told them things that were beyond their imagination as to what Len had done. At one point Jake was all for jumping in the lorry and driving up to Leicester to 'blow him away.'

"I'd like to see if I can do something by myself," I said as I explained my master plan to them. "I know this sounds selfish, I love you both," I went on. "You make me feel so special when I'm with you, but would you mind if I stayed here whilst you carry on to the other sites?"

Jane smiled at me as she asked, "Did you really spent all that time locked in a cupboard under the stairs?"

I looked up at her to recall Gethin profound words. "The trouble is with atrocities, is no one believes them until they've visited Belsen themselves," I said.

"So I have no need to answer that, as I know that you know I would never lie to you."

"Gethin's your teacher, isn't he?" she chirped up again.

"Yes. But for him I'm fairly sure I wouldn't be around today," I replied. I knew that they both felt for me, and as I sat there between them with my arms around their necks, I whispered, "You've both saved me as well."

I'd never seen Jake shed a tear, not even one, but he did on that morning, "I'm proud of you son, I'm proud of who you are," he said. "I'm not a soft bastard, but you're very important to us both, you're like a son."

"You can go on your adventure as long as you call us every day," Jane said softly. "And we'll pick you up on the way back. But just you remember! Without you, takings will be way down and a part of our lives missing without our *Pretty Boy,*" she said trying to lighten the mood.

CHAPTER SIXTEEN

"The core of a man's spirit comes from new experiences."
... Chris McCandless

It was hard that day as they readied themselves to go off to Penzance, and at one point I nearly changed my mind, and would have, but for Jake looking at me with his intense powerful eyes, charging me with energy again. Jane was being all Mumsy, making sure that I hadn't forgotten anything and that everything was packed in my case. They had given me over a hundred pounds, which I knew I hadn't earned, but she just smiled and said, "You're worth it."

Jake all but forced the bike on me but I refused, insisting that he'd need it and anyway I wasn't really legal to ride it. Saying goodbye took forever and it wasn't until almost an hour later that they pulled away to race down the road and join the convoy, and I began walking down the long winding road to Newquay. It took ages to get there; much longer than I had expected, a trait that has stayed with me to this day. Finally I arrived, and as I walked along the beach and under the strange bridge that linked the mainland to a large chunk of rock, I looked up to see an isolated house perched high on top; the suspension bridge its only means of access. I breathed deeply taking in the clean and fresh air as I walked along planning my next move, keen to find my feet; when suddenly a big hairy dog appeared out of nowhere. It was very angry, growling at me through a mass of hair that all but covered it's eyes. I was startled and to be honest a little scared, but in an effort to calm him I knelt down to match his height and remembering Jane had packed some biscuits I cautiously opened my case to retrieve one and offered it to the beast. He tipped his head and looked at me, although how he managed to see was a complete mystery. By this time, I was on all fours and tipping my head from side to side squeaking like a puppy with the biscuit hanging out of my mouth. It came closer and I could smell a strong salty smell with a tinge of seaweed,

"Do you want something to eat?" I squeaked, gingerly at first, then, "good boy," and he seemed to be pleased with my efforts to calm him down.

I'm not sure why but I lay down on the sand flat on my back with the biscuit sticking out of my mouth. He slowly came over whining and took the biscuit from me and then lay down flat beside me too. His breath stank, and he had no collar, so I assumed he was a stray. Leaning over I held out my hand and he whined again then began to lick it with a sense of urgency. I have no idea why, but the dog nudged closer and closer until his breath stung my eyes.

"What do you want boy?" I asked him softly, and he tipped his head and licked his lips again.

I was so involved with the dog that I hadn't realise the time and jumping up to carry on, I left him, only to find that he just kept following me. Wherever I went, he went, and as I rang the bell on a Bed & Breakfast house he turned up and sat beside me.

"Have you a room for the night?" I asked. To which they took one look at the dog and immediately declared that they didn't take animals. "He's not mine, he's a stray," I declared whilst the dog looked up at me as if we had been together for years.

I tried about six in all and the answer was always the same. On one occasion I even found a piece of rope and tied him to a drainpipe around the corner, but he escaped, and as I rang the bell his shaggy form sat down beside me with perfect timing, and almost grinned as they responded, "We don't take dogs!"

It was getting late and I found myself heading back to the beach again as I had seen a wooden shed with canoes piled up against it, which would provide me with some shelter. I knew I had a sleeping bag in my case and plenty of money to buy food, but I quite fancied the idea of sleeping on the beach with my new found friend, who was by this time following my every step, whining and groaning as he went. The shed was dull and very dark but nevertheless functional, it was well kept and would definitely keep off any rain. I opened the door to look in with extreme caution and a torch-light flashed.

"Who's that?" a young female voice demanded; closely followed by another voice as three torches illuminated the night air.

"Sorry! I was thinking about bedding down for the night," I said. "I can't get a room because they don't take dogs."

"Come in what's your name? said a ginger haired boy. "I'm Billy and this is Bridget," he went on and pointed to a girl next to him who was sighing and grumbling, having been disturbed from her sleep. Three other kids came into view as the torchlight flickered, drawing sinister lines on their faces.

"I'm Tom, and this is John and his chick Deborah," said another of the boys. "What's your name?"

"David," I replied, "and this my dog who I said hello to and now he won't go away."

Tom shone his torch at the dog, "Christ! It's that fucking mad bastard that attacked those Hells Angels last week," he said. "Are you sure you know what you're doing mate? You're lucky to still have your arm on.

It's that old English sheep dog, the one who's completely psycho" he called out to the others. Then turning to me he said, "The cops have been trying to catch him for days now but he's too bloody fast for them."

"He's been ok with me," I replied. "He hasn't tried to eat me yet. He's probably completely misunderstood."

I could feel a strange understanding floating in the warm clean air, like I had just found a long-lost family who were scanning my brain to be sure they weren't making any mistakes.

"Are you sure it's ok if I stay?" I asked.

"Yes fine," said Tom, "but keep that bloody dog out the way. We don't want to get eaten in the night."

The floor of the shed was really smooth, so I rolled out my sleeping bag ready to climb in, I was completely exhausted and looking forward to a good night's sleep, as yawning I slipped into the bag and zipped it up for the night. I closed my eyes clutching my money in my hand fearing someone might steal it from me, when suddenly I felt a large bulk pressing up against me. My heart started to thump as I thought I was about to be mugged but as the smell became stronger, I realised it was the dog who had decided to sleep with me.

First thing in the morning I'm going to get you a bath, clean your teeth and cut your bloody hair," I whispered, as he sighed deeply, rested his head on the sleeping bag and went to sleep.

Morning came, and I was woken by the sound of waves gently rolling in on the changing tide. I opened the door to let in the warm soothing rays of sunshine that were so bright they made me squint. Turning to open my suitcase I looked through it to find the sunglasses Jane had brought me; insisting they were *cool*. There's something about wearing sunglasses that's endearing and I felt good wearing them. The dog was nowhere to be seen but soon returned with a string of uncooked sausages, obviously stolen from the local butcher, hanging precariously from his mouth swinging back and forth as he ran. My analysis of the source proved to be incorrect as a Chinese man came running up the beach waving a meat cleaver shouting out in a broken English, "You fucking bastard give them back to me." The dog was almost grinning, and I could see how he'd earned his reputation, but he just ran off trailing the sausages with him as he went.

Luckily the Chinese fellow didn't realise that he was vaguely attached to me, and I smiled as he ran by using all manner of Chinese profanities. Eventually the dog returned again with only half the stash he'd started with; I could only guess what happened to the rest of them.

Tom was the first to appear at the door wearing a very old wet suit that was ripped at one knee, "Hi Tom, I called out, "Nice day."

"Yes," he replied, "Crap surfing though, no waves."

Bridget and Billy rose next and staggered out into the sunlight, "Hi guys, cool morning, but crap surfing," they both called out in almost perfect unison. They lit a fire and opened a cool-box which had chunks of meat and cases of eggs inside.

"Do you want something to eat David?" sparked Billy.

"Yes please, if that's ok," I replied, "but I don't eat meat."

"Oh I see, fussy, are you?" he said.

"Long story," I replied.

“We’ll have to swap notes at some point,” Billy said, looking at me and I could see shading around his eyes.

“You’ve not had a very good time in the past, have you?” I said.

“How did you know that?” he said with a grin.

“Takes one to know one,” I said knowingly.

While Billy and Tom made a start on preparing breakfast, I set about planning how I was going to clean the dog, creating a mental inventory of the items I would need. He was sat beside me again as close as he could get, grinning as he panted to cool his body down. It was getting hotter as the day went on and I could see his only way of cooling down was to bathe in the sea which was probably why he stank so much. Tom was an expert chef as the food was cooked to perfection, and keen to show my appreciation I offered to cook something for dinner later on.

“Ok, so you’re staying then, are you?” Tom enquired.

“Do you mind?” I asked.

“No not at all, I think we have a lot to talk about,” he said. The other two were locked in a fond embrace clearly more concerned about passion than food. “Don’t mind them, they’re always at it, helps to drown the pain.”

“What pain?” I asked. “

We’ve all had a bad time, but I’m guessing you know that because so have you.”

“No, I’m fine really. I’m very lucky,” I said.

“Oh! Then why are you prepared to sleep on the beach with perfect strangers?” he shot back at me.

"Good question," I responded with eyes wide open but hidden behind my sunglasses,

"Don't hide and don't lie to me," Tom snapped, "or we'll fall out, which would be a shame because I like you."

"Ok," I said, "what mucked up your life; I'm guessing bad parents?"

"That's the understatement of the world," he said. "I'm talking about total bastards."

"Go on tell me then," I said, sensing Tom needed to talk. We sat down together whilst he told me his life story, which involved abuse, violence and a complete mental breakdown. I was a little suspicious about what he'd said as I didn't understand how he could talk so freely about it, as I found it very difficult to talk about my problems to anyone let alone a total stranger.

"Why are you telling me this? I asked him. "It's not easy to talk about."

"You're not very old, are you?" he said. "What fourteen maybe fifteen at a pinch? I'm telling you because anyone who can tame that mad fucking dog has to be good. It's amazing what you've done, and dogs know who's good and who's bad don't they? So you must be good."

"Are you good at surfing?" I asked him. "I'd like to learn."

"Fair," he said, "it's very relaxing though and it takes away the pain," and I noticed it was the second time he'd mentioned pain in just a short time.

I began to think that he was a plant who'd been employed by Gethin to keep an eye out. "Christ Gethin! I haven't called Gethin, and I haven't called Jane!" I shouted out loud.

Jane had given me the number of a phone box in Penzance, with instructions to call at a specific time in the morning before the fair got busy for the day. I pulled the paper from my pocket and she had written eleven o'clock, so I made my excuses and went off to look for a phone box. "Can I leave my case here?" I asked Tom.

"Yes fine! You're coming back then?" he said. "Who you ringing; your parents?"

I smiled, "Sort of," I said, and off I went with the dog glued to my side. "What do you see in me Growler?" I whispered. "What did I do to deserve you?"

I eventually found a phone box and checked my watch, which was another gift from Jane. It was almost eleven, so I carefully dialled the number she'd written on the paper. The phone rang, and I pushed the button to be greeted by a jubilant Jane.

"You remembered!" she cried excitedly, "you do love me then, my *pretty boy*!" and I could hear Jake laughing in the background.

"Are you Ok, where did you sleep?" she asked like a mother hen fussing around.

"Err, on the beach. Well in a shed really, with three other lads," I replied. "Well one of them was a girl, I corrected myself. I've found a dog and it won't go away it's glued to my side all the time," I told her

"What kind of a dog?" she enquired.

"A big hairy one," I answered, as the beeps went, and she insisted that I called her back when I'd found some more change. I dug deep into my pocket and found several shillings and dialled the number again; she answered straight away.

"We miss you Dave," she said, and I could hear her voice breaking as she spoke to me.

Jake grabbed the phone and in his deep voice spouted, "What she really means is that we both love you. So you be careful."

Jane snatched the phone back and demanded to know if the dog was safe, "It's not got rabies has it?" she asked, and I could hear the worry in her voice. To be honest I hadn't given the dogs health any thought but realised it was a clever question as the truth was, I had no idea.

"He's fine," I said. "Just a bit smelly," and she laughed. She asked me for the number in the phone box to save me spending more money and called me back five times.

In the end Jake took over and barked, "Call us tomorrow mate. If you don't, my life won't be worth living. Now we'd best get on, bye."

"I will," I said, as the beeps went, and the phone went dead. I placed the phone back on the receiver and looked out of the window to see three people standing there slightly annoyed as I was hogging the phone.

"Are you going to be long one?" of them shouted, so I pushed the door open to let myself out knowing that I hadn't called Gethin yet. Growler, as I'd named the dog, had insisted on being in the box with me and had made it stink. However, he scared the hell out of them which meant they didn't complain at me as much as they would have if he wasn't there. I waited for them all to use the phone, which I think was sped up by Growler growling and showing his teeth at them. One bloke asked me, "Does he bite?"

"Yes, he's mad," I answered scaring him so much that he aborted the use of the phone altogether and I moved further up the queue. Something inside me felt very guilty when I finally dialled Gethin's number, and heard him answer with his usual Welsh accent, I instantly felt as if I had deserted him.

“Are you ok? he enquired.

“Yes” I’m fine,” I said.

“Do you have enough money?”

“Yes,” I replied again, “and I’ve already started planning what I’m going to do, to make some more.”

“Where are you sleeping?” he started to say but I interrupted him to ask… “Have they been round again?”

“Yes,” he replied, “but I told them you were away with friends. They insisted that it was their right to know who you were with, but I didn’t take any notice.”

“Well me being away will stop any wagging tongues, won’t it?” I said, “And stop any of the inevitable accusations, even though they just aren’t true.”

“It’s quiet here without you,” he muttered, “if you need anything just call me.”

I promised that I’d call every two days and was just telling him that I would take care of myself when I was interrupted by Growler, who had started barking at an innocent passer-by.

“What was that all that barking and growling? It sounded as though it was in the box with you?” said Gethin, sounding more than a little alarmed.

I froze for a moment, then managed to say, “Err I found a dog! He’s really big and hairy and for some reason he won’t go away. I’m the only person he seems to like, and he attacks anything or anyone that comes near me, so I feel quite safe with him around.”

I had been going to tell Gethin I was sleeping on the beach but cancelled the thought, as I needed time work out exactly how I would tell him. I decided it could wait until my next call in two days’ time.

The beeps went, and I quickly hurried my goodbye. "I miss you too Gethin, but I really need to prove that I can support myself," I told him, and the phone cut off.

On the way back to the beach Growler decided to pounce on a greasy looking biker bloke wearing a studded leather jacket. Tom had warned me he didn't like Hells Angels, which was not only accurate but inconvenient as Growler really meant business this time. I pulled him off and looked at the bloke, "What did you do to make him do that?" I shouted at him, secure in the knowledge that if he attacked me, Growler would take care of him. He brushed himself down and I apologised as I realised he hadn't done anything.

"Is he your dog?" grumbled the bloke.

"Sort of," I replied.

"Well keep him away from me," he snapped.

"No! You keeping away from him would work much better," I said, and he walked away.

We both trudged along the damp sands and realising that washing Growler was probably pointless I was thinking about cancelling the idea. Then seeing a holidaymaker hosing down his dingy near the slipway, I stopped and asked if I could use it to wash the dog and he kindly agreed.

I looked at Growler, "You're not going like this," I said, getting ready for him to moan and grumble, but he just sat down tipping his head to one side with his tongue hanging out. Then seeing how he was suffering from the hot sun beaming down on his back, I pointed the hose right at him, the cold water jet hit him with considerable force.

"I've got some soap if you want," the man said, and I gratefully accepted his generous offer, as to my astonishment Growler rolled over on his back for me to rub the soap into his tummy.

"You soppy idiot," I whispered leaning forward to rub it in; coming a bit too close to his mouth as I did so, and he nearly drowned me with his tongue.

"Who are you?" I whispered, not used to such affection, "Why are you being so kind to me, did someone send you to look after me?" Somehow, I knew that he'd found me because he knew I needed him.

Chapter Seventeen

"The word 'happy' would lose its meaning if it were not balanced by sadness."
... Carl Jung

We arrived back at the shed as Tom was talking to the owner of the canoes and peddle boats; he'd obviously done a deal with him as I heard the owner thank him for looking after his equipment and hand him a ten-shilling note. I hadn't realised just how switched on Tom was until then and I smiled with admiration at his attention to detail.

"You've set up a deal, haven't you?" I said.

"Yes, but it's not enough to keep us all going," he smiled.

"All," I commented with wide-eyed surprise, "there's only three of you, isn't there?"

"No! There's seven of us in all," he said as I walked over to him. We sat down together I told him about my money-making plan to draw and paint for the holidaymakers.

"You think the grockles will buy them, do you?" he said.

"Yes I do, I tried it out on the fairground and there were queues waiting to have their sketches done."

"What fair? You never mentioned a fair. Whose is it, not yours?" he asked.

"No, not mine. but I'm sure I mentioned it, you must have forgotten," I said. "We should talk, I owe you that much. Maybe tonight if that's ok?"

"Yes," he said, "and you're cooking remember? You promised!"

"I know, big surprise," I said as I walked over to the shed and opened the door to find my case, but it wasn't there!

"It's in the big wooden box in the corner," Tom shouted after me instinctively aware of my thoughts.

"Strangers. How strange," I thought, and I knew that my life was about to take on a sparkling new adventure.

Growler and I walked up the hill to a field that I'd spotted on my walk into Newquay; it was full of vegetables that were separated by plastic domes and I knew that the farmer wasn't far away as I could see his home on the edge of the field. I wandered into the field and as if by magic a short man in overalls appeared with a shotgun over his arm, it was broken but fully loaded.

"What do you'm want? he barked with a deep Cornish accent.

"Hello sir," I said, "I'm holding a party for abused kids on the beach tonight at about seven, and I was wondering if I could buy some vegetables from you?"

"You b'aint much more than a kid yourself, are you?" he said. "Haven't I seen you at the Perranporth fair?"

“Yes you have,” I replied.

“You one of they there Pikeys?” he asked.

“No, just working there to earn some money,” I said, and I could see that he was a kind man, camouflaged by a gun and a growl.

“Where d’you come from? Your accent’s midlands isn’t it?” he rumbled.

“Yes that’s right, I’m here for the summer holidays,” I explained, “and I met a group of kids who have all had problems growing up in this world.”

As I spoke, his face told me he was impressed with my attention to detail, and putting his gun down he said, “D’you fancy a cup of tea? I’ll get the missus to brew one if you like, and you can tell me all about yourself.”

My mind shot back to the farm where I’d hidden in the egg boxes as a child. I could see something about me had intrigued him, I wasn’t sure what, but I instinctively answered, “Yes please.”

“Bring your dog as well,” he called after me.

“Err I’d have a job as he won’t leave me alone,” I answered.

“That’s the mark of a good person and I’ve a feeling you’re good,” he said. “Come along and meet the wife,”

His cottage was very close to the field and it was only seconds before he pushed the red stable-door, and it creaked open to reveal the most beautiful place I’d ever seen. There was a big Aga in the corner that was bellowing out heat with the most exciting smells rising from the pots that were full of boiling vegetables.

“Merryn!” he shouted, “come and see what I’ve found in the field.”

I'd never seen such a kind face smiling at me as she held her arms out as if she had known me for years and she greeted me with, "Hello, my lover," and her voice echoed around the room as she kissed me on the cheek.

"Where have ee come from then?

"Must be a great place cuz you'm an ansom lad," she said as she bustled around and pulled out a chair for me to sit down.

"Make us a brew, will you?" said the farmer.

"Do it yourself Alan, you lazy bugger," she shouted, and he got up to fill the kettle.

She smiled at me, "Only joking! He's a fine old bugger really,"

Alan sat down and so did Growler, sitting as close as he could with his newly washed coat all fluffy and smelling of fresh soap, almost sparkling as a sudden beam of light from the window shone on him.

"He's very protective," I said, "So don't make any sudden moves will you."

"Sensible fellow, I can see why he'd want to protect you," said Alan. "So, tell me all about yourself."

I didn't want to come over as a damaged kid, so I told him a little about myself skipping over most of the points. "Why do you want to know?"

"Well it's the difference between ee having to pay for my vegetables or me giving em to you," he said with a smile.

"I do have some money," I said.

"I know you do, but I'm not after your money; so carry on," he said.

His comment made me feel strangely comfortable and I went on to tell him about Len and the bad adoption, even telling him about the tuberculosis that Len had infected me with. I explained how I came to be on the fair; but finished off by saying that I considered myself very lucky and wanted to do something for the kids on the beach, as they were broken and lost, and I knew I could help them.

"How you going to support yourself for eight weeks," he asked me, so I excitedly pulled out my crumpled pictures and darted around the principals of my plan as I could see that he was keen to help.

"It ain't often us meets an 'ansom boy that's smart as well! Is it Merryn?" he said.

"No, you're right my lover," she replied in her thick Cornish accent, "he's a rare boy indeed."

Alan looked at me and smiled, "Take what you want, on one condition."

"What's that?" I asked.

"That you'll come visit us on a regular basis, and if you needs a place to sleep, this is the door you knock on; cus it might get cold. Ok?"

Merryn smiled and added, "Sometimes you have to follow you heart and it led you straight into our field didn't it?"

"They're not conditions, they're pleasures," I said

"For both of us too Dave," he said as he rose up from the chair. "now you're going to need a spade."

I went out to the fields with Alan but didn't dig up loads; just enough for seven people. I put them into the box that he'd provided for me and we walked back to the house.

"What you going to do with them?" asked Merryn.

I was momentarily stopped in my tracks, then answered, “Well, I was reading about how you can wrap them in tin foil with a knob of butter and throw them on a hot fire.”

“You’ll be needing both of these as well then, won’t you?” she said, producing a packet of butter and a roll of baking foil.

“Alan take Dave to the beach please. He can’t lug that box all that way on his own.”

I said my goodbyes to Merryn and walked out to Alan’s Land Rover. Growler had been really good and not said a word up until then, but at that point Alan decided to try and stroke him and he growled and hissed at him.

“I see what you mean,” he chuckled, “that’s quite a bodyguard you have there."

We arrived at the shed more quickly than I’d thought because Alan had chosen to drive along the beach, rather than the road. He helped me with the box and shook my hand fearing that Growler might attack him if he did anything more. Dusk was beginning to fall and already the campfire was burning really well. It was almost magical as I watched the darkening sky start to block out the daylight with its night-time cloak, and the horizon came ablaze with colour. I just knew that tonight would be a very special night indeed.

Tom walked over, “Well, what are we eating?” he barked, clearly expecting me to have broken my promise to him.

“I have it all in the box,” I said, “I’ll sort dinner out, just as I promised.”

“I knew you would really,” he smiled, “so want do you want me to do?”

“Nothing,” I replied, “my promise, my job.”

Then knowing I'd get a reaction I said, "Oh and by the way, I forgot to tell you. No meat tonight!"

"Fuck me!" he declared, "there's gonna be a revolution!"

Growler sat by my side and guarded me with astonishing dedication as I carefully wrapped each vegetable in the baking-foil and placed a knob of butter on it before I twisted the package together. I was aware that Growler hadn't eaten yet as he was too busy taking care of me, so I prepared one for him not really knowing if he'd eat it or not, as he was very partial to meat. I completed every package and started to throw them on the fire, knowing they would cook very quickly and that if I left them too long it would end up as a disaster. Somebody produced some knives and forks and tin plates, just as the vegetables were ready to eat and I started to load them up with specific instruction on how to tackle eating them.

Everyone went really quiet; I think on purpose, and I could hear the knives clicking on the tin plates with no accompanying grumbles. Tom looked up and declared that the food was "Fucking marvellous," in his rebellious speech that I had grown to appreciate but above all understand, and everyone clapped in agreement.

"Dave turns up and we all start eating grass," he chuckled, "it won't be long before we start mooing! But well done Dave, good to know you're around us with that mad bastard that won't leave your side."

Then turning to everyone he said, "Please note that Growler will have your fucking arm off if anyone tries to stroke him. So don't try," and we all fell around laughing.

Everyone had finished eating and some bottles of beer appeared; I wondered where they'd come from as I knew all the kids were skint. I was guessing that it was contraband all stolen from the off-licence down the road.

"Where's this come from Tom?" I shouted.

"You don't want to know mate," he answered. "Ask no questions get no lies."

Being keen to fit in, as I totally knew all about rebellion and frustration, I said nothing, but my mind was uneasy, as the last thing we needed was the cops turning up with a hit squad. We all sat around the fire, each face illuminated by the flames, when a guitar was produced from nowhere and a guy called Lenny started to strum on it; but to be honest he was a bit crap. I had played around with a Spanish guitar at Gethin's house and learned several, well quite a few chords, so I polity asked Lenny if I could have a go and he said yes. My time on at the fair had brainwashed me with lots of music and I found it easy to find the notes to most of the popular songs of the day. I was particularly keen on Elvis and started to play 'Return to Sender,' hoping that everyone would join in. At first no one did, but after about five minutes everyone was screaming, "Return to sender, address unknown; no such number, no such zone," at the top of their voices, their smiling and laughing faces distorted by the light from the fire which illuminated the camp with its dancing flames. We played until the early hours, singing everything from The Everly Brothers, to Cliff Richard and Elvis Presley, until the entire group fell into an exhausted heap and slept.

As if by magic the dark night had passed to be replaced by sunlight peeping through the cracks in the shed door and it was morning again. Tom was already up and preparing some food.

"My turn now," he muttered, "a bastard's work is never done."

I staggered over to him a little worse for wear, "I know all about bastards!" I said, "I'm one as well, and it's always those who aren't, who love telling you."

"You're a strange guy Dave; everyone likes you, yet they really don't know who you are?"

"Well," I responded, "I'm not sure that I know yet. It takes a long time to mop up the psychological blood."

"You see! You've an answer for everything; and it always makes sense. Where did you learn to play a guitar like that?" he asked, not waiting for an answer.

"You're probably younger than me and yet you act and speak like you have a dictionary stuck up your arse. Your parents must be great, over the top great; yet here you are away from them all on a beach in Cornwall with a load of tormented Kids."

I stared at him and could identify with the pain he presented every time he spoke.

"My father tried to stick his dick up my arse so many times I can still feel it now," he said.

"I bet he used to say, "Now look what you've made me do!" I said smiling sympathetically.

"How the fuck did you know that?" he shouted. "Has someone been talking to you."

"No," I said, "I just know what sick people say to young kids to make them feel guilty."

Suddenly six more faces appeared, one by one, all worse for wear and wincing at the bright sunlight. "Hi guys," he shouted You all look like shit!"

"It's Dave's fault, he caused it," they all shouted in unison.

"A good night causes a bad headache; but what the hell it was worth it," piped up one of the group.

I looked at Tom enquiringly, "I've been thinking, I said. "I'm guessing you'll all be here for the rest of the summer, right? And the group will all grow. I'm here for at least another six weeks or so and I'd like to help you make it all good for these tortured kids…"

"What do you know about tortured kids," Tom snapped before I could finish.

"More than you think," I answered, "much more than you think."

He pulled the boiling water off the fire and threw several tea bags into a large metal jug. "I'm just trying to help them, I know what they've all been through; every one of them," he said.

Before he had time to take another breath and carry on, a young girl ran frantically up the beach crying and wailing as she went. I couldn't help jumping up and running after her as she was grey and shaking from head to toe.

"Hey, come on let me help you," I called out.

She looked up with an astonishing look of fright, "Get away from me," she screamed, and picked up a stick that was nearby.

Growler came bolting up teeth bared and glaring at her. "No," I shouted, at him, thinking he might eat us both if I pissed him off, but to my surprise he stopped in his tracks and licked her face. "Christ," I thought, "lucky he didn't attack her."

"Good boy, Growler," I called out to him as I ran over to give him a hug.

"You see he likes you, doesn't he?" I said to her, seeing the desperation and fear in her eyes.

She was very young, ten years old at most, and covered in bruises. I could see blood dripping down the inside of her leg but had no idea where it could be coming from. Growler was licking it away, but I was getting scared that she might be ill.

Tom had run over by his time, “It’s Lucy,” he snapped, “that bastards raped her again. Look at this,” he shouted pointing to the blood on her legs.

“What bastard,” I asked, as the whole thing was getting scary, and I’d never seen Tom so angry.

“Her father,” said Tom, “he lives just down the road from where I lived. The whole road is full of fucking nut cases!” he screamed.

“Well, let’s help her and then decide what to do,” I said. “She’s obviously been hurt.

“Split more like,” shouted Tom, “He’s done it twice before; I’ll kill the bastard this time she’s only nine!”

I looked at her, “Do you mind if I carry you over to the shed,” I said softly.

She was streaming with tears and I could see that Growler was getting confused. “It’s ok boy,” I said to him, “she’s fine,” but I could see he didn’t believe me as he was squeaking and grunting as if he was about to go on a mission.

Lucy was shaking with fear when I picked her up, “I’m going to take you to the hospital,” I whispered, but for some reason she freaked out again, which sent Growler back into a frenzy.

Tom looked at me and we both agreed that she would be better off in the shed until she’d calmed right down, so I carried her to a camp bed that slid across the floor as I tried to lay her down on it. She was still weeping, and Growler continued to be confused; I drew him closer to me, “It’s ok boy,” I said, and he tipped his head to one side and lay down.

Tom came in and announced that he’d rung the hospital, which set Lucy into a screaming fit again. “Please sweetheart,” I whispered, “You need to get fixed up, you’re obviously hurt.”

She started to shake again, "Please don't leave me," she pleaded, and I sat down beside her.

"I won't," I said smoothing her hair, "I'll come to the hospital with you, shall I?" I asked, and she nodded her head, calming down again.

In a flash there were several people in the shed with white coats and stethoscopes.

"What's her name?" asked one of them.

Tom gave them all the information they needed, and they put her on a stretcher, and we walked with her along the beach up the slipway to the waiting ambulance.

"You can't take the dog mate," said one of them.

"Well if he can't come, then I can't either, he'll go nuts if he can't see me; strange I know but true. He gets a bit loopy if he's away from me," I said.

"Sorry mate if you want to come, you'll have to leave the dog behind," he said and started to pull the doors closed ready to drive off.

I looked at Growler and hugged him while he licked my face with amazing energy, "Stay here boy, I'll be back soon," I said.

Tom called out from the back of the ambulance, "It's not a problem Dave, you just stay here with him, I'll go with Lucy. He might eat someone if you leave him behind."

But my heart was bleeding for this young girl, and in a that split second, I realised I'd be letting her down if I didn't go with them. I pushed the dog away from the door, jumping into the back of the ambulance as the doors closed and it sped off at great speed, ringing its shiny bell as it went. I held Lucy's hand all the way, constantly telling her that it wasn't her fault; remembering what Len had said after he'd finished with me.

After a short journey, the ambulance arrived at the hospital which was much smaller than I'd expected. To my astonishment, as I climbed out of the back doors, there was Growler was sitting up smiling and whining with his tongue hanging out, panting faster than I'd ever seen him do before.

"How the fuck did he get here?" shouted Tom when he saw him. "He must have run all the way." Even the medics were astonished,

"That's a loyal dog you have there," said one of them, walking over to stroke him.

"Oh no! Stay away he'll attack you if he thinks you're getting too close to me!" I called out just in time. "I wasn't joking he's completely mad," I said as the ambulance driver managed to pull back before Growler pounced on him.

I looked at Growler, realising just how special he was; he could sense a person in trouble, but everyone else he saw as a danger. "We're going to have to do something about your bad attitude boy," I said, but I half understood why he had it.

"He can't come in the hospital," said Tom, as we both started to follow the trolley as it bumped its way through the swing doors of the entrance. "It really is ok Dave," he said again, "I'll stay with her."

But I'd made up my mind; I was seeing this all the way, this little girl deserved all the support and understanding we could give her. I looked at Growler, "Stay here mate, please!" I pleaded, as I hugged his neck, and for the first time I was sure that he'd listened to me.

I ran along to the doors shouting "Stay," as I went, and as I finally looked around, he was lying on the floor panting.

"Hey, mate," I called to the man on the door as I ran past, "can you keep an eye on that dog for me, and tell everyone to keep away from him, he's not very keen on people."

No problem," he replied, "neither am I!"

The medics took a statement from Lucy and we had to leave the room whilst they checked her over, and I guessed it wasn't very pleasant as when she re-appeared at the door, she was in tears again. Running to me she gripped my hand so tight it was almost frightening.

"Here we go again! You ain't the pied piper, are you?" snapped Tom, feeling somewhat put out that Lucy had placed her trust in me and not him.

I looked at him and offered my hand, "You're one of the most genuine guys I've ever met," I said, "It's a privilege to know you Tom."

I'd never seen him smile before, but he did then, as we both walked out of the main door clutching Lucy's hands, one of us on either side. "It doesn't stop here mate," he said to me, then more softly he said to Lucy, "Don't you worry girl, well sort the bastard out." I could see that Tom meant business and my mind went into overdrive wondering what he might be planning.

Tom declared that Lucy was staying with us and I could see that it would be good for her to be amongst other victims. Because of Len, I knew exactly what she'd be thinking and how vulnerable she would be feeling, so when we arrived at the shed, we both sat down in the semi-darkness and I talked with her for several hours, making her feel as comfortable as possible. What really surprised me was that Growler sat in between us and allowed her to stroke him; which was the start of her healing as well. I knew that if anyone came near her again, he would attack them without a second thought.

The following day Lucy came out into the sunlight having slept between Growler and me that night, it had been very hot, and I'd had trouble sleeping. Seeing Lucy in such a state had unsettled me and Growler had been snoring which added to the problem. So I left them together and sat outside in the sea breeze, thinking and planning my days before the summer holidays were over, surprised that Growler hadn't followed me. I was still very keen to try my drawings out down at the inner harbour, but I needed some time alone and the shed kids were taking up too much of it. The fact was that my life had taken an amazing turn, as I had been put amongst people who were just as broken as I had been, but nowhere near as lucky as me and I knew that I owed them a huge debt of gratitude.

My mind suddenly jumped into action as I remembered I hadn't called Jane yet and Gethin would be silently disappointed with my forced silence. It was almost nine o'clock when Growler came bounding out and jumped on me with what he thought was real affection.

"Where's Lucy?" I whispered to him, "You're supposed to be looking after her."

He looked at the shed, then turned his head back to me, gazing out from under his shaggy fringe wriggling as close as he could get, panting like a steam train.

"Well what shall we do today mate?" I whispered again. "Let's have some fun, shall we?" I said, thinking about the drawing pad in my case and the full supply of charcoal pencils. My mind was excited at the thought of sitting with the grockles and drawing them and I couldn't wait to get started. Suddenly Lucy came to the door looking bleary eyed as if she was really having a bad time. "You will stay with me, won't you?" she whimpered.

"Of course we will," I responded immediately.

Tom came over with Billy and both had dark scheming faces.

"We're going to sort that bastard out. Are you in?" they asked.

"In what?" I answered.

"Sorting him out!" they both replied in perfect time.

"By that I guess you mean hurt him, right?" I said.

They both looked down at me and without a blink, barked out, "You scared or something?"

"No not at all." I said, "But won't the cops be going around there. You did report it didn't you?"

"Yes, but they don't do anything, he just keeps on getting away with it. He's a fucking pervert," said Tom.

I knew just what they meant, as Len had also been protected by the system that was reluctant to admit that civil servants could get so much wrong, and as such they easily manufactured excuses to protect their flimsy existences and their privileged positions.

"Yes I'm in, we owe it to Lucy she's just a child," I said uncomfortably, "but what do you intend to do to him?"

"What do you think we should do?" they both snapped back.

"I think you should plan your actions very carefully. And when you've planned them, I'll tell you what I think. We could all get ourselves into a whole lot of trouble if we're not careful." I knew they were inclined to act on the spur of the moment and I just wanted them to think things through.

"Good Idea," they both spouted out in unison again, "Let's plan then."

"I have to make some calls at eleven," I said, "so can we do it after?"

"No. Now!" barked Tom who was more hot-headed than Billy. "We need to do it now," he said as he grabbed my shirt sleeve.

"Don't do that!" I snapped, "take your hands off me."

"Why? What you going to do about it?" he said poking me with his outstretched finger. Growler true to his name was soon growling beside me, and to be honest I was surprised he hadn't attacked Tom already; but I knew he was very close to it.

"Stop now or you'll be sorry!" I shouted, and then Growler snapped and grabbed hold of his arm. He was really angry, and I knew he wouldn't stop until the job was done, so I tried to pull him off, but he still hung on to Tom's wetsuit sleeve. By this time, I was getting scared that someone would be really hurt.

"STOP!" I shouted, "Bad boy!" and tugged at his fur.

He finally let go of his grip and Tom stopped screaming, I think he was sure that the Growler would kill him.

"You're the one who declared him mad, and now you've proven it!" I shouted at Tom; angry at the way he'd behaved.

"Huh!" he snorted, "It's a good job he's with you. Wonder how you'd be on your own?" he said, threateningly.

"I wouldn't even think about it?" I replied, "He never leaves my side, but I can look after myself. I don't want to fight you Tom, I like you."

I got up and walked away with both Growler and Lucy stuck to me like glue. "I'll be back when you've cooled off," I called back over my shoulder, and we three unlikely companions set off to make our way to the telephone box.

As we arrived, I looked at the time, "It's still quite early, do you want something to eat sweetheart?" I whispered to Lucy.

"Yes please," she answered, and we made our way over to a café across the road from the telephone box.

I was a bit shaky at what had happened and felt very let down. I looked at Lucy as she gobbled up her breakfast. I'd chosen eggs for her thinking that everyone must like eggs, and it looked like I was right as she didn't leave anything on her plate.

"I'm sorry you had to see that, it wasn't fair sweetheart," I said looking down at this poor pathetic little child who had latched on to me.

"It's alright," she said bravely, "he got just as mad the last time and threatened to thump him hard then."

"How many times has this happened," I asked her.

"Five," she answered with astonishing and immediate accuracy, and I began to understand how Tom was feeling. Len's tirade of attacks on me had lasted for years and I couldn't help wondering what had really happened to Tom and the rest of the guys. We were all sleeping on the beach, but the reasons were invisible; hidden behind a wall of silence.

It was almost eleven and I raced across the road to the phone box and dialling the number I was glad to hear Jane's voice on the other end, as I had half expected her not to be there as I hadn't called the day before.

"Are you ok? I'll ring you back," she sparked, "stay where you are."

After a few moments, the phone rang, and I picked it up to tell her what had happened to Lucy the day before and why I hadn't called. She was fuming and at the same time very proud of what I'd done. When I told her Lucy was with me, she asked if she could talk to her.

"Yes of course," I answered and handed the phone to Lucy. I've no idea what she said but Lucy started to laugh before she handed the phone back to me.

"You're amazing, Davey" Jane sighed, "I'm so proud of you," and I could hear Jake's deep gruff voice by her side, agreeing with her.

Jake came on the phone, "Do you need any help?" he immediately asked.

I knew exactly what he meant by *help* and I said, "Maybe, but you have work to do. I need to sort this out myself, she's just a kid and I hurt for her. But I'll let you know if I do."

Jake was quiet for a moment; "I'm bloody speechless," he finally said, "and for the record, I know you will, but if you do need some help you know where I am son." He passed the telephone back to Jane and I could hear here pumping more money in, so I was guessing she meant to talk for a while.

"Listen Davey" she said, she always called me that when something serious was coming, "We both miss you terribly and we have another booking at Newquay next week, so we can be with you for a week."

I knew they hadn't really, because I remembered looking at the calendar dates before they left for Penzance. She must have juggled stuff about, and her words made me feel so proud and I welcomed the chance to be with them again. The fact was that deep down I'd learned what being loved was all about and I was really proud of both of them. She finished talking and asked, "What do you think then?"

"Can't wait, I miss you too Mum."

The word Mum slipped out before I could stop it. She didn't say a word, but I could feel her joy. "You Davey, are a very special *pretty boy* and we both love you very much," she said.

"I know," I whispered and we both started whimpering.

"Go on bugger off we'll see you next Monday," she said to break the tension. I wanted to say, "I love you," back to her, but before I could, she said it for me and I heard Jake shout out, "You soft buggers," but deep down I knew that he felt just the same.

"See you next week," I said, "And don't forget I have this dog that he won't leave my side; so when I see you don't make any sudden moves, or he'll try and eat you."

"I know!" she said, "We sent him to protect you."

"Oh yes!" I grinned, "how did you do that then?" but half of me was wondering if it was true as I always thought she was a bit psychic.

"See you next week," Jane said again, and the money ran out before I could say "ok."

Lucy was getting hot in the phone-box and Growler was making the windows steam up, so I pushed the door open to let some air in. I then called Gethin and he too made me feel like I was very important. My life now was so different from when I was with Len and Margaret, that my time with them was slowly vanishing into the dark depths of my brain where I had been pushing the horrors away; now I was able to use them as a cure rather than anger.

We walked back to the shed and I could see Tom sat down by the fire, "Sorry mate I was out of order," he said.

"And so was I," called out Billy, "way out!"

I said nothing but sat down between them and put my arms around both their necks. "Why don't we ask Lucy what she'd like us to do?" I said.

They both stared at me, "Yes, good idea," replied Billy.

Lucy was sat on the sand and I could see she wasn't comfortable with the situation, so I sat her between my knees and stroked her hair as I asked her what she thought should be done about her dad.

"The police don't believe anything I say; and it's my fault he keeps on doing things to me," she said; the words slipping out of her mouth like excrement, which made me angry.

"It's not your fault," I said bitterly, "You deserve to be loved and cared for."

"Do you love me?" she asked.

"Yes we all do," I answered in a gentle slow slightly embarrassed voice.

"Can I stay with you then?" she asked.

I was forced to point out that we were only there for the summer holidays, and that she would have to go back to her parents at some point. I looked at Tom and remembering Jake's offer of help.

"I think someone should pay this guy a visit; and I know the very person. Do you trust me to sort this out guys?"

"Yes completely," they both answered.

"Then leave it to me and I'll sort it. I promise you, he'll never hurt her again."

"You know her mums on drugs, don't you?" Tom said.

"I had a feeling that she might be but trust me I'll get it sorted."

I had it all figured out in my mind; I knew that Jake would be with me on Monday and he would know exactly what to do.

"I'm off to work now then," I said.

"Can I come, please," said Lucy.

"Yes, you can help me if you like," I said and as I looked at her, I could see the pain in her eyes. Deep down I knew it would take years for her to bury the damage that had been done, and the anger would stay with her for the rest of her life unless she was given proof that not everyone was as bad as her father.

We arrived at the inner harbour later than I had planned and a bloke came up and asked me if I wanted to rent a chair.

"How much do you want mate?

"I can sit on the step and draw so I don't really need one," I said, thinking it was an expense I didn't need and not realising that the clients would need something to sit on.

"Draw what?" he asked.

"Sit down and I'll show you, pull up a chair, they belong to you!" I grinned.

He sat down, and I started to draw him, distorting the prominent features of his face, grinning to myself as it took shape. It was clear that I needed the chair, so I called out, "What's your name?"

"Ron" he answered.

"Well Ron, how about this? If you like the sketch you get it for free, and I get the chair for the week. Deal?"

"Deal," he replied.

I pealed the paper from the thick sketch pad and turned it to face him. It had taken a lot less time to complete than I had imagined, and I was nervous he might think it was crap.

He started to laugh, "That's brilliant!" he snorted, "hang it on the rail, you'll need a sample. What's your name?"

"Davey," I replied, for some reason choosing to use Jane's name for me.

"Well Davey, pleased to meet you. I reckon you'll do well here," he said, and he wasn't wrong.

Lucy took the money and Growler sat very still next to me all day tipping his head from side to side and squeaking. I had spoken to him and warned him that he wasn't allowed to eat the clients and for some reason I think he had listened to me as he hadn't growled once all the time we were there. We made about ten pounds by the end of the day, and three people asked me if I would draw their dogs as well. I was keen to do it but realised that Growler might pick a fight and so I insisted on drawing from photographs only, telling them I would copy and deliver them back the next day. We didn't finish until half past six and judging from the look on her face Lucy had clearly enjoyed every second.

"Well, let's count the money now sweetheart, shall we?" I said, as I could see that she hadn't had the chance to shine at school yet.

We laid out the ten-shilling notes on the chair and counted the half crowns and odd coppers, and she wrote it all down on a piece of paper with surprising difficulty.

"Well done!" I exclaimed, keen to bolster her confidence.

"We'll need to help you with your adding up and writing, won't we?" I said, as I pulled her on to my knee and kissed her cheek. We returned the chair and Growler lifted himself up off the paving slabs that he had been lying on as he kept guard over us; one eye open all the time.

"Hi Guys," I called out as we arrive back at the shed, "I need to visit Alan's."

"Who's Alan?" squeaked Lucy, "can I come please Davey."

“Well I guess so,” I said, “but it’s a long way up the hill and your feet will hurt.”

“I’m not a baby,” she shouted and had a temper tantrum, but knowing what she’d been through I could totally understand and waited for her to calm down again before we all set off up the hill to the farm. We arrived at Alan’s and he predictably wanted to know why I was trailing Lucy along with me.

“I knows where her comes from,” he whispered, “and they’m not nice people, not nice people at all!”

He understood why I’d wanted to help her though, but made me promise I would send her home as soon as possible. I hadn’t told him about Jake or Jane, but his words made complete sense and I could see that he was concerned.

Chapter Eighteen

"There is nothing on this earth more prized than true friendship."
... Thomas Aquinas

I made over fifty pounds by the harbour that week and that didn't count the money I was charging for the dog sketches. I hadn't had one comment other than smiles and astonished looks when I produced the drawings to the clients. We both went back to the shed completely exhausted every night, except for Growler who had abandoned his one eye open protection job, in favour of full on sleeping; but I knew that if we needed him, he'd jump back into life.

Lucy was still with us, and the slightest thing sent her into fits of tears and rage, but we persevered with her, knowing the trauma she had been through; nevertheless, I was keen that she should return home, as Alan had suggested. I was slightly nervous that no one had come looking for her until Tom told me that he'd looked after her in the past, as he was loosely related to her, and her parents were pleased that she was out of the way for a while.

It was Monday and I had arranged to meet Jake and Jane at the field on the edge of town, not that far away from Alan's farm. I woke up early that morning with excitement as it seemed like ages since I'd seen them both. I had also spoken to Tom to ask him if he would take care of Lucy and gave her a convincing excuse as to why I needed to be on my own. Growler had chosen to stay with me which didn't exactly surprise me, and we set off to meet Jake and Jane. We eventually reached the field which had a large sign erected on a wooden frame advertising the fair, and as I looked across the field I could clearly see their lorry parked up in the furthest corner.

I knelt down by Growler and had a really long talk with him, explaining that Jane and Jake were very special and that he mustn't try and eat them. He always seemed to grin when he understood me, and I was reasonably confident that he knew what I had said. We made our way over to the lorry which was parked next to their caravan and Jane came running out to greet me, throwing her arms around me and smothering me with kisses. Astonishingly, Growler just looked at her and sat down, which not at all the reaction I'd been expecting; "Perhaps he really does understand me," I thought. Next to appear was Jake who jumped out from inside the lorry to put his arm round my shoulder and declare that he'd really missed me, complaining that his turnover was down.

I was so overwhelmed with excitement at the reunion, I hadn't noticed Jane going up to Growler with some biscuits. "Be careful! He's a bit mad," I called out when I spotted what she was doing, but to my amazement he rolled over presenting his tummy for a tickle. "How did you do that?" I shouted.

"He's not mad!" she laughed, "he's just very smart. One of the smartest dogs I've seen in a long time and I understand why he's so loyal to you.

"I've been dealing with animals all my life," she said, "I'm just thanking him for looking after you for me."

By this time Jake had already approached Growler with some food as well, and again he just rolled over whilst Jake rubbed and patted him with the most astonishing effect.

"Well!" I laughed "So much for my empty warnings!"

"He's amazing Davey, where on earth did you find him?" Jane asked.

"I didn't. He found me," I replied. "I was told later on by someone, that he had a reputation for killing people"

"Did he have a collar on him?" she asked.

"No, he just stank!"

"He has a ticket," she said, "sounds to me as though he got too much for his owner and so they dumped him."

I didn't know what she meant by ticket, but I later learned that she meant he wasn't a mongrel and that he was a thoroughbred. She'd been around animals and dogs for so long that she could tell, and the ticket she referred to was his pedigree papers. Not that I didn't know it already, I started to realise just how special Jake and Jane were, much more special than I'd ever given them credit for.

"Well come in," Jane went on, "Sit down and tell me all about your adventures Davey."

Jake had already taken up a front seat position with Growler perched awkwardly on his lap. I sat down and grinned, "Well you know that hundred quid you gave me… its nearly two hundred now," I told them.

"I've been painting and sketching by the harbour and the grockles love it."

“Where’ve you been sleeping?” Jane lovingly asked.

“In a canoe shed on the beach,” I told her, and began to pour out what had happened whilst they had been away. When I told them how I’d tried to find a bed and breakfast, and that the dog kept appearing every time I rang a doorbell, they both howled with laughter. It took me ages to explain everything in detail and both looked at me with total pride; even Jake was clearly moved at what I had been up to. I told them about Alan and his shot gun and how kind he and his wife Merryn had been, Jake was astonished.

“I’m going round there to thank him,” he declared.

“But they think I don’t belong anywhere,” I said, worriedly, thinking that if Alan thought I had Jake and Jane in my life he would think I’d deceived him. “That’s why he gave me the vegetables,” I said.

“Yes you do, you’re our son and we are both very proud of you,” snapped Jake, “so I’m going.”

Jane suddenly asked about Lucy and the atmosphere become more serious, and my face sharpened as I told them what had happened. I had never explained my own background in detail to them, but it now became relevant to what had happened. I began to explain some of what Len had done since I was three years old, most especially what he had said after virtually every attack. “*Now look what you’ve made me do!* he used to say, blaming me for his actions.” I told them.

They were not as shocked as I thought they would be, but I could see how very angry they were as every detail I relayed obviously confirmed what they had suspected but never quizzed me about. The painful memories that I had tried to bury, came back to me all too clearly and I started to shed tears as I remembered what had happened. Jane was crying, and Jake had a tear appearing on his cheek as I concluded by saying, “That’s why I wanted to help her.”

I continued with my account and told them about Tom and Billy who wanted to go and hurt her father, and how I talked them out of it.

"I know she'll have to go back," I said, "and I need to scare the bastard so much that he will never do it again, but without physically hurting him."

At that point Jake jumped up shouting, "Not just him, but Len as well!"

I was quite taken aback by the sheer anger I had never seen in him before. It hadn't really dawned on me that being part of the fairground, he and the others were often looked down on by the system, who considered them to be gypsies, and often failed to help them when called. This meant they often took the law into their own hands, and it looked like this was just what Jake was intending to do now.

"No, I'll sort it out myself Jake," I said hurriedly, worried at what might happen. "I don't want you to get involved, it's been reported to the Law, they'll deal with it."

I wanted to lighten things up, so I looked at Jake and asked, "Can I go for a ride on the bike please? Oh, and will you take care of the money for me?"

Jane looked at me, "You not sleeping in that shed tonight, you're staying here with us," she said.

Jake grinned and added, "Only if he works on the rides. We need our *pretty boy* back on the Walzer, to wow the women and pump up the takings." With that the atmosphere lightened, and I could worry about Lucy's dad later.

"What about him?" I said pointing to Growler who was licking Jake's hand with astonishing affection.

"He's not going anywhere," said Jane, "He can sleep with you, although I'm guessing he'll insist on doing that anyway."

I was immediately taken aback, as I knew that Jane kept her home spotless and he was bound to make a mess, "He'll drop hairs all over the place," I squealed.

"Well you'll just have to wash and brush him," she said, "he is looking a bit scruffy, isn't he?"

For the first time in several weeks I left the Growler to ride off on Jake's bike, he looked a bit upset as I started the bike up, having first promised him that I would be back soon. He had barked and wined but Jake calmed him down and he eventually accepted the deal. Like me I think Growler was feeling secure for the first time in his life. I tore off down to the canoe shed and showed off a bit in the sand as I had developed some really cool skills. Tom was sat by the fire with Lucy, who looked like she had been crying but I didn't ask why, for fear it was my absence that had caused it.

"I won't be back tonight, I have to work with my parents," I told them.

"I thought you didn't have any fucking parents," Tom snapped back with his usual choice words.

I sighed, "It's a long story which I haven't told you yet."

"Well does this mean that you're gone all week!" he asked, not looking too pleased.

"No I'll be back every day if that's ok." I could see that he was fretting and that my absence was taking away something that was important to him.

"Look mate I can't let my friends down," I said, "They've given me so much and I have returned so little. The least I can do is to stay with them for the next week."

Tom glared at me, embarrassed at showing his feelings, "I'll miss you, you're a mad bastard! Now bugger off or I'll nick your bike."

“What about Lucy? Will you look after her,” I said.

“Of course I will,” he snapped, “She’s family, like you.”

I attached my case to the bike with some bungee straps and kick-started the engine; “I’ll be back tomorrow,” I called out.

Lucy came running up, “You will be back, won’t you?” she pleaded, making me feel guilty.

“I will,” I promised her, “Every morning. I just have to work that’s all.”

I let out the clutch to pull away but on seeing her sad little face, I spun the bike round to go back and reassure her. I got off and sat down pulling her onto my knee, to give her a hug; “I just have to work sweetheart. I’ll see you in the morning; I promise.”

Just as she was giving me a weak smile, Tom shouted out, “Thought you’d already buggered off bastard!”

“I’m off now,” I replied, “Make sure you take care of Lucy.”

“Will do,” he said, “Be careful, see you tomorrow.” I jumped on the bike ready to ride off again, just in time to see Growler come running up from nowhere, launching himself at me in his excitement.

“That mad bastard! He’s never far away from you, is he?” shouted out Tom, laughing at Growler’s antics as I finally rode off with him running close behind me.

I sped off back to the field where Jake and Jane had parked their caravan, feeling total pride as Growler came bouncing up behind me, nearly knocking me off the bike as I slowed enough for him to catch me up. Jane came running out to greet me as if I hadn’t been round for years. “You are staying here tonight, aren’t you?” she shouted over the noise of the bike.

“Yes of course,” I said, “is that Ok?”

"Ok! It's essential!" she laughed as I climbed off the bike. "Right then Davey, you need to wash the dog and then go and help your Dad."

I smiled, "You really mean that, don't you?" I said, feeling warm inside at the thought of Jake being my Dad.

"Yes, I do, we're both very proud of you, so get on with it we've a busy night ahead,"

"What about Growler when I'm working?" I asked.

"Let's just take it one step at a time," she sighed, smiling as the words slipped out of her mouth. She produced a tall bottle of green shampoo and some sticks for Growler to chew on, which she assured me would clean his teeth and freshen his breath.

I connected the hosepipe to the caravan and sprayed him all over as I knew he liked the cold water. As I started to rub the green soap into his coat, the water ran almost black at first until it ran clear and a clean rather handsome Growler emerged. Gone was the muddy grey mess of fur to reveal a beautiful shiny coat and a gleaming milky white face. I was so pleased with the result that I spent a long time brushing him and by the time I'd finished he looked spectacular.

"Christ! *two pretty boys* instead of one," came Jane's voice as she stepped out of the caravan. "How are we going to cope?"

I looked at Growler, as proud as punch with my efforts and gave him a hug, while he licked my face.

"Just going over to help Dad now," I shouted testing the water to see if anything had changed.

The open show of affection from them, was like nothing I had ever experienced before, and I was slightly scared it might go away. I could feel her smiling as she said, "Yes, go and help your Dad, you know what to do."

Walking over to Jake, I found him bolting the Waltzer together with a big spanner and I stood there watching him, with Growler next to me.

"Come on *pretty boy*, don't just stand there. Come and hold this for me," he barked, and I jumped up and started work. Growler took a great interest in what we were doing, following me every time I went to fetch tools from Jake's toolbox and listening to his every word. Thinking it was some sort of a game Growler set about fetching tools from the box, one-by-one when we weren't looking and before long, we looked up to see the contents of the whole box spread around us; Growler sitting in the middle with a big grin on his face.

"Sorry Jake," I muttered, "Told you he was mad."

"Not mad Davey. Bloody smart, that's what he is," said Jake.

At last the rides were tested and we went back to the caravan to eat. Jake was totally in love with Growler and couldn't get over what he had been doing. Jane had been cooking and I can't remember a more perfect meal, Growler was sat by my feet and had eaten some vegetables, well a lot of vegetables, when Jane said, "What's the matter with him, doesn't he like meat?"

I giggled, "Err not now, not really sure why? He used to before he found me though," I said, remembering the Chinaman's sausages.

"Ok its time!" Jake shouted, and we all went out to the rides. "You know what to do Davey," he said. "And watch that dog we don't want him attacking anyone."

Growler sat down at the bottom of the steps that led to the Waltzer, the music had already started, and a bloke called Keith ramped up the speed from the control box in the centre of the ride as I took up my regular position looking *cool*. There were only three people on the ride, but I expected loads more later on when night drew in and the lights became more vibrant and hypnotic in the dark. I looked in amazement as I saw that Growler had followed me onto the ride and was balancing on the boards as they moved him up and down.

"Keith!" I shouted, "Move it up to Mac One."

I knew how stubborn Growler could be and I didn't want to shoo him off the ride, so I thought the extra speed would make him do it of his own accord. I couldn't have been more wrong as he not only managed to carry on balancing perfectly but looked like he was enjoying it.

Jane had been watching us and was in stiches at the sight of this new balancing act as the ride went round and round at full speed with the music booming out. Word soon got around that there was a dog on the Waltzer that was running around and just about everyone queued for a ride as Growler started to jump up and down moving as fast as he could to keep up with me. Even Jake was staggered and just stood there shaking his head in wonder. The takings went through the roof that night as Growler became the star attraction and I did my best to look *cool* for the women. As midnight passed the crowds dispersed and we all heaved a big sigh of relief, except for Growler, who was annoyed because the ride had stopped, and he just stood there complaining because it wasn't moving any more.

We all staggered into the caravan on the verge of collapse, glad that it wasn't far. It had been a hot sticky night, so I had a quick shower and flopped into bed, closely followed by Growler. I had been feeding him the sticks Jane had given me and his breath smelt really quite sweet as he curled up beside me.

Jane knocked on the door, "Are you two ok?" she giggled.

"What a night! Where did that dog come from," she said as she came up to the bed and kissed me on the forehead. "Night sweetheart, see you in the morning."

Jake poked his head around the door, "Well done mate, good to have you back. I want to talk to you tomorrow, I have an idea," he said, and with that we all fell into an exhausted sleep

The next day dawned all too soon and I crawled out of bed leaving Growler still sleeping, he was always slow at waking up but when he realised I wasn't there he quickly caught up with me. We were all sat round eating breakfast when Jake looked up and said, "Tell me about your pictures Davey. Will you do one of me?" he asked.

"Yes of course," I said, although I had no idea what he was planning. "I need to run down to the shed first, is that ok."

He knew that I'd promised to see the kids every day and that once I gave my word nothing would ever change it. Jane smiled at me, "You be careful on that bike," she said.

"Can I leave Growler with you?" I asked.

"No, I don't think so," said Jake, "He'll be off after you as soon as you leave.

"I also need to see Alan the farmer," I told him, and he immediately sparked up "Yes, I'd like to meet him myself."

"That would be great," I said. "We can both go over when I get back from the shed." And with that I kicked the bike into action and sped off with Growler following.

I rode out of the field and back down the hill towards the beach and sped along the sand to the shed; Growler seemed to run faster that he had ever done before as there were times when he overtook me. We arrived in no time at all and I spent some time with Tom, Billy and Lucy who were not happy at my absence, but Tom realised the position I was in and compensated his speech accordingly.

Eventually I said my goodbyes promising to return the next day and set off for the fairground, arriving with Growler just seconds behind me. Jake was waiting for me, so I got off and handed control of the bike over to him, then hopping on behind him we both set off for the farm. We rode up the road and through the farm gate and I could see Merryn at the window waving. We both got off the bike and walked over to the door, and before I could lift the brass knocker, I heard Merryn's voice.

"No need to knock, you just come on in."

"Well now, who's this my lover," she said in her broad Cornish accent. I was just going to introduce her to Jake when the door opened, and Alan walked in. "Morning Dave," he said, "How's you keeping my boy? Who's this you have ere with you?"

I introduced both of them to Jake properly, and the we all sat down to talk. Jake told them how he had first met me, saying, "He just banged on the door and said *I need a job*; simple as that. There was something about him, we just couldn't say no and he's been like a son ever since."

"He's a brilliant salesman," Jake told them and embarrassingly went on to say, "My wife calls him her *pretty boy*, as all the ladies at the fair love him. Takings are always up when he's on the ride."

"Yes, I know!" said Alan, "He impressed me as well. I thought I'd recognised him from the Perranporth fair when he turned up in my field with his dog. He's a fine lad, we're all very proud of him too."

Merryn asked if we would like some tea but Jake declined saying, "Thanks, but no. We have to get on, there's loads to do before tonight."

We got up to leave and Jake thanked them both again. Just as we got to the door, Merryn rushed over, saying, "Don't ee forget to come and see us will you Dave?" and threw her arms around me to give me a big hug.

"Of course not," I said, returning the hug, "see you soon," and as I looked at Jake, I saw a fleeting glimpse of jealousy cross his face.

"If you do need any more vegetables, just ee come up and pick em. You'm welcome anytime my boy," called out Alan as we rode off, and I couldn't help thinking about Jake's reaction. We arrived back at the caravan with Growler bounding after us, and as we went inside Jake mentioned my sketches again.

Remembering that he'd asked if I could do one of him, I opened the case and asked him to sit still for a few minutes and I began to draw. I was always scared that my work was crap; probably due to Len ripping up everything I did, so I was pretty nervous as I turned it round to show him, but I needn't have been.

"That's amazing! Where did you learn to do that?" he burst out all smiles. "No wonder you did well by the harbour. Do you think it would work at the fair?"

"Not sure," I said, "People don't have the time to sit still do they?"

"Perhaps you right," he said, pinning the sketch up on the wall.

Jane walked in and passed on her own euphoric complements that I knew were drowned in love. I just smiled and looked at Growler who was by this time glued to my side again.

For the next two weeks I worked every night and Growler became a total star, people were coming from miles away just to see him on the Waltzer and I was keen to do as well as I could for Jake. It would be difficult to stay behind this time when they moved on, I had another week to go before I needed to head off back to Gethin's and I planned on staying in Newquay. It was the last night before they had to leave for Plymouth, and I sat down with both of them knowing exactly what they were going to say.

"Will you come with us to Plymouth?" Jane pleaded. "We can't imagine being without you," she said, "Growler has settled down with us and he's part of the family too."

"Yes, of course I will," I responded realising that it was unfair to expect them to come all the way back from Plymouth to Newquay to pick me up for the journey back north.

"I'm a bit bothered about Growler when we get back to Leicester though!" I said. "He won't want to be away from me when I go back to school, and I can't keep him at Gethin's. Even if I could he'd probably try to follow me to school."

"We'll sort something out," she said. "So you are coming with us then?"

"Yes, I am but I need to say goodbye to everyone at the shed. I want to come back here again next year and I really need them to all to know how I feel."

Jane looked at me and smiled, "You will come back next year, and everyone will remember the happy times," she said.

The fair was almost packed up, so I set off to say goodbye, and my first stop was the shed. When I arrived, Tom was sat in his usual place, but he was looking glum and despondent.

"I've come to say goodbye," I called out. "I have to leave now, as I won't be able to get a lift back to Leicester if I don't.

"I'll be back next year though," I added.

Billy came up and boomed, "Your off then Dave?"

"Yes I am," I said, "But I wanted to tell you guys that I'll be back next year. Where's Lucy?"

"She's in the shed crying! I think she knows your off," he said, and I went into the shed to find everyone was sat there as if the end of the world had come.

"What's up guys?" I said, "What's happened to make you all so gloomy?"

"You're leaving, aren't you? No one wants you to leave. You've held us all together; you and that mad dog of yours!" said Billy, looking over at Growler who had turned up and plonked himself down next to me.

"There's only another week to go before I have to be back to school," I said, "but I do understand, I'll miss you lot as well."

They all lined up, some with tears in their eyes and others clearly wondering what comes next in their life and I either kissed or hugged everyone.

"I still haven't told everyone my whole story yet, because I didn't want to hide in my fear. But I will when I see you all again next summer, as long as I get to know yours too," I said to them.

Lucy was still crying as she looked up at me, "Please don't go Davey. Please, not yet," she whimpered, fighting to speak through the tears.

I sat down with her and whispered, "When you go back to your family, he won't ever touch you again, I promise."

"How do you know?" she squeaked.

"I just do," I said, concealing the fact that Jake had visited the pervert the night before and scared the hell out of him, making it very clear what he would do to him if he ever did it again; and Jake didn't make idle threats. Apart from which, the police had taken him to task, and he had been summoned to court, and with the evidence from the hospital he was almost certain to be locked up for a minimum of five years. From what I had been told criminals don't like paedophiles and he would be in for a very tough time.

Tom was listening, and I could see him grinning, "Crafty bastard! I knew you'd do something," he said.

"Yes," I said, "you're smart, I'm sure you can work it out. Next year I want you to teach me how to surf if that's ok."

"Bugger off and take that mad dog with you. I heard he was performing on the rides last week," he said laughing and chuckling whilst he spoke.

I climbed on the bike and shouted, "Look after the little one please, you know how to do that. Don't you?"

"What do you mean?" called Tom.

"It's easy," I said. "Just forget yourself."

"Yes, ok you clever bastard, now bugger off!" he said again. I knew that he was hurting and that he was hiding his true feelings by using colourful language, so I revved up the engine, making the wheels spin as I let the clutch out to do a perfect *wheelie* that was worthy of any showman. Growler sped along behind me then speeded up, and as I changed gear to go up the hill, he came thundering past me; then he suddenly stopped to look back and I had a feeling that he would miss the kids as well.

The nights were getting longer as it was nearing the end of August and dusk had fallen by the time we set off for Plymouth. We all climbed into the front of the lorry, and despite Jake preparing a bed for Growler in the back, he decided he preferred the seat I was sitting on.

"I told you he'd be trouble!" I said, and Jake laughed.

"You don't have to be smart to know that," he said.

Jane was sat scrunched up by the door and I pushed Growler to try and make some more room for her. “Move up mate!” I said, but he just dug his paws in and licked me. He seemed to think it was a game, as the more I pushed and asked him to move, the more he seemed to like it and licked me even harder, his soppy expression looking just like he was laughing at us.

“Is he allowed on the ride again?” I asked Jake, grinning. “I’ve taught him a new trick!”

“What trick?

“Well he doesn’t just balance on the boards of the Walzer, he can jump over the waves now. When we tried it out last time the entire ride went mad, they loved it so much,” I said excitedly.

“I noticed!” barked Jake. “He’s a showman and loves every minute of it; of course he’s allowed, the takings went skyward because of you two.”

The road to Plymouth was long and bendy with tall hedges everywhere, and it was difficult to see what might be coming around the corner and Jake had to concentrate. Jane quietly pulled a packet out of her bag and handed it to me.

“What’s that?” I asked.

“Open it and see,” she whispered.

I looked at her whilst I opened the box; she was so excited, grinning like a Cheshire cat, as I broke the seal. Inside was a collar for Growler, it was the most amazing thing that I had ever seen. It had gleaming sparkling jewels set all around it and a big brass clasp that was highly polished,

“He’ll need one in Plymouth,” she said. “He’ll be classed as a stray if he hasn’t got a collar and disk, and the cops will seize him, and we don’t want that.”

I looked a Growler, sure that he wouldn't like it, and expected him to go nuts as I wound it round his neck. But to my amazement he just sat there with his doggy grin, as if to say, "There you are, I belong somewhere as well," then he turned around to Jane and licked her face as though he knew she'd bought it.

"One of these days that dog will start talking!" sniggered Jake. "I've said it several times before, and I'm going to say it again; he's not mad, he's just very very smart," and we all agreed.

After a journey that took longer than it should because of the country roads, we pulled into a field on the edge of Plymouth, ready to un-hitch the caravan and bed down for the night. We were all completely knackered apart from Growler who was scratching his neck to try and remove the collar.

"I thought he would try that Jane," I said, "it must feel strange to him."

"He'll soon get used to it," she said, "so don't give in. We don't want any trouble with the dog cops."

The moonlight was reflecting in the gemstones on his collar as he moved his head around trying to scratch it, and the colours reminded me of the rides.

"It's really *cool*!" I shouted.

"What is?" asked Jane.

"The collar, it reflects the same colours as the ride doesn't it?"

"Yes," she said "That's why I bought it. It will look great when he starts performing again tomorrow night." But I also knew she'd bought it because she absolutely loved anything that was shiny and sparkly.

We all got ready for bed, and Growler jumped up with me resting his head on my chest. "Goodnight" I whispered to Jane as she came over to adjust the sheets. Jake called out, "Goodnight mate, sleep well. Loads to do in the morning," and I drifted off with the sound of Growler snoring in the background.

After what seemed only a few seconds, I woke up with a start to see daylight streaming through the curtains. Jake and Jane were already up, and Jake was outside talking to one of the ride operators.

"We'll need to check it!" I heard him say.

"The bearing's knackered; I told you about it months ago."

He didn't sound at all happy and I assumed that he was talking about our ride, so I needed to get up and get going. I was just slipping out of bed when I heard him shout out, "Davey! Come on, I need your help mate."

Growler was still snoring, and I was a bit nervous that he might not like his new surroundings; so I brushed his hair back and whispered, "Are you ok?" He grumbled and turned over again having given no response at all to my concerns. "What's up mate? You aren't sick, are you?" He grumbled again and then licked his lips as he smelt the aroma of breakfast slipping through the air. Food was the one thing that moved him and like a flash he was up, pushing the door open to sit by the table tipping his head from side to side.

"Morning young man how are you today," said Jane, speaking to Growler. And I guessed she was feeding him a sneaky sausage as I heard a squeak and a sharp flap of his tongue, which was a good sign that he was on top form and ready to do his thing. After visiting the bathroom, which was huge and always smelt of sweet perfume, I dressed and slid the door open to greet the new day. We had breakfast and I followed Jake outside where I could see he was obviously concerned about the ride.

"We need to fix it as soon as possible. Are you ok for it Davey?

"You're about the only one I can trust round here."

I put on some overalls and slipped under the platform, as there wasn't enough room for Jake. As I slid under, I could see the housing that held the bearing which had a huge bolt that held the drive shaft in position.

"Can you loosen it Davey?" called Jake.

"Don't know, but I'll try," I answered as I crawled nearer to the main shaft and the mega bolt. The spanner was really heavy, and I had to drag it with me along the grass.

"Right mate, put the ring over the bolt and pull as hard as you can," said Jake. It wasn't easy but eventually I slipped the ring over the bolt and put my entire weight on it. But it wasn't enough, and it didn't move one bit.

"Wait a minute, I'll throw a chain through the gap and you can hook it over the spanner," said Jake, seeing that it wouldn't budge.

"Ok," I called back as I lay there with only inches of room to spare. "Be quick Jake, it looks as though the casing might be cracked, but I'm not sure."

I had listened to everything that Jake had taught me since I'd known him, and in an effort to impress him even more I had also read up on the mechanics of the ride, so I was quite clued. As I waited for him to bring the chain, I was happy to see Jake was impressed with my efforts as helping him was a good way to repay all his kindness. The end of a big chain suddenly appeared through the hole in the platform and I hooked it over the spanner.

"I think you'll have to take it to bits again, Jake! This looks a bit bad to me," I called out from under the platform.

"We haven't got the time," he snapped, "so we'll have to remove it from under there and slip a new one on."

Through the gap I could see Growler was patiently waiting for me to come out from under the ride, tipping his head from side to side as if to say, "Are you sure you should be doing this."

As Jake wound the chain around the winch and started it up, I could see the pressure building. Suddenly there was a huge bang and several thick boards sprang loose, landing on my legs and pinning me to the ground. I had a moment's panic as I registered that my legs were trapped; but then realised I could still feel them and could move them slightly, but looking down it was clear that I was bleeding. Growler went mad, I could hear him howling as he scrambled to try and get to me. Eventually he managed to poke his head under one of the boards, which provided a degree of movement to one of my legs but the other was still stuck. Jake was already undoing the top boards and had physically pulled several up with his bare hands to uncover me.

Before anyone else could come and help me, Growler crawled underneath to join me, panting and puffing and started repeatedly pushing his neck up against my hands. Realising what he was doing, I grabbed hold of his new collar and edging backwards he began to pull me slowly out from under the broken ride. I have no idea how he did it, but he pulled me the whole way out, instinctively knowing that my legs were badly hurt and that I couldn't crawl myself.

When we reached the unbroken light of day, several of the other fairground workers had gathered round and started clapping. I could see that Growler had blood coming from his back, having caught himself as he rescued me, but he wasn't bothered, he just licked me and plonked his head on my chest whilst Jake inspected my legs.

"It's not as bad as I thought," he shouted as Jane came running up with a load of bandages.

"What the hell happened Jake! What were you thinking?" she snapped at him and it was the first time I had ever seen her angry with him.

"It's not that bad Jane, but Growler is hurt can you have a look at him please?" I asked her

She pulled back his coat and exclaimed "It's only a scratch!" as she massaged some antiseptic ointment into the cut.

Then looking down at me again she said, "We need to get you to a hospital, there's something sticking in your leg."

I started to realise that my leg really did hurt, and I could see that Jane was panicking as they bundled me into a small van and raced to the hospital. The hospital staff were adamant that Growler had to stay outside, but he just refused to listen and eventually they turned a blind eye, pretending that he wasn't there. A big bloke in a white coat threw the curtains back and asked what had happened, but before I could answer Jake told him the entire story.

He unwound the bandages that Jane had applied and after a brief look he said, "Yes there seems to be a foreign body embedded in his right leg. We will have to remove it."

"Nurse!" he called out, "Freeze his leg and I'll be back in just a minute."

I had expected a woman to come in from behind the curtains, but another bloke turned up with a big needle.

"Have you had a tetanus injection?" he asked.

"Not sure," I answered.

"Well, we'll give you one after we can get this splinter out," he said and stuck the needle in to freeze my leg. Jane was wrecked, and I could see tears building up in her eyes.

"It was no one's fault Jane; I was just unlucky. If it hadn't been for his new collar Growler couldn't have pulled me out," I said.

She started to laugh, "Oh I see! It was my gift that saved you was it?"

"Yes it was Mum," I said, "your kind thoughts save a load of problems. Not just now but always." And I really meant it.

The hospital removed the splinter and bound my leg, and it was nowhere near as bad as I had thought, even the bandages were really easy to wear as they didn't pinch at all. I pulled my jeans up over them and looked at Growler who had stopped fretting as he could see that the shine had come back in my eyes.

"Are you really ok Davey?" whispered Jane.

"Yes I'm fine," I said, beaming as I walked out of the hospital and into the carpark without so much as a limp.

"Are you ok boy?" I said to Growler as I looked down at his back, which looked a bit sore. He looked at me and tipped his head,

"*Yes, I'm fine as long as you are,*" I could hear him say, as he climbed back into the van and we headed off back to the fair.

"You're not working tonight Davey," Jane said firmly.

"I'll be fine, it hardly hurts at all," I said.

"Now don't worry, let's just get on and forget it. These things happen don't they, and no one was seriously hurt."

Chapter Nineteen

"There is only one happiness in this life,
to love and be loved."
... George Sand

I did work on the ride that night, as did Growler; and as usual the takings went through the roof again. The crew had rebuilt the ride in record time and to be honest it felt much smoother that it had ever done before. The week flew by with every night even more successful than the previous one. Growler was drawing in the crowds to what was by then 'The Amazing Waltzer,' with people coming from miles around to see the ride and the strange balancing dog. It was my last week of the summer holidays and I knew that I would be at school the following week with nothing but memories of my summer adventure; and sadness overflowed my emotions.

As promised, I called Gethin every day, and as the time for my return came closer, his zeal had grown. On the last time I called he told me that Len and Margaret had visited him again, but he had managed to get rid of them, albeit they had left almost accusing him of lying to them.

"They didn't believe that you weren't living here," he said, and went on to tell me that they had threatened legal proceedings against him. There was a slight edge to his voice, and I knew that he was a bit concerned about it, so I told him I would go and see them when I got back. I put on a brave act but in my heart the thought of seeing Len still terrified me for some reason. The mere thought of him flooded my brain with fear and I had no wish to poison my life with him again.

Finally, the day came for our return and we were packing up ready to drive up the M1 to Loughborough and I began to feel scared again.

"You can stay with us Davey, there's always a place for you here," Jane frequently murmured, sensing my turmoil.

"I know but I need to study and there are loads of books at Gethin's which I need to read."

"Will you still do the Lorry darling?" she asked.

"Yes, every Saturday at five, but I'm worried about Growler he won't like being away from me."

Jane and Jake had offered take care of him as I couldn't take him back to Gethin's, but I was still worried.

"So what do you want to do?" she said. "You know he can't really stay at Gethin's, can he? There's no other solution."

"No," I said, "I'll just have to come and see him every day, after school, he can't come with me!"

Jane was starting to realise just how dedicated Growler was and whispered, "What would we do if he ran away to try and find you?

“I don’t know, but I do know that’s what he’s likely to do,” I answered uncomfortably. “I haven’t the foggiest how to solve the problem. I’m worried he won’t stay, and once he gets something into his head he’s gone.

“You’d have to chain him down and he wouldn’t like that. Not one bit,” I said, getting more and more concerned with every thought.

We finally pulled up at Gethin’s house at around three in the morning and I could see there was a light on as he opened the front door to greet us.

“Good morning!” he muttered with such a look of pleasure on his face. “Good to have you back David.”

I hadn’t been called David for ages and it felt strange, his words hit me with a thud, and I knew that I was back to reality. I climbed out of the lorry and ran up to him, and he polity smiled and shook my hand,

“It’s good to have you back, I’ve missed you being around it’s been very quiet without you,” he said in his stilted slightly old-fashioned way. And although he didn’t show his feelings in the same way Jake and Jane did, they were no less sincere.

I could hear Growler trying to escape from the lorry, and as a long shot I said, “Err, I don’t suppose I could keep my dog here could I Gethin. It’s a long story, but could I?”

“What dog?” he burst out, just as Growler broke free and bounded up to me.

“This one,” I said as I pointed to him; “he’s also quite large.”

“No, He’s too big and we couldn’t leave him in the house all day,” he said.

“Your quite right!” I muttered, “stupid question really. Sorry.”

Jane jumped out of the lorry closely followed by Jake who nervously walked up to Gethin and greeted him with an out-stretched hand. I could see at a glance that Gethin didn't like my friends at all as he politely said, "How do you do."

I could almost hear Jake thinking "*pretentious idiot*," but I kept a straight face and allowed the visitation to continue.

"How did he get on with you, was he a pleasure to be with?" asked Gethin.

"Oh yes!" Jane replied, before Jake could utter a word.

"Yes," said Gethin, "he is exceptionally aware, and I am keen to see him do well. Would you like to come in? I know it's late, but I'd like to speak to you both."

I could feel something brewing and I was becoming nervous as I thought "Jake is not the best person with whom to pick a fight." Then taken aback, I thought, "Good God! I've only been here for ten minutes and I'm already thinking in more eloquent speech," and for the first time I realised that my stuttering had completely vanished, due only to the long hours and dedicated training by Gethin.

Jane looked very uncomfortable when she sat down, "He's been like a son to us," she remarked.

"I understand exactly what you mean," Gethin went on in his precise Welsh manner, that I could see made them feel uncomfortable.

"And life skills are very important. Especially as his childhood was virtually unspeakable. Spending hours locked up underneath the stairs in a cupboard hardly expands the mind, does it?" he said. "Has he mentioned his past to you?"

"He's told us some of his past, but not all the details," Jane said, trying hard to fit in with Gethin's deliberate profile.

"I thought not," Gethin grunted, and I looked up into the air avoiding eye contact with them.

"The reason it hasn't been mentioned, is because he is too busy considering other people," he went on. "Were you aware that only last year he could barely utter one word without stuttering?"

Jane looked at me in horror, "Why didn't you say? We would never have put you on the back of the lorry if we'd known!"

"That's the very reason why I didn't say anything," I replied.

"How did you stop?" asked Jake.

"Gethin spent hours with me, whilst I looked in a mirror and pronounced the words properly," I said; but I could see that Jake was getting hot under the collar.

"You think we're stupid, don't you?" he burst out at Gethin.

"No I do not," said Gethin. "Very much to the contrary. In fact, I think you are essential for his future mental health."

"Why is that?" asked Jake.

"Because you both love him properly, and he now understands the true meaning of life as a consequence of your gifts to him."

"You didn't want him to go away with us, did you?" said Jake

"Yes I did, and we made a deal for a variety of good and sound reasons," said Gethin. "I also want you to understand that in my own way I needed to gift him with knowledge, and that any overlap in our thoughts is relevant.

"He's had a bad time and school is very important to him; so I just wanted you to know that my thoughts are just as dedicated as yours and that we will need to work together.

"Also you should know that his adopted parents keep on coming round and threatening me if doesn't return him; which is pathetic if you knew the whole story and I think you have the right to know what is going on as it could affect you too."

I had sat there in total silence at what Gethin was saying, and Growler had frozen by my side as if he knew that I was uneasy.

"May I say something please," I said.

"I'm not a kid anymore; Len stole my childhood from me a long time ago. What I am, is very determined not to let anyone down. When I look at the dog and each one of you, it is obvious that someone is taking care of me up there.

"I don't want to hide behind what happened to me. I don't want to feel sorry for myself and if I can't cope with any damage that I haven't identified yet, I have all of you to rely on. I'm really very lucky you know; so stop, please stop this. Just promise me one thing."

"What's that?" they all responded in unison.

"That I will never have to sleep in the same house with Len again; until I can understand all of the reasons why he did what he did to me."

Jake looked up at Gethin, "Can I have your telephone number please, just in case we need to talk?"

I knew that they were going to discuss me in private and so I shouted, "No problem as long as no one feels sorry for me. I don't want to hide; I want to be seen."

"What are we going to do with Growler?" I said, changing the subject slightly. "I need to tell you how he found me Gethin; so, could he stay just for the night? Until we can figure out what to do with him?"

Gethin looked at me sternly, "He can't stay here, and we both have to be at school. You're just turned fifteen not forty and you need some discipline in your life."

My summer break had matured me, and my age was almost immaterial as I answered, "He protected me, he was essential; I couldn't have survived without him."

"Well I still say he can't stay here. But I'll let him sleep here for just one night, as we still have another day to go before school," he answered.

"I thought we were back to school tomorrow?" I said.

"I lied, in order to give you time to prepare," replied Gethin with a smirk on his face.

"Cool I understand. Good idea!"

Jake yawned and said, "It's getting really late. We need to get a move on," and they made their way out to the lorry. I could see that the arrangement was not at all what Jane wanted, so I reached up and kissed her on the cheek.

"See you tomorrow, be careful please," she whispered as the brakes hissed and the lorry pulled away.

"Call me! You have the number," I shouted after them, and they were gone.

That night Gethin was really nervous, looking at Growler as if he was an alien.

"I know he'll have to go somewhere else, but he's been protecting me for eight weeks, and he doesn't like being away from me." I said. "If I go anywhere, he will break out and follow me; I suspect even to school.

I could see that he thought I was exaggerating so I started to move around, and sure enough Growler mirrored my every move.

"I really don't know how I'm going to keep him away from school."

"How did you find him?" Gethin asked.

"I didn't, he found me." I said, "I know it's late, but would you like to hear the story?"

"Yes I would," he said, and we sat down as I told him how we'd met. I told Gethin how he had tried to attack me and how I'd made friends by putting the biscuit in my mouth, I told him everything. When I got to the bed and breakfast bit even Gethin had to laugh.

"Well! what are you going to do *Davey*," he said, smiling as he mimicked Jane's name for me.

"Where the hell did *Davey* come from? That's not you at all is it?" he said, and I laughed.

"Sometimes other people's thoughts are more important that your own," I muttered, and got up to climb the stairs dragging my case behind me with Growler shadowing me.

"Shouldn't he be sleeping downstairs," Gethin barked.

"He just won't," I answered, "you don't want him to eat your kitchen, do you?"

"I really am sorry about this; I didn't think it through correctly; this is all my fault!"

"I know," replied Gethin sarcastically, "but it's repairable. Good night lad, it's good to have you back."

Summer was over, and the nights were drawing in as winter was on its way, the next morning I woke to the sound of rain falling with tedious regularity. Growler wasn't keen on the rain; he had become a lot softer than when I first met him and had grown fond of his freshly groomed look. Jane had given me a really great brush that untied all the knots that accumulated over the day and I never missed the chance to use it on him, as I could see he accepted my diligence as a show of affection. As I pulled back the curtains the grey sky doomed down on me with a sickening disappointment; no sea air, no sunshine just smoking chimneys and partial light that seemed to strangle the day before it had begun. Growler was still snoring, and I wondered what I could do to make him understand that he wouldn't be able to stay with me. I turned on the light as the daylight from outside barely illuminated anything and Growler stirred and grunted. His eyes were still hidden under his hair, but I knew he could sense my mood, and wasn't happy. "Come here boy," I whispered, "we need to talk."

I knew that most teenagers of my age were preoccupied by acne, raging hormones and girls, but few were infatuated with a dog and I was guessing that Len's brutality had made me try and recapture my lost childhood. I had read one of Gethin's books by Alicija Englard, in which she discussed the problems that could loom up in later life. I was not at all interested in girls, but I had noticed the attention I was getting on the Waltzer, which was both pleasing and confusing to me. Every time I considered saying, "Hi," to a girl of my age, a dismal picture of Alice Oakley standing in the doorway, loomed in my head with disturbing consequences. I would then start to shake inside, and my speech would temporarily revert back to a moderate stutter.

I tried to understand why I could show affection to Jane and Merryn so easily and realised that I was building a bridge to take the place of Margaret. This made me feel guilty as I had always been sure that her feelings were genuine, save the influence of Len's conduct against me.

I lay down beside Growler and started to speak to him, "Look mate," I whispered, "I have to go to school and there's not enough room for you to stay here. So you need to stay with Jane; just for a bit till I can sort something out."

I knew he wasn't listening to me and that he would continue to shadow my every move no matter what. So I just hugged him and sighed, "If it wasn't for you, I'd probably be dead now."

I hadn't heard Gethin coming up the stairs and was so engrossed that his presence outside the door had escaped my attention. He knocked on the door, "May I come in?"

"Yes of course you can, it's your house," I snapped. He opened the door and immediately sat down beside me.

"I heard you talking to the dog and I totally understand how you feel," he said. "It's clear to me that the dog has protected you for the last eight weeks and that I have no right to separate you from him. But even if he stayed here, they definitely wouldn't allow him in school."

"I know," I replied. "And he'd only break free and follow me, so what can we do?"

"Maybe he could stay with Jake?" he said, not knowing that they had already offered to keep him. "He seems to get on well with him."

"That's because I am always there with him. I should have left him in Cornwall, it's all my fault," I snapped. "I'm really sorry that I've given you so much trouble."

"You haven't," he said, "we'll sort something out my lad so don't worry."

"I don't want to miss any school and I really want to stay here with you," I said, "did you get much trouble whilst I was away. I don't want Len taking any action against you."

"No not much, but Margaret did seem determined. I am sure that they will fling something at me before long. But as I said, we will deal with that when it comes," he replied.

"What did they say when you told them I was away?" I asked him.

"I don't think they believed me, but it did stop the accusations for a while. I've been expecting a visit from the police; the fact is, that you are technically a minor until you are twenty-one and they have the law on their side. I suspect that they may have had a visit from Mr Dick."

"Do you really need this Gethin? You don't deserve to be under any suspicion at all," I said.

"Look my lad," he responded, "the system is not likely to admit it had made such a large mistake; and we are too insignificant to make a difference."

He smiled and looked me straight in the eye, "You are not going anywhere, my lad," he sighed, "we will just have to brave the storm."

Growler grumbled and moved in between us both.

"You see! If I like you, he does as well," I said. "So be thankful that now he's your friend, he will protect you too."

The day went slowly by and the grey clouds cast depression on my every thought, even Growler was lethargic as he had spent all of his life in Cornwall breathing in clean sea air and I could see that the Midlands was not going to suit him. We had our breakfast and Gethin had seemingly relaxed around Growler who appeared to be keen to help him. Every time Gethin used the tea towel to dry the pots and replaced it back on the hook, Growler would un-hook it and bring it back to him again.

"I can see what you mean *Davey*!" he chuckled, "is he really as vicious as you've been telling me?"

"If he's here when Len knocks on the door! Just watch as he eats him up!" I said.

"But if he did that, the system would try and put him down."

"What you mean Len?" I quickly replied, and we both started to laugh.

CHAPTER TWENTY

"It is in our darkest moments
that we must focus to see the light."
... Aristotle

It was time for school, and I slipped from beneath the bed sheets to the sound of Gethin as he clanged a saucepan with a spoon to beckon me down for breakfast. The house seemed empty as Jake had taken Growler back with him last night, and I felt lonely and isolated; but I knew it was the only sensible solution. We had agreed that I wouldn't go to see them in the week, but that I would still work on the lorry on a Saturday as planned. I had reluctantly agreed, on the condition that they called me every day.

I sluggishly put on my shirt and tied my Windsor knot with extreme accuracy, combed my hair and brushed my teeth before slipping on my jacket. Gethin had already left by the time I set off, as we had rehearsed the rules. I was under strict instructions not to say a word to anyone about where I was living, for fear of a spiteful reprisal. The day was bleak and cold; the sun all but forgotten in the grey sky as

I walked up the hill to the school gates. The buzzer sounded, and the term began with Mr Griffin glaring at us from his elevated position in the classroom.

"Right then, class!" he roared, "I want you to write an essay to describe what you did on your holidays."

I had already heard people talking about their holidays in France and Spain and how they had had a wonderful time with their families. I pondered for a moment and considered what I had been doing; realising that no one would believe a word of it. So to protect Gethin, I had decided to pretend that I had been away with Len, Margaret and Paul, to North Wales. I recounted the visit to Tenby all those years ago when I was younger, pretending it was this year and adjusting it to fit. The idea of not being able to tell the truth was disheartening and I found it difficult to write such a terrifying *novel.* Recalling how I'd been locked out of the caravan and bitten to pieces by the mosquitos until the early hours of a disastrous morning. It seemed so wrong as I reluctantly etched my pen over the paper; my memories were crystal clear of what had really happened, and I felt as though I had abandoned my friends completely. I scribbled down several pages of rubbish which was clearly done with no enthusiasm at all, and we all handed in the papers to be marked for the following day.

I had not been surprised when Mr Griffin handed the papers back, and that my paper had the words 'Poor Effort!' scrawled across it in red with a mark of 3/10.

I wondered what might have been scrawled in red if I had told the truth; probably 'Fiction, stop dreaming!' and a mark of 0/10'.

That week went so slowly, and my mind was caught up in a mass of thoughts; some useful others not. On Saturday I rose at five and Jake picked me up to *do my thing* on the stage at the back of the lorry assisted by Growler.

"He escaped several times during the week," Jake told me, "but we eventually found him wandering around whining."

It was a relief to see him every Saturday, his eyes lighting up as soon as he saw me; as did mine. But with each passing week it became more and more difficult to say goodbye to him and go back to my school life with Gethin. The terms work became more intense and Mr Griffin never forgot my 3/10 mark, and always made snide remarks even if my present work had been marked flawlessly. That particular term seemed to be magnetically controlled as the days grew longer and the subjects less interesting; apart from Mathematics and Literature which involved reading books and remembering the content.

As the summer returned, I worked on the fair again after school, but as I matured the excitement seemed to fade and my enthusiasm faded with it. I think Jane had realised that there were changes around the corner that were not very palatable to her.

Len and Margaret had turned up at Gethin's house on multiple occasions, always threatening but never acting out their threats to sue him. I had called Margaret only three times since I returned to school; it was difficult for me and I always found an excuse not to. My enthusiasm for work was diminishing but I didn't know why, and Gethin had outlined his concerns as I must have seemed stagnant to him as well.

The summer came and went and as promised I had travelled to Newquay with Jake, Jane and Growler, but nothing seemed to glue the time together.

It was now autumn and Growler had escaped more times than I could count; his zeal for me had never faded, but even he was tired of the long dark days and I could see him yearning to go back to his carefree life in Cornwall. Jake always remembered to call me if Growler was causing trouble but on one particular day, he failed to make that call, and when I did receive one the next day, I knew in my heart that something was wrong as I heard Jane on the other end crying.

"What's up?" I asked

"It's Growler he went looking for you again and was knocked down," she managed to say, her voice breaking as she tried to hold back her tears long enough to speak.

"He's at the vets, but we've been told that he is close to death."

The words hit me like an arrow, I was gutted and collapsed on the floor sobbing uncontrollably. Eventually I pulled myself together for long enough to ask, "Where is he, can Jake take me to him?" and it wasn't long before I could hear the hiss of air brakes and I climbed up into the cabin to find Jane still in tears.

Trying to be brave, and with my logical brain kicking in, I whispered, "We actually don't know how old he is, Old English Sheepdogs don't live that long and he might be older than we think.

"Let's just go and see how he is and hope he's not too old to get better, we all have to be strong." I said, but as I uttered the words my heart was breaking, and I was fearing the worst.

Jake drew up outside the vets and walked through the doors to where a short man in a white coat was standing. Jake asked him to guide us to the room where Growler was laying. The door opened, and I could see immediately that he had been badly damaged, the side of his face was really grazed, and two legs were clearly broken. The vet told me that they had taken X-Rays and there was likely to be internal damage as well and recommended that he was put to sleep. I looked at him lying there.

"You silly sod!" I whispered, "I told you I would be back."

He half opened an eye, hearing my voice and grunted back at me obviously in extreme pain. I could see that he was in a very bad state and I knew that the kindest thing to do was to let him rest.

"Are you sure that he can't be saved?" I asked helplessly, knowing what the answer would be.

"No" replied the vet, "but judging by the look of him he's quite old, they don't live past much past ten or twelve, he's had a good innings," he said.

I was gutted, and my mind shot back through all the perfect times I'd spent with him. Remembering his total dedication to protect me no matter what, and I couldn't bear to see him in pain. What made it even worse was that I knew he was looking for me when it happened, and that I'd always thought I should have left him in Cornwall. The tears ran down my face like a waterfall and Jane was very close to collapsing on the floor when I agreed to let him be put to sleep.

The vet produced a long syringe with a thick pointed needle and pushed it into his flesh. I felt totally wretched as I whispered, "I love you.

"I'll see you again on the other side," I promised, and I drew his hair back to kiss his face. I can still remember his last breath as he blinked one last time before he was no more in this world. I knew that his presence would be in my heart forever and that I would miss the very essence of his magnificence.

"See you soon boy," I said, "wait for me! I need to laugh again one day."

Jane was so upset that I walked over to her and held out my arms.

"It wasn't your fault, it was bound to happen," I said bravely.

"He just had to look for me and he wasn't very sure of where he was," I said.

I had never seen Jake cry like this before, but he did, saying, "I'm so sorry Davey, can you ever forgive me?"

"It wasn't your fault!" I repeated sternly.

"He's gone now but we all have the memory of him. He saved my life and enriched the lives of everyone else that knew him; apart from those he tried to eat," I said trying to lighten the sombre moment.

I walked over to the vet, "I want you to save his ashes please, I need to take them back to Newquay."

Jake immediately responded with, "We're coming too!"

I managed a weak smile and said, "I know, you will … He's already running around up there looking for me. I shall speak to him every day," and with that we solemnly walked back outside to the lorry.

When I returned to Gethin's he could see that I was in a bad way and that I needed to talk.

"I know how much he meant to you and I should have let him stay here," he said, and I really think he meant it.

"You know that would have been impossible," I said, "We made the right decision; he was bound to come looking for me and because he didn't know the area the inevitable happened.

"If anyone's to blame it's me for not leaving him in Cornwall; that's where he was born and that's where he knew. I shall miss him Gethin he saved my life; I will really miss him," I said.

Ever practical, Gethin reminded me that the exams were close, and I needed to revise.

"This won't affect your work will it?" he asked.

"No," I answered, "if anything the revision will allow me to lose myself in learning and help me get through the loss.

I realised just how much Jake and Jane thought of me and how bad they felt about Growler, when the following week they missed the market, and instead travelled with me to visit Newquay with the jar containing Growler's ashes and we scattered them on the beach at exactly the place were Growler had found me.

I took the opportunity to visit all my friends who were still down there and wished them well; especially Lucy, who had not been attacked ever again just as I had hoped.

The months ticked by and I did indeed lose myself in revision, and the exams were finally here. Unlike the usual end of year ones, this time they were really important, as they would create my path to college and beyond. I had been working very hard and reading more than I had ever done before. The only break from revision had been each Saturday, when I still worked on the lorry with Jake and Jane, who were both as dedicated and supportive as ever in everything I did.

I sat the exams and like all my classmates I had to wait for the results. But I knew I'd revised well, and I was hoping to get the required results that would gain me a place at Loughborough College.

Len had visited Gethin so many times that I had lost count, and each time I had tried to accommodate his demands; protecting Gethin at every position. I was still registered as living at their address and was compelled to use it on the exam papers in order to keep the records straight. This meant that the results would be posted there. However, Gethin had somehow received the results early and came home one day to declare that I'd passed and gained my place at College.

I needed to go and get the letter from Len's house and Jake had kindly loaned me his motor bike, to which I was now fully licenced to ride and had been for almost two years. It was important for me to get the letter and also to see Len, as I was still not twenty-one and needed his signature to approve my application to the Royal Academy of Art in London; which Gethin thought I was good enough to apply for. I rode over to Birstall with extreme trepidation and parked the bike up outside the house before walking up the path and knocking on the door.

"Come in," came a voice from inside which I recognised as Paul.

"Sorry to bother you, is Len around" I asked politely.

"No but he's usually back about now; do you want a drink?" he answered.

"Where's Margaret? I whispered, thinking that she might be resting somewhere.

"She's out as well," he said. "You didn't answer me, did you, would you like a drink?" he repeated.

"Ok, thanks. How's things going with you?" I enquired trying to make conversation.

"Not bad, I'm doing ok at school, but I didn't make it to grammar like you," he said.

'I'd heard that," I said, "but it's nothing to be ashamed of. You were always good with your hands and I've a feeling that you'll make it into engineering or something along those lines."

He smiled and thanked me, "You always look on the bright side, don't you?"

"Yes, you have to, or not bother at all," I responded.

He went to the fridge and pulled out a bottle of milk and poured it into a tall glass before handing it to me, and I sat down waiting for Len feeling very nervous. At that moment he appeared at the door and stared at me.

“What do you want?” he growled.

“I need you to sign a paper for me as I’m not twenty-one yet,” I answered.

“Oh I see!” he barked, “You know where to come when you want something.”

I could see he was wound up like a coiled spring and I sat there hoping that things would calm down, when he suddenly saw the glass of milk in front of me.

“Who said you could have that?” he shouted, pointing at it.

‘S-sorry! Paul offered it to me. H-have it back if you want, it’s not a p-problem,” I stuttered, mortified that he had the effect of making my stammer return.

He strode over, grabbed the glass and literally poured it all over my head. Seeing red I rose up off the chair glaring at him.

“What did you do that for you bastard!” I shouted, checking myself so I didn’t stammer.

He proceeded to prod me with his pointed finger, “You’re not tough, you just smell strong!” he snarled.

Paul tried to calm things down as he could see my face was in a rage; but something snapped in me, I was no longer the helpless little boy that he could bully and scare. The memory of all his past actions welled up inside me, and in blaze of anger, I grabbed Len by the collar and hit I’m so hard that he went over the settee and crashed against the wall. I had a flood of feelings that collected and compiled all the tortuous memories, all the insults and all the pain from so many years. Part of me was panicking, as I knew he would later try and take advantage of the situation and use it to try and destroy me, but at that moment I couldn’t control myself.

The lounge door opened, and Margaret walked in to see Len in a heap on the floor; his glasses were broken and there was a cut at the side of his eye which was bleeding.

"Call the police!" he screamed, "the bastard's attacked me!"

Margaret come over and calmly asked what had happened and to my total surprise Paul butted in.

"He deserved it!" he said and began to explain word for word what had happened. It was the first time that Paul had ever defended me.

By this time, Len had picked himself up and was holding a tissue against his eye to mop up the blood. I was surprised that he hadn't bolted for the phone, but I was guessing that Paul's testament had thrown him off balance a little, and to be honest it was having a similar effect on me.

Margaret glared at Len, "Why did you do that to him. What's wrong with you?" she shouted out at him.

Then Paul looked at Len and added, "What did you expect, tipping milk over his head for no reason? Why did you prod him Dad, what was all that about?"

"He attacked me!" Len shouted again, "I'm going to call the police."

Margaret looked at him with an anger I'd never seen before, "You do, and you'll regret it," she thundered. Then she walked over to me and flung her arms around my neck.

"Sorry darling," she whispered, "he's bloody unhinged; and he's getting worse. God only knows what's going on in his head."

I looked at Len, "Why did you do that? I did nothing to you. Why do you hate me so much?"

He had no answer for me, and his lack of response made me even more mad.

“I have more reason to hate you that anyone,” I carried on. “It was you who infected me with Tuberculosis making my life hell as a small child having to go to Groby Road every week, being unable to play sport with the other kids at school. I’ve done everything I can to accommodate you. I did my best to keep out of your way, I tried not to cause any trouble and never questioned your assaults on me.”

He remained silent which only fuelled my anger.

“Do you remember?” I shouted.

The more I said, the more that poured out of me, “What do you think it was like being locked under the stairs, you bastard?” I screamed.

“A little boy of four locked under the stairs in the dark with no food, for no reason!

“Always making me feel as if it was all my fault! Do you remember buggering me, and do you remember what you used to say afterwards?

“Now look what you’ve made me do!

That’s what you used to say. Calmly whispering it so no one could here you! Do you remember?”

Margaret started to weep, “Are you serious?” she whimpered.

“Yes, I’m serious. Do you really think I’d lie about something as serious as this?” I snapped.

“I’m so sorry!” she said, and I knew that she truly was. She was broken, unable to look at me, her head downcast as she numbly stared at the floor.

"I know you are," I said. "You have no idea what he got up to, do you? But I don't blame you. He's mad and controlling."

I stared at him as he sat there looking dazed, watching the cracks appearing in his carefully constructed kingdom.

"Go on then. Ring the police you bastard!" I shouted at him.

"I'm done with this! Stick your signature up your arse, I don't need it. You'll never beat me, not ever."

I looked at Margaret and smiled over at Paul.

"Sometimes the truth comes as a big surprise," I said. "Thank you for telling the truth Paul. I know that it will cause you problems and for that I apologise."

Len was almost speechless as he sat there in disbelief.

"You see? Even your family will turn on you one day. Just be thankful you have them under your control or you would be worthless, you sick moron." I turned to walk out of the house for the very last time.

My mind was dark with rage and my head filled with images of my pointless childhood, as buttoning up my jacket I opened the door and walked out to climb back onto the bike; wishing that I had never gone there.

Margaret came running out pleading with me not to go.

"I'll call you soon," I told her, "I just need time to cool off, it's my fault I shouldn't have come. If I'd called you first, it wouldn't have happened."

I kicked the starter, let out the clutch and the bike burst into action as I pulled away.

I headed off, unaware of what I was doing or where I was going and found myself in a place called Frog Island; the opposite way to my intended destination. As I approached a set of traffic lights, I was still angry, and seeing they were on orange I revved up and tried to beat them; unaware of a Ford Zodiac at the left side of the junction impatiently waiting for them to turn in his favour. I went through the light just as it turned to red, and the Zodiac being in a hurry was hot off the mark and headed towards me. I slammed the brakes hard to miss the car and thumped down on the hard road using my left arm to cushion my fall. I could almost hear it snap as I rolled over and heard someone shout, "Call an ambulance!" But I was more bothered about damaging Jake's bike.

I had crashed very close to North End Coaches and in the confusion, I looked up and recognised a friend called Ron looking down on me.

"It was my fault," I grunted, "think I've busted my arm, can you pull my bike over the road to the coach park please Ron."

He lifted the bike that was thankfully barely scratched and wheeled it over to park it under the bridge. From nowhere a man in a white coat appeared just as I was scraping myself up of the ground.

"Don't move! Stay still!" he shouted; but it was too late, I already had. He took one look at my arm and ran for a splint, "This is badly broken," he mumbled as he wound the bandages around the splint and bundled me into the back of a waiting ambulance.

I don't really remember the journey to hospital, it was all a bit of a dream as time dripped by. The next thing I knew I was laying behind the curtains, thinking about what I had done, when a very tall nurse wafted in through the drapes.

"Hello there, I'm going to wheel you to the X-Ray unit," she said.

With that, the image of Len came flying back as I recalled the last time I was taken into an X-Ray unit and why. I lay there concerned that everything was flooding back; as if seeing Len earlier had poisoned my very existence, and the good times had been drowned with his personified evil.

"I'd rather walk if that's ok?" I whispered and then heard a bloke grunting behind the next curtain; an image and sound which also disturbed my thoughts.

"Why is that?" enquired the nurse.

"You don't want to know," I answered. "But just for the record; I'm walking anyway. Ok?"

My arm was really hurting as I walked down the corridor with the nurse. "What's your name?" I asked her, "It doesn't seem right referring to you as nurse."

"Janet," she answered without hesitation.

"Well Janet I've been a bit stupid … well a lot stupid, and I need to make a phone call to my family?"

"Haven't you done that yet?" she asked.

"No, and they'll be worried about me," I said as we walked into the room with a yellow and black sign on it. The image evoked the same level of fear as it had when I saw it previously after Len had attacked me all those years before, albeit I had since properly re-named it as a trefoil. "What the hell is going on!" I thought to myself as I shivered, it was like someone had woken up the past, as a fat woman with a heavy apron on smiled at me.

"What have we been up to then?" she said.

"Well it appears that *we* have broken our arm; but to be honest yours looks fine to me," I replied somewhat sarcastically. She didn't appreciate the joke and her face changed from a false smile to a more realistic frown. She slipped the strangely familiar plate under my arm and took cover behind the glass screen whilst the X-Ray was taken; clearly not knowing or ever having considered that Hiroshima was fairly close to what she was involved in.

"Right! All done," she said, and she bundled me out of the door where I found Janet waiting for me, smiling and asking if I was ok.

"Bit shaky but fine," I whispered as I walked back along the corridor and through the curtains.

"Can I make a call now, please?" I asked her, and she vanished, returning with a phone on a trolley with a huge plug that she connected to the switch on the wall.

I dialled Gethin because he'd known where I was going and why, and when I told him what had happened, he went mad at me.

"I told you that bike wasn't safe; but you wouldn't listen. Where are you?" he shouted.

"In the Leicester Royal Infirmary," I replied.

"I'll come and fetch you. And on the way home you can tell me how you have fallen in to yet another load of crap!" he said, chuckling as he said it.

"Can you get a message to Jake?" I asked.

"We can go round to see him on the way back," replied Gethin. "Is his bike badly smashed?"

"No, only me and it hurts quite a bit. But I'm guessing that it's supposed to. See you soon, I'll come and wait by the door,"

Janet was just about to sweep the curtains back for me to make my way out, when Margaret and Len walked into the room. I later found out that someone had checked my bike licence to confirm my address and as a matter of course had informed them that I'd been involved in a road accident. Len had a grin on his face, and I noted that his eye had already been treated and an overly large plaster applied; I was guessing for effect. Margaret had obviously been upset by the call, as she came straight over to the bed and held my hand.

"Are you ok?" she whimpered.

"Yes I'm fine," I replied. "It was my fault; I was still mad at Len. I should have stayed with you to cool down but as usual I didn't listen."

Len glared at me with a sinister smile, "Huh! Broken your *left* arm, have you?" he whispered to make sure that no one heard him. "You'll never draw again!" he snarled smiling as he said it. I looked at him with a burning hatred that was so uncomfortable and intense that my eyes wouldn't focus properly.

"Janet!" I called out, "They're leaving now. They have some urgent business to attend to, can you show them out please."

I think Janet had heard what Len said because she gave me a knowing smile and without hesitation ushered them both out of the door and down the corridor.

"Who was that?" she exclaimed on her return, in an enquiring voice.

"None of your business." I replied and blew her a kiss. She looked at me with strangely caring eyes.

"He wasn't your father, was he?"

"No, adopted father but I don't want to talk about it," I said, "It's a long story."

She picked up a note pad and scribbled down a telephone number, “Well if you ever decide you’d like to tell someone; I’m all ears,” she whispered as she handed me the paper.

Gethin came rushing into the room, “And what the hell has been going on,” he enquired, “are you ok. Is he badly hurt he nurse?”

Janet look at him and calmly asked who he was.

“I’m his...,” I felt sure that he was about to say father, but he paused, “guardian,” he snorted. “I’m his legal guardian and his tutor.”

“I see,” she whispered, “is that correct David?”

“More accurately, a life saver!” I spouted, “were it not for him I’d probably be dead now.”

Gethin smiled, “He has a way with words, doesn’t he? Unfortunately, not the words to answer my original question though!”

Janet immediately turned to him having clipped the X-Ray to the illuminated frame on the wall.

“He will need a cast, but the break isn’t serious. It should be healed in no time, but we will need to ask the doctor what he thinks,” she said. “He will be here in a short while.”

I was not keen to have a plaster on as I could remember the problems that the last one had caused me, so I lay there contemplating my reasons for refusing one. The doctor came floating into the room; complete with a white coat and several biros clipped to his breast pocket. He stared at the X-Ray and declared that it was a simple fracture and that the bone was perfectly in place. Then coming over to me he spouted in an eloquent voice.

“My name is Dr Morley and having looked at your X-Ray, it would be possible and probably better if we applied a thick bandage with a splint to support what appears to be a simple crack.”

To be honest I was neither keen on the white coat nor the fact that he appeared to view everyone as if they were stupid.

"I was watching you scrutinising the x-ray and I did hear your comments to Janet," I said to him.

"Janet who?" he exclaimed.

"Your colleague .... sorry I meant nurse. My mistake!" I said.

Gethin by this time had begun to grin as he knew just what was going on in my mind.

"I think you're right!" I declared, "a splint and strong bandage will be just what the doctor ordered."

Janet was given a sheet with some very strange writing which Dr Morley had inscribed with one of his ball point pens; she walked over to me grinning.

"You don't like him, do you?"

Gethin chipped in, "It's a long story."

It wasn't long before the door burst open again and in walked Jake and Jane who had noted that I hadn't returned on time and rang the police, who informed them that I'd been involved in an accident and taken to the Royal Infirmary. Jane rushed over and flung here arms around me.

"Is he alright," she asked.

"Who are you?" Janet enquired.

"I'm his mother!" she declared, "well sort of if you understand."

Janet started to smile, "I'm beginning to think that we have been blessed with a very important person, here" she said with a wink.

"Oh!" smiled Jane, "much more important than that.

Jake was talking to Gethin and I began to feel very guilty about his bike.

"Jake!" I called out, "your bike is at Frog Island and there's no damage … well very little. I'll pay for it to be repaired it was my fault!"

Towering above the bed he looked down on me and whispered, "As long as you're ok, I don't give a damn about the bike.

"What happened Davey? It's not like you to come off, especially around traffic."

By this time Janet was preparing the splint and bandages and moving the trolley closer to the bed.

"You can all stay," she smiled, "but I need to apply the splint correctly with just the right amount of pressure to the arm."

Jake was deep in conversation with Gethin again and I could hear him saying that I had been over to Len's as I needed his signature to confirm my place at the Royal Academy in London.

"Did he get it?" Jake boomed.

"I am not sure," replied Gethin. "I have not been here long myself, so I haven't had the time to ask yet."

Janet did her job superbly and as I looked up at her she smiled. "How does that feel?" she whispered.

"Fine," I grinned, "just fine."

"Well that's good, don't forget you have my number. I'd like to see you again, so call me. Promise?"

I was set free and Gethin and Jake grabbed hold of me on either side pretending that I was some kind of cripple.

"Come along old man," they sniggered, "let us help you into the car."

I had no idea that Gethin had warmed to Jake and Jane as they seemed to be in total harmony.

"We'll follow you back to your place," called out Jake, "damn the time. I want to know what happened."

On the way home Gethin kept on quizzing me and I had a feeling that he knew something had gone wrong.

"What happened, I really need to know. Was there trouble again?" he asked.

I started to run through what I had done, and how Len had become angry about a glass of milk, and when I arrived at the bit where I had whacked him, Gethin stopped the car and looked at me.

"Did he sign the paper?"

"No" I sighed, "but I think I was wasting my time anyway."

We arrive home to see Jake's lorry parked outside and both of them pacing up and down by the front door. It was quite late, but I knew that Jake would not rest until he knew what had happened. I climbed out of the car and walked over to the door and before the key was eventually turned Jake demanded an explanation.

"I just know that bastard's been at it again," he said, "there must be a reason for what happened. You're a brilliant rider, I taught you how to fall off.

"You were angry, weren't you?"

"Come in both of you, and sit down," said Gethin. "I want to know what happened myself as Len refused to sign the paper and that means he can't take his place in the LRA."

I sat down and stage by stage transcribed everything into an accurate verbal report of the events.

"What! You hit the bastard? You actually hit

him?" said Jake with more than a slight glint in his eye.

I wasn't very proud of what I had done so I embellished the reasons.

"He prodded me," I said, and revisited his words that were embedded in my mind.

"He prodded me and said *You're not tough! You just smell strong*, what would you have done?" I asked them. "I just lost it; all I could see was red. But I know I shouldn't have hit him."

"Yes you should!" sparked Jake, "and much more. But you should have stayed off the bike until you had calmed down."

"Yes, that's what Margaret said, and I didn't listen. Sorry Jake, I should have been more careful."

I spent the next hour trying to convince Jake not to visit Len, as he was fuming. Even Jane was screaming revenge but in the end we all agreed that it would be better to let things calm down and then Gethin would go back to try and get him to sign the paper.

Chapter Twenty One

"Problems do not go away.
They must be worked through or else they remain,
forever a barrier to the growth and development of the spirit"
... M Scott Peck

Gethin did visit Len several days later; to be told, that I *should find a proper job*, and that, I *wasn't worth the investment of government money*. Len knew he would be liable to sponsor me and declined, and even though Gethin had pleaded with him to sign the paper, he refused. I didn't ask about it again, as I could see that Gethin was disappointed and had done all he could to correct the problem.

I continued to work hard, as I had always done, and Gethin spent his time supporting me wherever he could. I was transferred to an Art College in a place called Williams Street, which provided a lesser but still adequate chance of success compared to that of the LRA. Somehow Gethin had managed to sign my admission form and support me without offending the law; at the same time destroying Len's wish to see me fail.

Several years later and suitably qualified I was desperate to pay him back and I applied for a job at Rank Xerox, who had been working in the document management industry forever. They were at the forefront of many office machines and copying equipment, and the job they were advertising required a good understanding of the technical functionality as well as a subliminal talent to understand why people would buy their products. The ideas would then be transferred into graphics and content, which I felt confident in doing.

I had considered the job very carefully before applying but pretty sure my qualifications would carry me forward, I supplied documented proof of them when I applied for the job and was subsequently invited to an interview with a man called Ray Briggs.

He was the manager of the advertising department and being a graduate, I appeared to fit in with his graphical and technical requirements. I had to wait for several weeks but one day a letter popped through the door telling me that I had been selected for the position. I was delighted and what was even better was that the wage would allow me to pay back Gethin; albeit it would take several years. But I was very keen to do so.

Jake had given me the motor bike and I had gratefully accepted it as he'd told me he was now too old to ride it. Although I hadn't believed that for a moment, as I could see the smile on his face every time he rode the machine.

I remember vividly my first day at work when Mr Briggs led me over to a desk with a large A0 drawing board and a set of very precise drawing pens lined up in the well beneath.

I was keen to produce some quality ideas, so I spent my time doodling before I committed the final work to the expensive cartridge paper; as they involved a lot of costly colour separations.

Mr Briggs had completely changed from the polite person I'd first met at the interview; he would visit me every hour, demanding to see what I had done, and he showed his disapproval of my doodles on almost every occasion. Nevertheless, I persevered and eventually committed my ideas to paper. One of the problems I was incurring was his tendency to use me as a mule, delighting in stopping me from my work to go and fetch coffee or sandwiches or anything else he fancied from the canteen; to later complain that I hadn't done enough work.

I remember on this particular day I had worked really hard to provide a design along with a set of full transparent separations, all with detailed psychological explanations as to why I considered that my reasoning was sound.

Gethin had always insisted that I sign my work for authenticity; which he said was pro-forma to intellectual property. I had made about seven trips to the canteen that day and I had delivered at least twenty cut sandwiches to other members of staff; so I wasn't feeling very happy about my day when I presented my work to him.

He looked at it and started to grumble that I had signed every page.

"Sorry," I politely answered, "it's the way I have been taught do things."

He snarled at me, rolled up the papers and carried them off to his own drawing board and I was immediately given another project to work on. It was for some new equipment called the Gestetner, which was to be launched the following year. The Gestetner was essentially a duplicator with huge potential to save a lot of time and intrigued by it my mind was exploding with exciting ideas as I started to doodle again.

It was three o'clock on a Wednesday afternoon as I remember, and we had all been summoned to a sales meeting with the upper management. There were to be presentations and awards given to members of staff, and I attended with trepidation as I knew that I was essentially zero in the rankings.

We all sat down on the rows of green fabric chairs, and an immaculately dressed man called Mr Frost appeared. He looked to be excited about what had been achieved in Mr Briggs' department and opened the drapes to present what he exclaimed was the best work he seen in a long time.

It was unveiled as a totally new concept in advertising, and as he turned through the pages of the presentation board I was astonished to see my work being displayed to the entire gathering, and Mr Briggs was invited to explain why he had done what he had done to the project. To my horror, Mr Briggs was using my notes to explain the reasons, almost word for word; at the end of which everyone in the room applauded him. We all filed out of the room and returned to our offices, and I sat there puzzled as to why he had chosen to steal my work.

Looking back, I could not have avoided my next action, as I rose and slowly walked over to his board and politely asked, "Why have you stolen my work?"

"It's not your work!" he snapped, "it belongs to the company, and I'm running the department."

"But you've removed my signatures from the separations!" I snapped.

He rose up from his tall chair and glared at me.

"Go and sit down now! Or I'll sack you on the spot." he snarled, and he pushed me away as though I was a piece of rubbish.

I was fuming and rushed back at him, "Why did you push me?" I shouted, "don't ever do that again."

He stepped forward and pushed me again, and by this time everyone in the office was aware of what was going on but said nothing. I don't know why, but something inside me snapped and I sprang forward and whacked him. I admit this was a very stupid thing to do but the fact is I couldn't control my feelings. He fell to the floor and I tried to help him up, but it was too late as he vowed to dismiss me on the spot.

I was shuffled to the director's office and asked why I had thumped him, and I could see that my actions would not be tolerated, even though he had stolen my work and presented it as his own, so I said nothing. They terminated my employment with immediate effect and essentially blacklisted me as being violent; making it quite clear that they would never provide a reference and that as far as they were concerned, I would never work in England again.

I went back to my drawing board and packed up my personal belongings, placing them carefully into a cardboard box. I glared at Mr Briggs who by this time was purring with contentment at what he'd achieved. I walked out of the office, down to the main foyer and left through the spinning doors, making sure that I pushed them as hard as I could. Then walking out to my bike I strapped the box onto the back with bungee straps ready to ride back to Gethin's, knowing that he wouldn't be very pleased with my actions.

On the way I called in to see Jake and Jane and parking the bike outside I went up to the caravan and banged on the door.

"I need a job," I said, as my knock was answered by Jane.

On hearing those words, Jake boomed out "Christ here we go again!" and we all started to laugh, although I knew it was serious really.

I went in and sat down to tell them what had happened and more importantly what I intended to do. I told them word for word what Mr Briggs had done and that I was relieved to have been sacked, as he was a particularly nasty person. But secretly I was aware that I had yet again attacked someone, which would badly reflect on my character.

Jane excitedly suggested that I came to work with them as the whole business would belong to me one day. I looked at her and started to explain what I had planned, warning them both that they wouldn't like what I was going to say.

"When I was at college," I told them, "I met a young guy who was called Peter Akando. His father is a North American Indian, and he's heavily involved with Graphics tablets in a new place called Silicon Valley, in California.

"He told me '*they are looking for artists with flair*' and insisted that I would fit in with the American lifestyle."

"I haven't asked him yet," I said, "but I think I need a change; and a new country would give me the chance to get away from all of this. I know I'm still screwed up or I wouldn't be thumping people all the time,"

"It's hardly all the time is it!" barked Jake "but I do understand."

"I love you both very much and I have no idea what I'm doing at the moment," I said to him, "but I have to do something."

"Well!" said Jake, "it worked in Newquay. So why can't it work in America. Go and show them son I have every faith in you.

"But just promise me one thing," he said.

"Yes I promise I'll call you every week," I said before he could say another word.

"Good," Jake replied, "coz we love you too, and I'm guessing that Gethin won't be too happy either."

"I'll bring the bike back when I've things sorted it out," I said to Jake.

"It's yours," he replied.

"Then keep it safe for my return."

Jane was already weeping, and I looked at her.

"You've been more of a mother to me than anyone. You've made me feel as though I can do anything! Thank you," I said to her and I think I hugged her more than I had ever hugged her before.

I climbed on the bike and pointed it in the direction of Gethin's house, "See you tomorrow," I called out, and sped off doing *wheelies* again.

When I arrived at Gethin's he seemed to know that something was wrong.

"What happened?" he asked, and I took a deep breath to tell him. I went through what had happened and apologised that I had let him down.

"You haven't let me down at all," he smiled, "I agree with you. What you did was right, but you will never fight the system. History proves that those who have, want more and more."

I told him about my plans, explaining how Mr Briggs had made it clear he would make sure I wouldn't be able to work in England for years.

"My only chance now is to try and prove myself elsewhere," I said.

He smiled and shook my hand. "I envy you, and I have every faith that you will succeed in whatever you try and do," he said, "the simple fact is that you are strong, confident and determined; which are the three ingredients that are needed to gain success.

"It has been a pleasure and a privilege to know you David, and you will always have a special place in my heart."

I knew that he was saying goodbye to me as he wasn't far off retirement and he was thinking that he wouldn't be around on my return. I looked at him and smiled fondly.

"Were it not for you, I wouldn't be alive to go anywhere, would I? You saved me Gethin."

The following day I went to see Peter who enjoyed the luxury of a large palatial apartment that was paid for by his father. He was a good friend, but I was always cautious about our friendship as it was rumoured around the college that he was *queer,* which was how gay people were referred to in those days. The age of consent was twenty-one for homosexual relationships, and as I neither wanted nor agreed with such an action I simply stayed away. There was a real stigma in those days, and I was keen to avoid any idea that I may also be gay, which by the way I'm not. But as I was still tongue tied when it came to girls and usually kept out of their way, it would have been all too easy for people to make the wrong assumptions. I was also brutally aware that any such rumours could damage Gethin's reputation especially as I was still living in his house at the time.

To be honest I really liked Peter, but I can't say that his inexhaustible supply of money didn't influence my decision. In a way I felt guilty when I rang his doorbell and he peered through the peep hole to identify me, before allowing me into his apartment. I sat down and without any polite talk or preamble I immediately asked if there were still any positions in his father's firm.

"Oh yes," he said, "several, and knowing how talented you are. I would recommend you without a second thought."

I didn't want to trip myself up, so I told him that I'd just been sacked and why, and to my surprise he grinned.

"I would have done the same if I'd had the guts," he said determinedly.

We both laughed, and I realised from the way he was looking at me that there was a distinct possibility that he liked me. So I opened my eyes wide and stared at him sternly, then made it very clear that I wasn't queer, and that whilst I really liked his company, I wouldn't like to go to the States with anyone thinking that I was. I think Peter was shocked by how blunt I was he took it on the chin. By the time I left his apartment Peter had promised to call his father the following day and let me know the outcome. We shook hands and I left, although I could see he would rather have given me a hug.

I set off back to Gethin's again to tell him about my meeting with Peter. Rank Xerox had given me two weeks' pay in lieu of notice and I wanted, or rather I needed to give some money to Gethin, as I felt sure that I would be off in just a short time; probably less than a week. I parked the bike up and opened the front door to see him sitting down reading a book and puffing on his cigar; I had always liked that smell and I knew that I would miss it.

"Well! It looks as though I will know tomorrow," I told him.

He looked up and smiled, "I will miss you son."

"Aren't you supposed to say that with a tear in your eye?" I teased.

"Yes. But I don't want you to see it," he said. "You have been like a son to me, and don't think that you haven't given to me as such. I have a host of good memories that I recall almost on a daily basis."

I could see that he was secretly upset, and I walked over to him.

"Don't get soppy, please! I'm too old for this," he said smiling,

"I know you're going, but please call me to let me know you're safe."

"Of course I will," I whispered, did you think that I wouldn't?"

"No," he said, "but this time it's important."

"I know," I replied, understanding what he meant. I opened the door to climb the stairs, knowing I was about to end what had been the most valuable time of my life. I needed to go to America if I was to make anything of myself. In my heart I knew that these next few days would probably be the last times I would see Gethin, but I also knew deep down that he would always be watching out for me.

I have no idea why but the next day I felt the need to visit Margaret and tell her what I had planned.

Peter had called me to say that his father had agreed to employ me, solely on his recommendation. I was both flattered and honoured; spending perhaps more time than I should have talking to him on the telephone, expressing my gratitude at his trust in me. From what I had gathered his father Mr Albert Akando was going to call me at 6:30 pm the following evening which was 10:30 am his time, for an introductory telephone interview. In preparation for the call I had been reading all about first generation graphic tablets and the interesting mathematics that lay behind the technology, so that I could impress him, and he would see that I would be useful to employ.

Knowing that Len would be at work I was reasonably relaxed about the visit to see Margaret and whistled as I opened the gate to walk up the to the back door. It was strangely comforting to note that Len's car wasn't parked on the driveway and I felt totally at ease as I called out "Mum, it's David. Anyone at home?"

In a flash she appeared at the door beaming with smiles at my presence.

"I've come to tell you that I'm going to America to work," I said,

"Oh!" she frowned, "why's that?"

I thought for a moment, and realised that I owed her the absolute truth, so I told her what had happened at Rank Xerox and how and why I'd thumped Mr Briggs, and that it resulted in my instant dismissal. She looked at me and her response took me by surprise.

"I understand exactly why that happened, and I don't blame you one little bit."

"You do understand that I thumped him, don't you? In pretty much the same state as when I landed Len?"

"Yes" she smiled, "and I'm surprised that you haven't done it more often."

I looked at her sternly and snapped, "Look Mum! What I did was wrong, both to him and Len. Violence never solved anything.

"I have a lot of respect for people who oppose violence, I'm just suffering from gross injustice," I murmured.

"I'm a bit mixed up because if violence is never justified, then why have I been subjected to so much of it? And why have there been two world wars?

"The simple fact is that I don't know if violence can ever be justified. But from what I've seen my violence has *solved* my problems one way or another. I doubt if Len will ever threaten me again, as he knows that he's run out of persecution time and that after all these years I am no longer a victim."

I paused for a moment and continued.

"I do know that those who insist on being entirely non-violent will eventually discover that everything they've ever done is at the sufferance of those who are good at it," I told her, "and therefore I don't intend to take anymore ever again.

"I will never agree with Len or his extended torture against me and I think that Briggs was wrong, or I wouldn't have whacked him; although to be honest he did push me first."

I smiled again, "Look I've come to say that I'm going away and I don't want you to tell Len, as he is likely to try and stop me because I'm still under age. I'm not even sure that I'll be allowed without the correct travel papers in place. I need a passport and I'm still under twenty-one, but we'll see. It's something that I will just have to work out.

"In any event Len should be delighted as five thousand miles seems like a pretty good distance to convince him that I'm out of his life for good."

Margaret had remained silent throughout my whole elongated speech to her.

"Send me the paper that you need to sign, and I promise you that I'll get him to sign it. I'm fairly sure that I'm allowed to sign for you if he won't, so don't worry I understand how important this is to you."

I rose up from the chair and kissed her on the cheek.

"I love you Mum, none of this was your fault, I whispered. "You had no idea how he would react, and to be honest it hasn't been great for you either, has it? Most of the time you've been torn down the middle."

As I went to the door she called out, "Please let me know your safe. Write to me from time to time, won't you?"

"I will. Don't worry though, I'll be fine you have no idea how determined I can be," I assured her.

The following day I was hovering around the phone like a bee buzzing around a honey pot, and Gethin was getting annoyed.

"Sit down! They will call you!" he shouted.

I was sure that he was sad at the prospects of my departure and so I sat down sighing and puffing. When the phone eventually rang, I picked it up to hear a deep growling voice with a very strong American accent on the other end.

"Hi, Mr Albert T Akando, pleased to make your acquaintance," the voice said. I gulped and in my very best English, I politely thanked him for the call.

"I understand that Peter thinks you're a very smart guy," Mr Akando growled, "and we need smart guys around here! So why don't you tell me what you can do for me, and what you know about graphics tablets."

I'd read up on his company and the embryonic Silicon Valley and had also spent hours reading up on tablet computers; which had appeared in several science fiction books I had been reading. So I closed my eyes and blasted everything at him, quoting from several sections of at least five books.

He was obviously pretty smart himself as he paused for a moment before exclaiming, "You couldn't have prepared for this meeting! How did you quote all that word for word, do you have a snapshot mind or is it prolonged?"

I had no idea what a snapshot mind was, so I just answered, "I'm able to remember things quite well Sir!"

"It's Albert, not Sir!" he barked, "and I have a feeling that you would fit in fine over here. What do your parents think about you coming over?" he asked.

I was keen to tell him the truth but said that, "the telephone was hardly the place to discuss it." He agreed, and I confirmed my willingness to come over at his convenience, reminding him that my parents were not able to support me and that my tutor had brought me up from the age of thirteen. He sensed him smile on the other end of the telephone as he muttered, "I've a feeling you and I will get along fine!

"I'll get things sorted with Peter; call him tomorrow I'm keen to see what you can do Dave."

I put the phone down and screamed at the top of my voice, "Cool! It looks as though I'm off to America soon!"

Gethin looked at me and mumbled, "I'll miss you," and I realised that what was good news for me, was cutting him in half.

I sat down and whispered, "Look Gethin, I *will* call you every day."

"No you won't," he smiled, "you won't have time. But I'll still miss you."

There were a thousand things bubbling in my mind but none of them seemed to help so I just looked at him and whispered.

"Thank you for saving my life."

CHAPTER TWENTY TWO

"A journey of a thousand miles begins with a single step."
... Lao Tzu

Two weeks had gone by when Peter phoned to tell me that he had received a contract and that once it was signed, a flight had been arranged from Heathrow to San Francisco, where I was to be collected and driven to a nearby apartment which was in the grounds of my intended work place. I rushed around to complete the paperwork which did involve Len's signature and was forced to visit for what I hoped would be the last time. To my astonishment he signed it and I was on my way.

Gethin, Jake and Jane came with me to the airport and I have never seen so many tears shed in such a short time, including mine.

I was scared very scared as I was leaving all that I had known to be good to me, and my insides were trembling when they allocated my seat number and handed me a boarding pass; putting a sticker on the carboard image of the plane to indicate that it was now taken. To this day I still miss the old-fashioned way that airline seats and boarding passes were handed out. I climbed the stairs to the aircraft, realising that I was about to take one of the most daring steps of my life.

Peter joined me onboard as he was also conveniently flying back to the States; and I suspected it was contrived to provide me with a level of security and comfort. It seemed like an age before it was announced that we were about to land at San Francisco Airport, it was the first time I had flown, and the landing was scary as the engines roared and the plane came to a standstill. Peter rose up from his seat and pulled his bag from the overhead locker, and as I did the same, I had a fleeting moment when I wondered if I'd made the right decision?

"It's too late now," I thought to myself pushing all further thoughts aside.

The Air Hostess opened the door and I started down the steps, with Peter next to me. The hot air hit me like a brick making it almost impossible to breathe; something I hadn't at all expected.

"Don't worry, you'll soon get used to it," he giggled, "it's very different to England. You can look forward to a nice suntan and a good life."

A huge limousine was waiting for us and I was taken to the apartment that had been arranged for me to live in. It too was huge, much bigger than anything I had ever seen, and I began to feel a little overwhelmed, and realised that small felt more secure. Jake had given me a telephone number and time to call, and Peter said I could use the telephone to call whoever I wished. So, calculating the time to be almost exact, I dialled the number and Jane answered. For some strange reason I burst into tears shaking and wailing like a baby.

"I miss you mum!" I blubbered, as It suddenly dawned on me that I was five thousand miles away from all that I knew and loved.

We both calmed down and I could hear Jake muttering in the background, "I told you he should have stayed with us. I miss him already and he's only been gone for twenty-four hours."

He came to the phone and said, "Look mate if it doesn't work out, were all here for you. I know it's not what you want; but you'll always have a home and money and security with us." His words soothed me, and I calmed right down.

"Tell mum I love her," I said, "I have to go now, but I'll call you tomorrow at the same time."

It was Monday morning, but I had no idea what the time was as my head had been playing strange tricks. Last night I had tried to sleep and in the pitch black of night a little bell had rung in my head to tell me it was time to get up. I didn't know about jetlag, all I knew was that I'd lost several hours, and it seemed strange that I was calling Jane at 10 am and they were answering me at 6 pm. *No wonder my head is muddled,* I sighed. Suddenly the doorbell rang and a tall man in a black suit beckoned me to a huge car.

"God!" I shouted, "are you sure we need one that big?"

"Sorry" he growled in his American twang, "it's the only size we have around here!"

It was only ten minutes to where I was about to start work and as we drew up to a huge building, I couldn't miss the largest sign I'd ever seen, which read, ATA-Tec Inc, Albert T Akando, CEO and Founder.

I walked into a mega room with computers mounted on every wall. There were magnetic tapes spinning and so many lights flashing that it reminded me of the Walzer when I was a kid. I sat down at a desk that again was huge, to see it had a computer terminal linked to what I had read all about; but I knew very little about its practical use. I was given a tablet and several styluses and instructed to copy a scenic picture which was taken somewhere in the Yukon. I was keen to doodle on paper, but they were keen for me to do everything on the tablet.

I had been working at it for several weeks when a big man with a Stetson walked up and started to talk to me.

"You've been doing some pretty *cool* work," he sniggered, "how do you like here?"

I told him I had been reading all about a computer programmer called Grace Hopper who had developed a simple mathematical compiler, which was used in COBOL and surprisingly I almost perfectly understood what she was up to. The maths had become more interesting to me than the artwork and I commented, "I've been playing around with the compiler to see if I could turn the graphics through 360 degrees, which isn't easy, but I'm making some head way."

I had no idea who I was talking to, but I had a strong feeling that it was no less that Albert T Akando himself, and so I looked at him and asked, "Are you Mr Akando?"

"I am indeed!" he proudly stated, "sorry I haven't visited you sooner; been very busy," and that was my introduction to Albert.

As he walked away, he shouted back, "Keep up the good work. I think you're on to something," and he was gone.

I was under a man named Shaeffer who often visited me to see what I was doing; there were only three people in my room and neither of the other two spoke English so to be honest life was all about work which I didn't mind at all. I had tried to speak to Chikuma who was Japanese and appeared to be very clever, but I had no success. The other was German and not very responsive at all. Chikuma was keen to speak to me as I advanced in my mathematical adventure, and I suddenly realised that Mathematics was a universal language and that there was no barrier if I wrote everything down before I tried to say anything. I was keen to share my thoughts with him, as by then I had mastered simple programming, and my graphic designs were layered and detachable and considered to be valuable by Chikuma who had given several thumbs up signs as I had advanced.

I rushed home that night to call Jane and write to Gethin, when I suddenly had a eureka moment, and jotted down my thoughts in symbols and a simple schematic.

I was really keen to try it out the next morning when I noticed a large three-phase cable had been fixed to the wall leading to Shaeffer's office. Something inside me reminded me of Mr Briggs and his ability to steal my efforts, so I sat there for a moment and considered my position as I had a strong feeling that the cable was there to clone my for someone else would take the credit.

I had become competent with Cobol and had learned how to compile or translate my maths to machine code, which was not far away from what I was doing to communicate with Chikuma. As we sat there drinking coffee, I pulled out my schematic and placed it on the table for Chikuma to look at. He went wild and offered me his hand to shake with extreme excitement. It was then that I realised that what I was doing was important, and that America was no different to England; they just used a different dialect. I had long been suspicious of Shaeffer as on almost every visit he had taken my notes and filed them in his personal folder which he carried wherever he went.

I sat down and worked out what was to be possibly my greatest plan; I knew that the code I had mastered fell into a pattern, and that the compiler translated it to work to the required hardware. I knew that once my code was compiled, it would be readable on the system, but not until then. So I started to write some cryptic comments which I hid in the code, taking my inspiration from the German enigma machine that I had read about in Gethin's library, then I fed the data to the tapes, knowing it would be intercepted by Shaeffer. It must have taken hours for him to translate my messages, which became visible after he had spent hours compiling the code.

One message read, *if you want to know; why don't you just ask instead of stealing*. I wrote dozens of encrypted scripts some of which were very insulting, until one day Shaeffer came down the stairs and officiously stated that he was interested in my coding talents,

"Especially as you were taken on as an artist and appear to have caught on very quickly," he said.

I looked at him and quietly replied, "Well if you want to know what I'm doing, I'm going to want something in return."

"What is this?" he stumbled in his broken English.

I paused and smiled, "I want a yellow Mustang and I want you to sponsor me to Harvard, as I'm fed up with guessing the basic stuff."

"We will see what we can do," he chuckled.

"Oh! And one other thing, I want $2000.00 a month, or I go back home."

Albert came to visit me the next day in a much less official manner, smiling all the time.

"I like you Dave!" he grinned, "I understand you've been speaking to Shaeffer and you made certain demands!"

"Yes," I answered thinking that I was about to be sacked.

To my amazement he said, "Well you have everything you wanted. With one condition."

"What's that?" I asked nervously.

"You move in with my family. As I don't want to miss a second of your extraordinary mind. Peter was right! and I've a feeling that you'll do some amazing stuff in the future."

I sat back in my chair and pondered for a moment; my mind raced back to Gethin who had taught me so much, I had read every book in his house, probably twice. He had taught me speak properly and spent hours teaching me to play the guitar, determined that I would master it; without any benefit to himself at all. He had given up hours, days, months of his time to show me the wonders of artistic creation, and his quotations were ringing in my ears like bells summoning me to a perfect world. *The access of the ellipse is always at right-angles to the axis of the cylinder*, thundered through my mind and a thousand more pieces of wisdom came flooding back.

Jake had Jane had gifted me with confidence and shown me the true meaning of dedication. From the first time I knocked on their caravan door they never ever let me down. I recalled the hours I spent on the Waltzer and the days I stood on the back of the lorry selling pots; when only months before I couldn't speak a word without stuttering. Jane compensated for so much, she taught me what it was like to be loved. Jake was strong and towered above me teaching me what it was like to be safe. And then there was Growler the dog whose only purpose was to protect me, his devotion was extraordinary, and I wondered how I had ever stopped crying when he died.

My mind flew back to Alan and his wife Merryn and their kindness. Then to Tom, Billy and Lucy all suffering yet filled with caring and decency; disregarding their own problems completely. I felt guilty that even though I had travelled down to see them for several years afterwards to sit and listen to them, there were many important points that had been skipped over especially in my own story which has always been difficult to talk about.

And finally, I thought about Margaret who had been trapped in an impossible situation having little or no idea of what Len was like, or why he did what he did. She had known some of what he was, but in part refused to believe it.

My answer to Albert was "Yes!"

I went back to visit Margaret and Len seven years later and I never forgot to call any of my extended family during my time in America.

Writing this book about my formative years and thinking about the years I had spent in the US and my time after returning to the UK; I have been inspired to make a start on writing a second book.

Jake had taught me so well to ride a trial bike and as a consequence I raced in the Isle of Man. You see he was right! he had taught me well and I never rode my Honda RC30 on the TT course without thinking about him.

I am seventy years old now; Gethin is waiting for me, as are Jane and Jake who could not live without each other in this life. I will never forget what Margaret had said to me, when we sat by the light house on Berry Head in Brixham only twenty minutes' walk from my house. Len had virtually ruined her life and I was delighted to offer her accommodation to give her a break from his strange ways. We had decided to take a walk to the light house as the night had stolen the daylight by illuminating the sky with a mass of twinkling stars.

"David," she said holding my hand tightly, "I'm so sorry to have put you with him, you never deserved it!

Please forgive me."

Upon returning to Leicester she died the following week, and I know that her last words in this world would have been good and kind words and I look forward to walking with her again knowing that she is waiting for my call.

I have so much more in my heart that I know will inspire anyone that is in this position although I must admit the culture has changed so much since I was a kid and there are not many like Gethin, Jake or Jane about these days.

Printed in Great Britain
by Amazon

62439022R00179